D0847990

Ghost Towns of California

Ghost Towns of California

By
Donald C. Miller

PRUETT PUBLISHING COMPANY
Boulder, Colorado

Library of Congress Cataloging in Publication Data

Miller, Donald C., 1933-
Ghost towns of California.

Includes index.
1. Cities and towns, Ruined, extinct, etc.—California—History. 2. California—History, Local. I. Title.
F861.M56 979.4 78-7788
ISBN 0-87108-517-8

First Edition

1 2 3 4 5 6 7 8 9

Printed in the United States of America

Note: Town locations on the map are very approximate and are intended to depict only general distributions.

Hawkinsville
Cottonwood
Happy Camp
Henley
Hamburg
Greenhorn
Scott Bar
Sawyers Bar
Etna
Somes Bar
Orleans
Forks of Salmon
Callahan
Black Bear
Trinidad
Carrville
Old Denny (New River City)
Election Camp
Castle Crags
Stringtown
Dedrick
Trinity Center
Canon City
Hayden Hill
Minersville
Del Loma
Deadwood
Big Bar
Summit City (Meadow Lake)
Junction City
Ingot
Kennet
Hayfork
French Gulch
Carriers Gulch
Whiskey Town
Ruth
Shasta
Douglas City
Cottonwood
Ono
Anderson
Weaverville
Indian Creek
Igo
Lewiston
Susanville
Taylorsville
Meadow Valley
Pulga
Oroville
Downieville
Wyandotte
Forest City
Hamilton
Yuba City
Marysville
Plumas
Grass Valley
Natoma
Colfax
Forest Hill
El Dorado
Cool
Woodfords
Plymouth
Silver Mountain
Drytown
Coloma
Folsom
Placerville
Clarksburg
Diamond Springs
Amador City
Fiddletown
Sutter Creek
Volcano
Monitor
Markleeville
Butte City
Railroad Flat
Mokelumne Hili
Douglas Flat
Masonic
San Andreas
Murphys
Cameron
Melones
Angels Camp
Bridgeport
Tuttletown
Columbia
Dogtown
Bodie
Copperopolis
Shaws Flat
Lundy
Chinese Camp
Sonora
Tioga
Monoville
Jacksonville
Lee Vining
Big Oak Flat
Groveland
Mammoth City
Mountain House
Coulterville
Second Garrote
Mill City
Benton
Bagby
Snelling
Bear Valley
Pine City
Mt. Ophir
Mt. Bullion
Owensville
Hornitos
Agua Fria
New Almaden
Coarsegold
Mariposa
Bishop
Confidence
Mormon Bar
Academy
San Carlos
Bend City
Kearsarge
Leadfield
Chloride
Soledad
Lee
Bartlett
Swansea
New Indria
Keeler
Cerro Gordo
Furnace
Cartago
Harrisburg
Darwin
Greenwater
Old Coso
Lookout
Millspaugh
Los Burros
Gorda
Ballarat
Tecopa
Klau
White River
Kernville
Cambria
Lake Isabella
Keysville
Bodfish
Ivanpah
Havilah
Claraville
Johannesburg
Crackerjack
Mescal
Garlock
Vanderbilt
Randsburgh
Copper City
Barnwell
Hart
Atolia
Red Mountain
Tehachapi
Coolgardie
Bismarck
Mojave
Calico
Providence
Rosamond
Goffs
Daggett
Ludlow
Essex
Orogrande
Victorville
Stedman
Bagdad
Belleville
Doble
Old Dale
Twentynine Palms
New Dale
Dale III
Perris
Julian
Banner
Cuyamaca
Picacho
Tumco
Buckman Springs

"The story of one mining-camp was the story of mankind; and to follow it after death was the story of the gods."

—Hubert Howe Bancroft

Introduction

California gold! It was a wild call, a clear and ubiquitous call that many could not deny.

All "pilgrims" sought bonanza. Many found only borrasca.

California was the first of a spectacular series of gold discoveries in western North America in the nineteenth century. The process was to be repeated time and again: in Colorado, Nevada, Arizona, New Mexico, Utah, Idaho, Montana, British Columbia, Washington, Oregon, Wyoming, and the Black Hills of South Dakota.

As one writer phrased it, "The founder of American California, the George Washington of the Golden State, was a Swiss wanderer, John A. Sutter."[1] The first gold discovery in California is often erroneously[2] credited to James W. Marshall, whose discovery of placer gold in the tail race of Sutter's undershot water sawmill on January 24, 1848[3] led to the gold rush of 1849. The discovery site was at Coloma, about forty miles up the American River from Sutter's Fort, New Helvetia (Sacramento).

When Sutter[4] was informed of the discovery, he tried to keep its secret in order to protect his fragile agricultural interests from hordes of destructive miners and prospectors. But such earthshaking news could not long be suppressed; and when the word spread, virtually every adult male resident of California headed for the diggings.[5] During that first year of 1848, perhaps $10 million were taken from California's placer deposits. By 1852 large-scale hydraulic operations were undertaken. Lode mining became important in the 1860s, and between 1884 and 1918 gold-quartz veins became the major source of California's gold production. From 1848 to the present, more than 100 million ounces of gold were wrenched from state placer and lode deposits and as byproduct gold from other mining efforts.

The gold and other treasures came from northern mines in the Redding and Yreka areas; from the sinuous Mother Lode Country, with its confusing "dips, spurs, angles, and variations" stretching from Auburn to Mariposa along its one-mile width and 120-mile length. The eastern and southern desert mines and forbidding Death Valley[6] lured countless treasure seekers.

The rainbow chasers came from throughout the world, but mostly they were Americans who scrambled to the gold fields by numerous trails over prairie, desert, and mountain.[7] Some came by sea routes via Cape Horn. Some came in sailing vessels to Vera Cruz then traveled overland to Mazatlan, Mexico, and up the coast by ship, mule, or horse. Some crossed the Isthmus of Panama, or Nicaragua, and continued to California.

No matter what the varying routes taken, the aims were the same for the scrambling fortune seekers — to get as much gold as could be gotten in the least time possible.

Most of them probably didn't intend to stay in the "golden land" once they had "made their pile." When the dust settled, some returned home; some couldn't afford to go home again; some didn't want to return; and some wouldn't admit failure by returning with an empty poke.

The theoretical attractions were understandable — free riches for the taking to float a man above a maelstrom of downward-sucking poverty. Others were very likely lured by adventure.

Profiles are available of those who came to the new Eden. What they endured is recorded. When they came is known. Where they went is amply chronicled. Perhaps because the record is so rich and relatively plentiful, it is also diverse and often contradictory. But it needs to be examined, for these firsthand and after-the-fact reactions form the skeleton of the California gold saga and give substance to the unique and significant body of information on western americana lore.

Descriptions of the gold seeker's character were as variable as night and day. Mercurial miners arriving at Sacramento in 1850, hot on the heels of the gold discoveries, were described in the *Sacramento Transcript*[8] as being "a sea whose tide knows no law." Another observer[9] thought the miners "as fluctuating and unstable as the waves of the sea."

A differing opinion was that "A more kind and hospitable people are nowhere found,"[10] while another observed that California miners became "a race of sybarites and epicureans."[11] Still others opined that the miners included "Indians, Mexicans, runaway sailors, disbanded soldiers, Conacers from the islands [Hawaiians], and men and monsters."[12] Others commented that "The Adams of this Eveless Eden were dirty, bewhiskered, and cheerful."[13]

Prospectors and miners were frequently pictured as hard working, "habited in their red flannel shirts, rough as the grisly [*sic*] bear, long beards, long hair, old hats, no shoes, or shoes variously patched,"[14] but "like the gold they seek, surrounded with dirt, rough looking, yet often possessing that sterling worth which will give them currency among the good, the gifted, and the beautiful."[15]

California gold seekers were even likened to chickens. "They followed the track of it, in '48 and '49 and '50, like you'll see chickens follow a trail of corn, pecking and scratching away after it."[16]

The new land held great promise. J. Ross Browne, in *Adventures in the Apache Country,*[17] wondered, "Could it be that a grand mistake was made in Mohammedan history — that Paradise is nothing more than a faint attempt to delineate the beauties of California?" But Browne bemoaned that in California "we have had gold manias, and silver manias and ranch manias and fruit manias, and all other sorts of manias, till it really seems as if nothing could be done without a special insanity . . ."

In the rush toward elusive riches, many miners apparently forgot promises made to others, to themselves, and to God. One miner lamented, "Here all my promises vanish from my mind about leading a Christian life."[18] The same pilgrim hoped to make short his visit to California. He hoped "to find a place where we can make a little & then leave California for a place to settle down on & live like a Christian."[19]

That writer was not alone. Another[20] wrote, "Men forgot home, happiness, and heaven; forgot the training of childhood, manhood, and the fear of God. They madly threw all the past of life to the four winds, and literally changed the words of Holy Writ and the highest maxims of human morality, and declared in every act, that 'the love of money was the best policy, and honesty the root of all evil.'" Yet, he also thought the miners to be "good fellows, true to each other, and generous to a fault."[21] But he lamented the amount of whisky, brandy, rum, gin, wine, ale, porter, and beer used in California, which, he calculated, totaled forty-two gallons to each man, woman, and child.[22]

The average forty-niner knew little of mining. Once he found gold, he also found it difficult to keep. One diarist[23] wrote: "Not only is the digging of gold the most uncertain of all employments, it is also one in which science and all past experience are at fault. No rules can be given, no evidences furnished for finding the concealed veins or opening the rich deposits. The miner is not sure of his gold till he holds it in his hand, and then it seems very difficult for him to hold on to it. One of our coins is very properly denominated the eagle, since it seems endued with wings, and is so apt to fly away."

And when the men found gold, it wasn't always where it was supposed to be. One chronicler[24] wrote, "it is a notorious fact that the gold defeats all calculations, and with a strange perversity, is generally found just where it ought not to be."

The camps established by the forty-niners varied greatly. Tent towns, wickiups, lean-tos, and caves were common residences for the gold seekers. Some "homes" were made of adobe, some of stone, some of lumber, some of logs; some were permanent, some transitory, and some died a' bornin'. They were settled by what has been called a "thriving, go-ahead"[25] population.

These are nostalgia pieces of something of the lusty, brawling mining camps built out of adobe, brick, mortar, log, milled lumber, nails, canvas, dreams, money, mining stocks, swindles, avarice, and sweat.

What remains tells much of what was. It has been written, "There is something infinitely moving and sad about a deserted mining camp."[26] A respected mining historian mused, "The saddest of all possible sights in the old mining region is where there are not even half a dozen miners to keep each other company, but where, solitary and in desolation, the last miner clings to his former haunts."[27]

True, there is sadness in mining camps. But there's also excitement, virility, intrigue, cheating, murder, mayhem, baseness, love, beauty, humor, greed, and well . . . read on!

The Academy school, probably built in 1872. Principal James Darwin Collins was later Fresno County sheriff (1898-1906) — *Fresno County Historical Society.*

The Academy post office — *Fresno County Historical Society.*

Academy, about twenty-two miles northeast of Fresno, is not usually included on the roster of California mining camps. Perhaps it should be, however, because granite was mined in the area.

The "Academy," a private two-room school built there in 1872,[28] was regarded by some as the handsomest structure in Fresno County. It was torn down in 1920.

Acton was founded by the Southern Pacific Railroad in 1875. The camp, about twenty miles north of Los Angeles, attracted miners to the Red Rover and New York mines, which did not close until the 1940s.

Adamstown was established about two miles above Oroville by George Adams in 1848. This camp on the Feather River has also been known as **Adams Bar** and **Adamsville.**

Early-day Agua Fria — *The Huntington Library.*

Agua Fria[29] (Spanish: cold water) was an important southern California mining settlement that served as Mariposa county seat from 1850 to 1854.

It boasted one dozen stores, several saloons, and an assortment of other structures, including houses roofed with slate.[30]

One of the mysteries of Agua Fria revolved around J. F. A. Marr, Mariposa county treasurer, who testified against certain liquor dealers in November 1851. Marr apparently swore that the dealers didn't make required payments to the county for liquor licenses. The men were fined and became determined to avenge their accuser.

On December 28, Marr, with county money in his possession, took a stage for Stockton. Unfortunately for Marr, the stage plummeted into flood-swollen Mariposa Creek. His body was later recovered, but the $25,000 in gold was missing.

The area, including Marr's garden, has been thoroughly searched by treasure-hunters. After the county seat was moved to Mariposa, the gold-hungry picked among the ruins of the county courthouse, even panning the ground on which the building rested. The money wasn't found.

In their mad scratching for treasure, miners eventually undermined the town site so badly that it washed into Mariposa Creek. Only a marker and a few foundations remain.

The historic marker for Agua Fria stands on the site of **Carson,** where a tannery existed in the 1850s. The camp was probably named for trailblazer Kit Carson, who led explorer John Fremont through the region in December 1845. Nearby was **Arkansas Flat,** a now-vanished mining settlement which saw a resurgence of mining activity during the Depression of the 1930s when out of work men scoured the area in and around Godey Gulch. **Logtown** was a short-lived placer camp along the creek below and to the west of the Mariposa cemetery.

Albany Flat was located between Angel's Camp and Carson Hill. By 1851 the camp along Six Mile Creek may have had 1,500 people. The nearby Marble Spring lode mine was apparently not particularly productive. The town site is marked by the James Romaggi home, built in 1852. One report has it that this building is one of the best in the Mother Lode country for size, excellence of construction, and elaborateness.[31]

Algerine Camp was settled in 1853. The settlement, south of Sonora, was first called **Providence Camp,** then **Algiers.** The camp probably never exceeded 1,000 people.

Alleghany has been the center of placer, lode, drift, and hydraulic mining beginning with gold discoveries on Kanaka Creek by a party of Hawaiians (Kanakas) in May 1850.[32]

The better-known Alleghany area mines include the Ruby, the Kenton, the Bald Mountain, the Twenty One, the Oriental, the Plumbago, the Rainbow, the Knickerbocker, the Brush Creek, the Yellow Jacket, and the Sixteen-to-One. The Sixteen-to-One, located near Kanaka Creek, was probably discovered in 1876[33] and proved to be the principal producer in the district[34] until it was closed in the mid-1960s.[35]

After locomotives replaced mules for pulling underground ore cars, one of the beasts, named Mae West because of her "big rear end and a slow, lazy gate [*sic*]," became an attraction in Alleghany. The mule ended her retirement days bumming around the settlement, wandering from house to house begging apples and carrots.

More ephemeral, and perhaps more exciting, were the "ghosts" within the depths of the Sixteen-to-One mine. One was known as "The Man From Five-Forty-Two" because he exclusively haunted the 542-foot level of the Sixteen-to-One. "The Man" was supposedly dressed in his burial clothes: a black suit, white shirt, and bow tie. The story goes that he probably wasn't a miner, because he was a "solemn figure." More likely he was a storekeeper, clerk, or schoolteacher. The distinguishing characteristic of "The Man from Five-Forty-Two" was the manner in which he wore, or didn't wear, his head. Sometimes he carried his head under his arm. Although he never harmed the miners, they refused to work that level of the mine alone. A more feared phantom of the Sixteen-to-One was the "Ghost of Twenty-Six-Hundred," an apparition who was believed to have killed three men. One was pushed down a shaft, another was crushed beneath a boulder, and the other was frightened to death. Unlike "The Man from Five-Forty Two," the "Ghost of Twenty-Six-Hundred" was never seen.

The closing down of the Sixteen-to-One properties signalled the finale of an era — the last of California hardrock gold mining.

Altaville was founded in 1852. The settlement at the junction of Highways 5 and 49 had first been called **Forks-of-the-Road**, then **Winterton** (for popular miner Bill Winters), and then **Cherokee Flat** before finally being dubbed "Altaville."

The B. R. Prince and D. Garibardi building in Altaville dates to 1857.

Some of the better-producing mines in the area included the Wagon Rut, the Belmont-Osborne, the Golden River, the Slab Ranch, and the Vallecito Western. Still another "precious treasure" was "mined" in the Altaville area; more specifically, in the Calaveras Central mine — on Bald Hill or Bald Mountain. In 1866 the "Calaveras Skull" hoax was perpetrated on State Geologist J. Whitney. The human skull was much touted by Professor Whitney, and much controversy raged as to its authenticity. Bret Harte's story to the "Californian" called "To the Pliocene Skull" was one of many viewpoints on the so-called significant scientific anthropological find of the remains of a prehistoric man. But as it turned out, the skull was most likely planted as a practical joke. The Pliocene skull either belonged to an Indian or may have been the laboratory skeleton of nearby Angel's Camp dentist, Dr. Kelly.[36]

Some relics of Altaville's past remain, including the 1857 Prince Hotel, the 1857 Prince and Garibardi store, the Demarest foundry dating to 1854, and an 1858-vintage brick school, used until 1950.

Old markers in the graveyard tell of men dying by falling "of" river banks.

This is probably from an early 1850s daguerrotype showing the first quartz mill in Amador City — *The Huntington Library.*

Amador City.

The Amador Hotel in Amador City.

The founding date of **Amador City** is uncertain. It is known that prospecting was carried on in 1848 along Amador Creek and that the camp was probably established by the following year. The town was most likely named for soldier and Indian fighter Jose Maria Amador.

In 1851 Reverend Davidson and three other ministers made the first quartz discovery in the region on what was known as Ministers' Claim (or Gulch). The preachers prospected for gold on weekdays and for men's souls on Sundays.

By 1869 the Keystone mine, which had been formed from the consolidation of several existing claims dating to 1853 and 1857, had become the best producing mine near Amador City. It continued in that role until 1919, and then again from 1935 to 1942. Total production may have reached $24 million.

A number of reminders of Amador City's lusty mining days remain, including the 1851 stone Fleethart store, the 1856 Amador and Imperial hotels,[37] and the Mine house, a two-story brick building that once housed the office and residence of the Keystone mine superintendent. The Mine house has since been converted to a motel.

Within two miles of Amador City were the camps of **New Chicago** and **New Philadelphia.**

Amalie was a Kern County camp north of Mojave. It had a post office from 1894 to 1900.

American Hill is now a part of Nevada City. Some claim it was here that the hydraulic giant was invented or improved by Edward Matteson.

Anderson, south of Redding, is hardly a ghost town, but at one time it served as a transportation center to the Trinity River mines.

It is uncertain when Anderson was founded, but its beginnings probably coincide with that of the American Ranch, bought by Elias Anderson in 1856.

Anderson's main street in 1915 — *Shasta Historical Society.*

Angels Camp was founded in 1848 by Henry (George) Angel, who discovered gold while working with Colonel J. D. Stevenson. Some authorities believe that James H. Carson was co-discoverer of the gold; but he probably left Angel, moved a few miles south of Angels Camp, and discovered Carson Hill. Still other sources indicate that Bennager Raspberry found gold in the area, although he probably was not the initial discoverer. In any event, Angel established a trading post, and the camp that sprouted up around it became known as Angels Camp.[38]

About 1895 the Utica Mining Company constructed a hydroelectric plant on Angels Creek that supplied Angels Camp and the area mines with electric power. The plant was later updated and continued in operation until 1954, when it was replaced.

Early mining centered around placers, but when they petered out, quartz mining was initiated. By 1857 eleven[39] quartz mills were operating there.

Both Mark Twain and Bret Harte are associated with Angels Camp. Twain's short story "The Celebrated Jumping Frog of Calaveras County" may have been inspired by a tale he had heard in the Hotel Angels barroom in 1865. Twain was critical of the food and drink at the French restaurant. He described the coffee as "day-before-yesterday's dish-water."[40] His notes of February 3, 1865 noted dining again at the French restaurant and having "beans and dish-water" plus "Hell-fire" soup, one of four varieties served there, in addition to the "General Debility," "Insanity," and "Sudden Death" soups, but he lamented, "it is not possible to describe them."[41]

Angels Camp may also be the setting for Bret Harte's stories *Mrs. Skaggs' Husbands* and *The Bell Ringer of Angel's.*

Angels Camp — *Society of California Pioneers.*

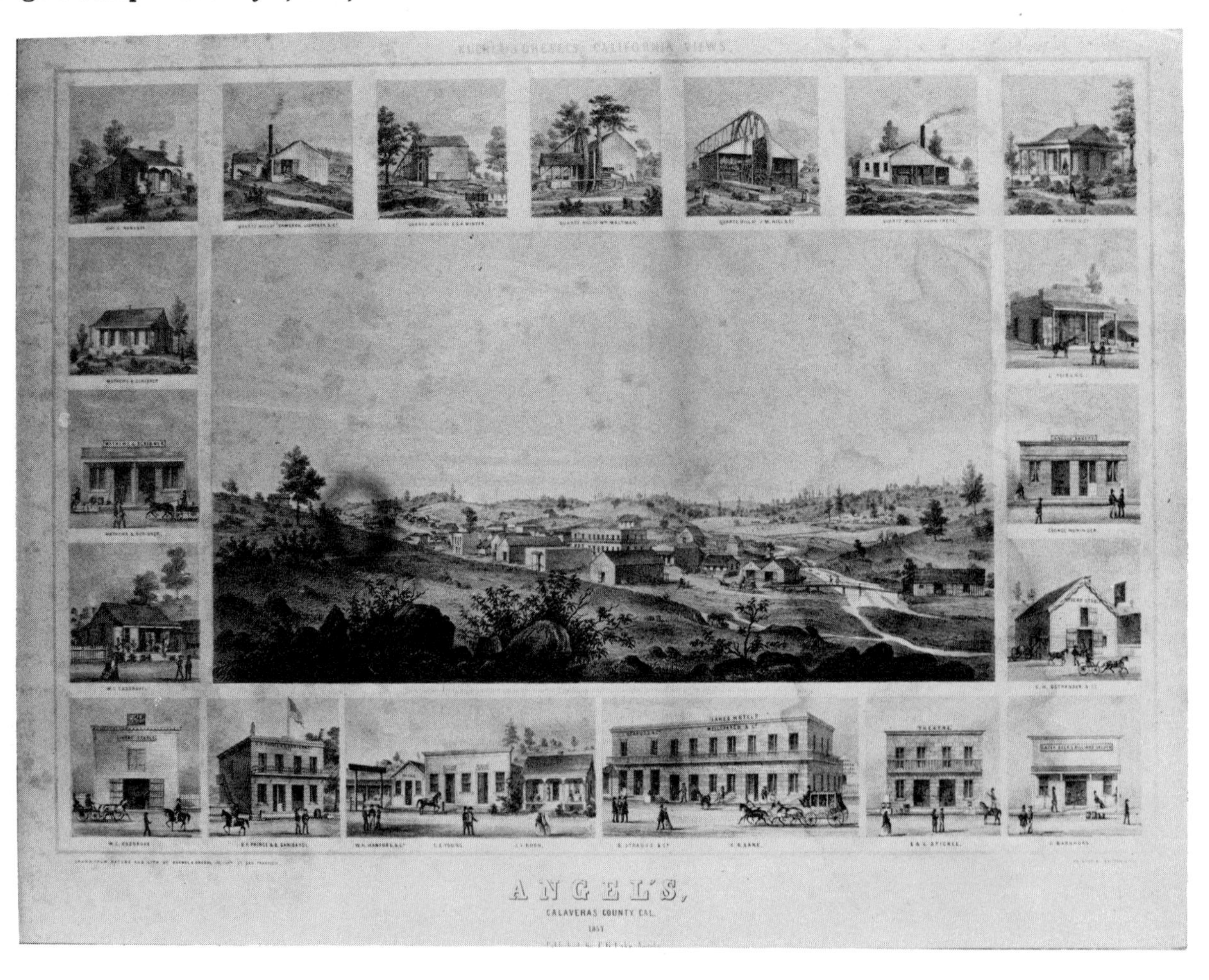

Equipment from the Lightner mine located near Angels Camp in 1855.

Mark Twain circa 1869 — *The Huntington Library.*

Although disastrous fires leveled Angels Camp in 1856 and 1885, a few original structures remain, including the 1885 Angels hotel and remnants of the Angels quartz mine.

A monument to Mark Twain and the "jumping frog" is a relatively recent addition to the "history" of Angels Camp. Remains of machinery used at the Lightner mine are situated near the Twain statue, and part of the story of its $6 million production is told on a nearby historical marker. Other mines included the Marshall, the Mother Lode Central, and the rich Utica.

Antelope may have been a Sierra County camp, but its location is not known. **Antelope Spring** in Butte County and **Antelope Ravine** in Placer County may also have been gold mining camps.

Aquaduct City was built three miles south of Volcano, probably in 1850. The mines were exhausted in less than twenty years, and the camp collapsed.

Arastraville was established a short distance north of Tuolumne. **Arrastre Flat** was east of Belleville in San Bernardino County; **Arrastre Spring,** also in San Bernardino County, was a mining camp, probably first settled by Mexican miners.

Argentine, one dozen miles east of Quincy, was apparently known first as **Greenhorn Diggings.**

Ashland (Amador County) was near Volcano. As many as 100 miners may have lived here. Another Ashland was located northwest of Folsom. It appears to have been called variously **Big Gulch, Bowlesville,** and **Russville.**

Atolia grew up southeast of Randsburg following rich tungsten discoveries in 1905. By 1907 the town had blossomed to a boom town that peaked at a population of 2,000 by 1915.[42] During World War I the Atolia tungsten mine helped supply Allied war demands. However, other less-expensive ore sources were later developed, and Atolia atrophied. Tungsten is still mined in the area.

A reproduction of an early 1850s daguerreotype of mining at the head of Auburn Ravine — *The Huntington Library.*

Flourishing **Auburn** began as a mining camp because of placer gold discoveries made by Claude Chana[43] and a party of Indians in May 1848.

The camp had been known as **Wood's Dry Diggings,**[44] **North Fork Dry Diggings,**[45] and **Rich Dry Diggin's**, but was renamed in 1849 by miners who had originated from Auburn, New York. By 1850 the town's population may have been as high as 1,500 — or at least that many were probably digging in Auburn ravine west of town.

But soon the rich placer deposits gave out, and Auburn seemed destined to join the lengthy list of expired California placer camps. However, with the coming of the railroad in 1865, the moribund town revived — this time as a transportation center.

The original section of Auburn, known as Old Town, still retains vestiges of the settlement's pioneer days despite serious fires which destroyed parts of the town in 1855, 1859, and 1863.

Present-day Auburn has been described as a town that "spills over hill and hollow, encircled by orchard-covered knolls."[46]

Euchre Bar, Double Springs, Virginiatown, Gold Hill, and **Ophir** were nearby mining camps.

Aurum City (Auram, Auram City, Arum) was just southeast of El Dorado. A quartz mill was established at the town, probably in 1852.

Austin may have been a camp south of Diamond Springs, in El Dorado County.

Ava Maria was immediately south of Mariposa. It was probably named for Mexican miners.

During the late 1860s and early 1870s, the **Bagby** area was a placer gold district where at least 50,000 ounces[47] of placer gold may have been garnered from such properties as the Virginia mine.

The townsite was originally the location of Benton Mills, named for Senator Thomas H. Benton, who was nicknamed "Old Bullion" for his stand on the maintenance of hard currency. In 1966 Bagby's structures were razed, and the site is now under the waters of Lake McClure, along with the camps of **Barrett** and **Pleasant Valley**. The camp of **Forlorn Hope** was east of Bagby.

Bagdad was situated just below Oroville on the Feather River. The War Eagle and Orange Blossom mines were among the best producers.

This Mojave Desert camp was virtually destroyed by a fire in 1918. Its parched remains are frequently buffeted by high desert winds.

It has been estimated that Bagdad receives less rain than any other place except one in or near the Mojave Desert, and that its annual rainfall is 2.3 inches. It is further estimated that in four out of twenty years no rain falls there.[48] However, these figures are to be approached with caution, since the National Oceanic and Atmospheric Administration has little climatological data for Bagdad.

The site of Bagdad is now a weather station.

Bairdstown was located in eastern Holcomb Valley. The San Bernardino County gold camp was named for Samuel Baird, an early prospector. Its post office survived for only about six months, and by one dozen or so years after its founding, the town had died.

Baker still survives along Interstate 15 northeast of Barstow.

This once busy mining camp was located at the junction of the Tonopah and Tidewater railroad lines to Death Valley.

Baker was on the line of march of the twenty-mule-team borax wagons from Death Valley.

The area is also remembered as a battleground where, under the command of Lieutenant Carr, the United States Army fought Indians. The army also maintained a camp on the floor of nearby dry Soda Lake.

Balaklava Hill was south of Vallecito. It was named for the Black Sea seaport of the same name. Copper seems to have been the major precious metal mined in the area.

Ballarat was probably named for Ballarat, Australia, the site of what some authorities believe to be the world's largest gold nugget — the Welcome Stranger — a 2,280-ounce nugget originally valued at $42,000 but currently worth much more.

The Ratcliff was the chief mine in the area. Located in 1897, it produced gold valued between $300,000 and $1 million by 1903. The

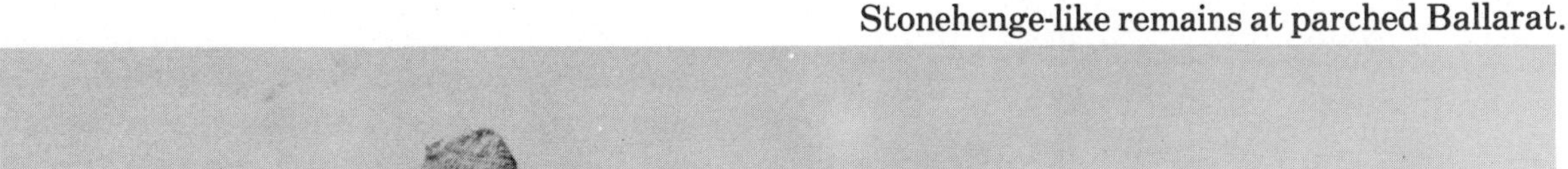

Stonehenge-like remains at parched Ballarat.

One of the more habitable structures still at Ballarat.

mine was apparently closed for a time, but known production figures of gold between 1927 and 1942 are estimated at $250,000.[49]

The area around the settlement abutting the Panamint Mountains was timberless, so most structures were made of adobe.

The town and its last inhabitant, "Shorty" Harris, died in 1934.[50] A few crumbling adobe walls mark the original Mojave Desert camp. A modern store and campground squat on the inhospitable alkali flats of Ballarat, now privately owned.

Baltimore City was a short-lived Nevada County camp probably founded in 1865 and named for a man named Wightman. Initially the camp was called **Wightman Camp.**

Bangor was founded in 1855 by the Lumbert Brothers, who named it for their hometown in Maine. It was located between North and South Honcut creeks in Butte County.

Banner is located east of Julian on Highway 78, at the foot of Banner grade. Gold was discovered in nearby Julian in 1870, and probably in the immediate Banner area at about the same time. Apparently the town was established in February 1871.

The richest mines were the Redman and the Golden Chariot.

A camp and picnic ground now occupy the original townsite near Volcan Mountain.

Interesting accounts of Banner can be found in Helen Ellsberg's *Mines of Julian* (La Siesta Press, 1972).

Bannerville was southeast of Nevada City.

Bartees Bar (Bardee Bar) was a mining camp along the North Fork of the Feather River, north of Oroville.

Bartlett grew up near Owens Lake as the center of operations for one of the nation's largest borax mining companies.

The lake was named for Richard Owen, a member of explorer John C. Fremont's 1845 expedition.

Bartons Bar may have been a Yuba County mining camp, or perhaps only the location of a store built by the Barton Brothers.

Bath was an important gold mining town located north of Forest Hill in Placer County. The camp was probably first christened **Volcano,** then **Sarahsville.**

Beals Bar was on the North Fork of the American River, northeast of Folsom.

Beartrap Flat may have been a mining camp in Kern County's Greenhorn Gulch.

Bear Valley was established by John C. Fremont as headquarters for his 44,000-acre Rancho de las Mariposas and his mines. The camp was probably first known as **Haydensville** for Charles, David, and William Hayden. The Haydensville post office was established in January 1851. By August 1852 it was closed. However, that same year the camp was known as **Biddle's Camp** for William C. Biddle. At about this time, the camp also seems to have been known as **Simpsonville** for Robert Simpson, a local store owner. In 1856 the town was surveyed and named **Johnsonville** for John F. "Quartz" Johnson. Finally, on June 21, 1858, the camp was renamed Bear Valley.

Fremont's wife, Jessie[51] Benton Fremont, wrote that Bear Valley "stretched haphazardly along a dusty road in a trough between Mt. Bullion and the chapparal-covered hills,"[52] and that it "was a scattering of unsubstantial frame and canvas buildings on a

A sagging Bear Valley building that will soon topple to the ground.

single untidy, unattractive street."[53]

Fremont built the elegant Oso House to serve as headquarters for his enterprises and as a hotel for travelers. Among the guests was Ulysses S. Grant. Some of the wood for the building was even shipped around The Horn. Although the mid-1850s structure was described by Jessie Fremont as the architectural showplace of the town with two stories, pillared porch, and balcony, she admitted that "Its less bravely dressed interior walls, however, were of cotton sheeting."[54]

North of Bear Valley can be found Fremont's Josephine mine and his Benton stamp mill. His Mt. Ophir mill and mine were located south of town.

The town probably grew to a population of 3,000.[55]

Fremont, who is accused of grabbing land and mining properties not legally his, instigated a small armed conflict to oust miners from what he considered his lands. Court costs, lawyer's fees, mining property investments that failed, and other misfortunes plagued Fremont, and he lamented bitterly, "When I came to California I hadn't a cent. Now I owe two million dollars."[56]

The Fremont residence (variably called "The Fremont House" and the "White House") with its goldfish pond and fountain[57] is gone, as is the Oso House, which was set afire by careless campers in 1938. But several adobe and schist slab ruins set in mortar and plastered with stucco dot the landscape, and several structures dating to the gold rush days remain. Vestiges of a Chinese settlement can still be found at the northeast end of town.

Beckworth (Beckwith, Beckwourth) was named for Jim Beckwourth, mountain man and trading post operator. It was located near Hawley, in southeastern Plumas County.

Belfort, northeast of Bridgeport, is near Mount Patterson. Nothing of its history was found. Its very tenuous existence seems to be proven by its appearance on United States Geological Survey maps.

Belleville was settled northeast of San Bernardino, in the Big Bear Lake vicinity near the Holcomb public campground. Little is known of this mining camp, named for Belle Van Dusen, daughter of a town blacksmith. In 1861 Belleville almost became San Bernardino's county seat, but the town's heyday was brief. Remains of an arrastre are the only reminders of palmier days.

Bend City is shrouded in a hazy past, although first gold discoveries were probably made near the Owens River in 1862 by a soldier from Camp Independence. The camp grew rapidly and eclipsed its sister camps of San Carlos and Chrysopolis.

Bend City became provisional county seat of newly organized Coso County, but by 1865 the camp was deserted.

The town — constructed almost exclusively of adobe — has almost completely disintegrated, and remains are difficult to find.

Bennettville was established high atop Mono Pass in 1882. The mining camp was named for Thomas Bennett, mining company president. Its post office lasted for only two years. A few structures remain.

Bensonville was immediately below Columbia. It was primarily a hydraulic mining camp.

Benton was a mining camp[58] dating to the 1860s. Silver was perhaps the most important of the minerals produced. The settlement still exists north of Bishop, near Benton Station. It was once a depot on the old Carson and Colorado Railroad connecting

An artist's conception of Bidwell Bar about 1853 or 1854 — *Butte County Historical Society.*

with Nevada.[59] The town was probably founded in 1865, with a post office being established in 1866.

Some original buildings and a cemetery remain in this sleepy little town, which at one time was perhaps known as Montgomery City.

Benton's two newspapers were some of the shortest-lived in the state. The *Mono Weekly Messenger* managed to publish only from February to April 1879 as a weekly. The *Bentonian*, on the other hand, published from 1879 to 1880 as a semiweekly, triweekly, and weekly.

Berdan, southwest of Inskip, in Butte County, was not a mining camp, but was a trading center for area mines.

Bestville was about one mile south of Sawyers Bar. The camp was named for Captain Best, although it probably grew up around the discovery site pointed out by an Indian.

Bidwell's Bar was named for one of John Sutter's aides, John Bidwell,[60] who discovered gold on July 4, 1848. With the help of friendly Indians, Bidwell built a log cabin on the site that served as a home and trading post. Although Bidwell was friendly with the Indians, he didn't have their complete confidence, for he was white and white men were fools — that is what at least some Indians thought. One Indian is reported to have said of the white man, "White man, he heap fool. Give Indian big handful beans, take yellow rocks, heap big fool."[61] But each must have thought he was getting the better of the other, for this barter continued for some time.

The camp must have struck some as inhospitable, for one visitor dubbed it a "rag" city lacking in suitable accommodations, commenting that "As there was nothing to sleep *in* but a tent, and nothing to sleep *on* but the ground, and the air was black with the fleas hopping about in every direction, we concluded to ride forward to the Berry Creek House, a ranch ten miles farther on our way, where we proposed to pass the night."[62]

The camp was probably the first on the Feather River and may have grown to a pop-

John Bidwell in his earlier years — *Butte County Historical Society.*

John Bidwell in his later years — *The Huntington Library.*

ulation of 2,000[63] by 1853. From 1853 to 1856 the town served as Butte county seat.[64]

By the late 1850s, Bidwell's Bar had become a thriving camp served by Whiting's Dog Express. Whiting had hit upon the idea of training dogs to pull sleds through snow-clogged mountains between Rich Bar and Bidwell's Bar. The mutts performed well in their mission of dog-delivering mail and supplies between the camps, and their success led to similar "canine expresses" elsewhere.

Bidwell's Bar is said to have boasted the first suspension bridge in the state. It supposedly looked like a pontoon bridge. The boat was linked to each shore of the Feather River by cables attached to anchors embedded in rock. Miners walked over the bridge on twelve-inch planks. It has been said that Saturday nights added to the work load of the bridge attendant, since he had to rescue "those victims of mining-camp jollification" who failed to properly navigate the crossing.[65]

The bridge was washed away by floodwaters in 1852. It was replaced in 1856 and still exists.

Flumes were constructed to carry water for mining and personal needs. Mining reached its peak in 1856–57. Soon after that, Bidwell's Bar was virtually deserted as miners and prospectors were tempted away, seeking new diggings in Oroville.

Big Bar (one of perhaps nine towns in the state with the same name) was probably settled as early as 1849[66] and grew to be the most important camp on the Mokelumne River by the 1850s. By May 1850 it had thirty to forty tents and shacks. Its prime *raison d'etre* was the ferry which moved men and supplies to the diggings and carried gold from the mines, although some believe that its main claim to fame is that it was the first place in Trinity County where an Indian-fighting female miner made dumplings,[67] or johnnycake.

Coal mining was carried on in the region from 1929 to 1934. Perhaps coal mining even took place in the nearby Willshire mine in the early days of the settlement.[68]

The town[69] still exists west of Weaverville.

Big Flat[70] blossomed in 1850 west of Weaverville near the Trinity River.

It was named for John Weaver, who is also credited with finding Weaverville the preceding year. Isaac Cox in *Annals of Trinity County*[71] mused about the naming of the two settlements. He wrote, "The apparent incongruity that this Big Flat was not called Weaver Flat, and the county seat of Trinity somebody else's ville, is perfectly open to the reader, to be compared to his heart's content, with similar occurrences in American history, as America and Columbus to begin with."

Cox appears content to write off the early years of Big Flat, claiming that "Big Flat thus discovered has an interregnum from 1850 to 1855 which may be tacked on to the wings of briefness, and thus dispatched without snaky detail, having few incidents worthy of lengthy remarks."[72]

Among those few worthy incidents: John Weaver and party built a flume from Little Weaver Creek at a cost of $10,000 in 1851, through which they were able to mine about $100,000 in precious metals. Little Weaver Creek was also the site of Yankee Sawmill, owned and operated by William Warrener. He built the structure of wood, excluding the saw, for about $200. Since going into production in 1854, the Yankee Sawmill produced up to 100,000 feet of lumber annually. In 1855 Warrener built the first bridge across the Trinity River at the site of Big Bar. The bridge connected what was then the Trinity and Humboldt trails.

By 1855 Big Flat boasted a population of about 250. By the following year it consisted of about 400 men, nine married women, and "three marriageable ditto."[73] By 1858 the population was probably 250 men, nine women, and "three pretties."[74]

Other California mining camps were called Big Flat — one in Calaveras County, another in Del Norte County.

Big Oak Flat was first called **Savage Diggings** by founder James Savage, who settled in the area in 1849 or 1850 with his Indian wives and several Indian servants.[75] The town's name was changed when a large[76] oak tree which squatted in the center of the camp was felled for gold that clung to its roots.[77]

The placers were rich, perhaps yielding more than $25 million.[78]

But the town of around 3,000 dwindled in size.

The Odd Fellows Hall stands as one of the most interesting remnants of the past.

Big Rock Creek is a Butte County mining camp; but little information was gleaned about its history.

Birchville was one of four hydraulic mining towns in the Nevada City area.[79]

It was probably founded in the early 1850s and survived as long as hydraulic mining was legal. But with the state ban on this mining technique, the town faded and vanished. Some hydraulic pits, most of them filled with water, can be seen at the townsite.

Bird was a Placer County mining camp founded about 1850 and named for a local storekeeper named Mr. Bird. One of the few scraps of information about the camp is that a thirty-three-ounce lump of gold was found there in 1855. **Birds Valley** was a Placer County camp near Michigan Bluffs. The camp hit its heyday in 1850 but died about 1855.

Bishop was named for Bishop Creek, which in turn was named for Samuel A. Bishop, a stockman who drove the first herd of cattle into Owens Valley and settled there in 1861. Two years later settlers came into Owens Valley in such numbers that the village of Bishop sprang up near Bishop's ranch.

Mining followed later, about 1916, with the discovery of tungsten. Mining continued until 1960, with the Pine Creek mine being the richest producer. This mine was also the principal source of gold in the district, as gold was a byproduct of the tungsten mining. Another mine was exclusively a gold producer, but it has been barren since 1938.

Total gold production in the Wilshire-Bishop Creek district through 1959 was between 75,000 and 100,000 ounces.[80]

Although no longer a mining center, Bishop continues to serve as a supply and outfitting point for the area. The lofty Sierra Nevada mountains tower nearby.

Bismarck was located near, and was contemporary with, the restored ghost town of **Calico.**

Colemanite[81] was found near Bismarck and was mined until more profitable deposits were found elsewhere. As mining ceased, so did Bismarck.

Bismarck is remembered by some as being the home of Dorsey, a dog who carried mail to and from neighboring Calico. Answers to questions of how, why, and when a canine substituted for a human mailman seem to have been lost in dim history.[82]

Black Bear was the name of a settlement that grew up near the Black Bear mine. Located between **Sawyers Bar** and **Cecilville,** the camp had a post office established in 1869.

The rich Black Bear quartz mine may have produced $3 million in gold before it was closed in 1932. The post office was discontinued in 1941.

The Black Bear mine — *Siskiyou County Historical Society.*

Blue Canyon was along Blue Canyon Creek, northeast of Dutch Flat. It was named for miner Jim Blue.

Blue Mountain City was on the Licking Fork, a tributary of the South Fork of the Mokelumne River. Silver and gold were mined in the area.

Blue Nose was a mining camp north of Somes Bar. It was named for the Blue Nose gold mine.

Blue Tent grew up northeast of Nevada City and created a mining flap for a while. Quartz and hydraulic mining were undertaken there.

Bodfish is situated northeast of Bakersfield on Highway 178. The settlement was probably named for pioneer placer miner Orlando Bodfish.

The extant town was a boom camp during the Kern River Canyon gold rush in the 1880s.

Bodie was located on the eastern side of the Sierras, north of Mono Lake, a few miles west of the Nevada border. Gold was discovered probably just west of the present townsite in 1859 by Waterman S. Body (or Bodye, Bodie, or Bodey) and three companions. A mining district was organized on July 10, 1860. Controversy wages as to why the town was spelled "Bodie," but most authorities seem to agree that it was a deliberate change by town residents to insure proper pronunciation of the camp's name.

Lack of capital forced the sale and consolidation of claims during 1861-62. One result was the formation of the Bodie Bluff Consolidated Mining Company, with Leland Stan-

Part of the "ghost town" at Bodfish.

ford as president. When the company failed, the Empire Company of New York took control — but it failed, too. It seemed as if Bodie's death were inevitable.

However, in 1876 the Bodie mine was developed and the town was revitalized. By 1879 the population was 10,000 plus. Other mines, such as the Standard and Bulmer, became good producers.[83] During the late 1870s and most of the 1880s, Bodie became one of the richest mining camps in the West.

The need for wood as fuel in the mines required 45,000 cords per year.[84] Many of the wood camp laborers were Chinese. It is claimed that at one time Bodie had a larger Chinese population than any other California settlement except San Francisco.[85]

The town's founder met an unfortunate end shortly after discovering the gold. He headed for Monoville in the autumn of 1859 to stock up on supplies for the winter. On the return trip he and E. S. Taylor were caught in a blizzard, and Body became exhausted. Taylor left his partner wrapped in a blanket and went for help. When Taylor returned to where he thought he had left his companion, there was no trace of Body. The following spring the body was found, taken to Bodie, and laid to rest on the hill overlooking the townsite.[86] But Body's body was not destined to rest. The *Daily Free Press* reported on December 3, 1879 that "Someone left the gate of the cemetery open last night and let in a terrible draft of cold air. It was so cold, that Bill Bodey got up and shut the gate with such a slam that both hinges were broken off. The residents of that section state that his language, on the occasion, [was] frightful." It was probably about this time that the settlement was named, or renamed, in his honor.

The town blossomed, perhaps to 20,000 residents by 1878.[87] Sixty saloons, gambling halls, several breweries, and five[88] newspapers sprang up and prospered.[89] It was a wild town, spawning such well-deserved phrases as "Bad Man from Bodie" and "Shooters Town." Some have said that a hanging or a church will kill any mining town. Bodie had both — and much more. Most of the whorehouses were located along Virgin Alley, where such demimondes as Big Bonanza, Beautiful Doll, Big Nell, Bull Con Josie, and Rosa May plied the oldest of all

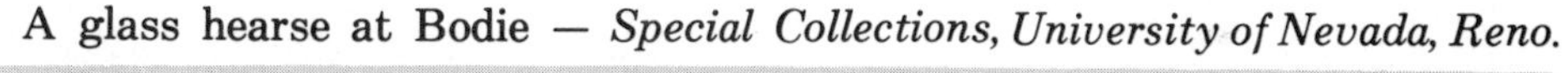
A glass hearse at Bodie — *Special Collections, University of Nevada, Reno.*

professions. Here "Madame Moustache" (Eleanor Dumont) dealt 21 and keno, and ultimately killed herself. The *Reno Weekly Gazette*[90] opined that Bodie had more saloons in a given length than any thoroughfare in the world. That same year (1879) a *Reno Weekly Gazette* correspondent described the settlement as a little city strung along "like an elongated banana on a cord."[91] The year 1879 was also when the Odd Fellows Lodge was established. The Miners Union had been founded two years earlier.

Although several writers have commented at length about Bodie and the people who lived there (including well-known correspondent J. Ross Brown[92]), others wrote *to* Bodie. A Bodie newspaper claims that a letter was written to officials in the town. It went like this:

> KIND AND RESPECTED CIR: — I see in the paper that a man named John Sipes was attacted and et up by a bare whose kubs he was trying to get when the she bare came up and stopt him by eating him in the mountains near your town.
>
> What I want to know is did it kill him ded or was he only partly et up and is he from this plaice and all about the bar. I don't know but he is a distant husband of mine. My first husband was of that name and I supposed he was killed in the war, but the name of the man the bare et being the same I thought it might be him all and I ought to know if he wasn't killed either in the war or by the bare, for I have been married twise and there ought to be divorse papers got out by him or me if the bare did not eat him up. If it is him you will know by his having six toes on his left foot.
>
> He also had a spreadeagle tattooed on his front chest and a anker on his right arm which you will know him by if the bare did not eat up these sines of it being him.
>
> Find out all you kin about him without him knowing what it is for, that is if the bare did not eat him all up. If it did I don't see as you kin do anything and you needn't to trouble.
>
> Please ancer back.
>
> P.S. — Was the bare killed? Also was he married again and did he have propty wuth me laying claim to?[93]

By 1893[94] Bodie's Standard Consolidated Mining Company had electric power. The Standard company built the facility to power

its mill and mine, but ultimately homes and businesses in town were allowed to share the electricity.[95] Later, a more modern hydroelectric system provided power for Bodie and other area towns.

But by 1883 the settlement had begun to decline, with all but two mines being forced to close. Gold production did continue, however, until 1955, totalling about 1,456,300 ounces.[96]

Lessees tried to mine during the 1920s, and the sometimes-successful Roseklip mine was worked from 1935 or 1936 until 1942. The Standard mine was sporadically operated until World War II.

A fire in June 1932 destroyed perhaps two-thirds of the business district,[97] accelerating the town's decline. In 1962 the State Department of Parks and Recreation was handed the responsibility of administering Bodie as a State Historic Park.[98]

Bodie, no date — *Society of California Pioneers.*

A portrait of Bodie.

A portrait of Bodie.

Bondville, east of Benton Mills, seems to revolve around Stephen Bond, the camp's storekeeper and postmaster. It was a placer camp.

Boulder Flat was probably a short-lived mining camp northeast of Bridgeport. The camp was named for the large boulders found in the vicinity. The gold and silver camp dates to the 1880s.

Bowling Green was a "here today-gone tomorrow" camp near Rough and Ready. What scant evidence is available seems to indicate that it was a gold mining camp.

Box (Letter Box) was a Plumas County trading center for miners located near the Butte County line. Its post office served miners for the five years of its existence.

Brandy City was a Sierra County mining camp on Cherokee Creek. Some evidence suggests that the camp was first known as **Strychnine City**.

Brandy Flat was a Nevada County mining camp near Alpha.

Branson City was established just east of Julian. It appears to have been named for Lewis Branson, a lawyer who founded the town.

Bridgeport was a mining town nurtured in part by the Dunderberg mine twelve miles to the south. The mine was discovered by Charles Snyder about 1870 and later passed into the hands of several persons from Carson City, Nevada.

A water-powered twenty-stamp mill, a concentrator, and chlorination and cyanide plants were operated on the property at various times. The real estate changed hands frequently, but mining was not successful.

Bridgeport deserves a niche in history, not as a mining town, but rather as a county seat. Apparently officials determined that the county seat of Mono County — Aurora — was in Nevada. Records were moved to Bridgeport, and a courthouse was built to house them. It still stands.

The bridge at Bridgeport — *Dick Elke, Compass Maps, Modesto, California.*

A view of Bridgeport, contrasting the automobile and the wagon — *Society of California Pioneers.*

Briggsville was west of Redding. Some gold mining occurred there, but the camp was better known as a lime producer.

Brown's Ravine was a mining camp of short duration north of Oroville.

Browns Valley was located about one dozen miles northeast of Marysville.

Brownsville was named for pioneer settler Alfred Brown. The placer camp near Murphys hit its heyday in the 1850s and 1860s. Besides this Calaveras County Brownsville, there may have been one so named in Siskiyou County on the East Fork of the Salmon River. Additionally, a Brownsville in Yuba County was a mining settlement.

There probably was a mining settlement just east of Grass Valley called **Brunswick.**

Buchanan Hill was north of Oroville, in Butte County.

Buck (Bucks Ranch) was a Plumas County camp on Bucks Creek. The site is now inundated by the waters of Buck's dam and reservoir.

Buckeye grew up north of Redding. It probably traces its founding to a Mr. Johnson, who discovered quartz in the area.

Buckman Springs is between Jacumba and Pine Valley, east of El Cajon, in extreme southern California.

Little was learned of the settlement's history, except that the town was named for Colonel Amos Buckman, who prospected for gold in the area in the 1860s.

There were two **Buena Vistas** in California: one in Amador County, south of Ione; one in Nevada County, on the Colfax to Grass Valley road. The Amador County camp was also known as **The Corners.** The Nevada County camp may have been also known as **Buena Vista Ranch.**

Buena Vista Camp was a gold mining town near Knights Ferry, in Stanislaus County.

Buena Vista Hill was northeast of Mokelumne Hill. It appears to have been primarily a hydraulic gold mining camp.

Bullard's Bar is a Yuba County mining camp on the North Fork of the Yuba River near Fosters Bar. It was apparently named for Dr. Bullard of Brooklyn, New York. The camp was probably established in 1849. Less than ten years later, only a few Chinese inhabited the camp. Bullard's reservoir has submerged Bullard's Bar into a watery grave.

Burns Camp was located southwest of Hornitos. It was named for John and Robert Burns, who settled there in 1847. Gold was found on their ranch, perhaps in 1849.

Burnt Ranch is a Trinity County town on Highway 299 west of Weaverville. It was probably named for an Indian village that had been burned by miners. The town still exists.

Butchers Ranch, east of Auburn, is also known as **Butchers.** A number of large gold nuggets were found in the area, including one which weighed twenty pounds.

Butte City was a roistering gold camp in the 1850s.

The settlement was named for nearby butte formations.

One report claims that building stones for Butte City were quarried in China, shipped by clipper ship to San Francisco, and hauled by mule to Butte City.

The old Benoist Store (later named the Ginnochio Store) remains, built in 1854 or 1856.

Gudde (page 54) points out that an August 15, 1852 issue of the Volcano *Weekly Ledger* reported some "non-English speaking" people building a store, which may have been the Ginnochio Store.

Butt Valley was a Plumas County mining camp south of Lake Almanor. It was named for early-day miner Horace Butts.

Byrnes Ferry was established at a ferry crossing where the Copperopolis–Mountain Pass road crossed the Stanislaus River. The mining camp was established in 1849 or 1850.

Calaveritas is southeast of San Andreas. Its adobe ruins indicate that it was once populated by Mexican miners. The camp was probably founded in 1849. By 1850 an Upper Calaveritas and a Lower Calaveritas existed. The former still survives; the latter has vanished.

Calico was spawned by silver mining although both gold and silver were mined in the area as early as 1880.

The town was probably named for the calico-like hills nearby.

Calico about 1890 — *The Huntington Library.*

One of the most unusual businesses in the mining town was a combination boot and shoe shop with adjoining bar.[99]

There were a few uncommon things about Calico: it was home for Dorsey, a dog who may have been one of the nation's few canine mail-carriers; and its "fun houses" were in the middle of the main business district rather than on the outskirts of town.

But it also had some typical places like the Hyena House Hotel, described as consisting of barrel staves on the outside and holes-in-the-rocks on the inside.[100] Here Bill Harpold served breakfasts of chile beans and whisky. And here, too — typically — the whites frequently molested the Chinese; but here — not typically — the Chinese once fought back and were thenceforth left alone.

In later years (just before the turn of the century),[101] calcium borate was discovered east of Calico, and the Borate & Daggett Railroad was built between Daggett and the Calico Mountains to bring deposits in for processing. As borate mining increased and then levelled off, silver mining declined, and the town began to die.

Calico has been "restored" to some semblance of its former self, and today is a tourist attraction.

Callahan (Callahan's Ranch) is at the south end of Scott Valley. It was founded by M. B. Callahan in 1851. First called **Callahan's Ranch,** it is now simply Callahan.

Callahan has the distinction of being the location of the first stage station in Siskiyou County. The station was erected in 1854, when the area was swarming with gold seekers, most of whom bought supplies at the settlement.

Much of the charm and many of the buildings of the gold rush remain.

Camanche (sometimes spelled Comanche) was once called **Limerick.** Much dredging was carried on in the area. However, with the filling of Camanche reservoir, the town went under water.

Callahan — *Siskiyou County Historical Society.*

Cambria can be found northwest of Atascadero. It was established as a copper camp, probably in 1863, and later became a quicksilver camp.

The extant settlement is along coastal Highway 1.

Cameron was a gold camp that reached its apex during 1882-83. The camp, twelve miles north of Bridgeport, was located in Frying Pan Canyon. The Mono County camp was in the Patterson mining district. The camp was first called **Newburg,** but when the post office was established August 6, 1887, the name was changed to Cameron in honor of Robert A. Cameron, who mined in the area from 1897 to 1900.

Little remains of the camp. Most of its structures were moved to Clinton and Bridgeport when mining failed.

Camp Cady, about twenty miles east of Daggett, was originally a military post; at one time it had a stamp mill.

Camp Opera was southeast of Ione. It's not known when the camp began, but by 1853 it was on the upswing, and by 1857 or so it was at its apex. The Mexican settlement, however, began to die in the late 1850s and early 1860s. Some claim it was a hideout for outlaw Joaquin Murieta.

The Mexican-born camp of **Campo Seco** reached its peak during the 1860s. The Penn copper mine was the largest producer, although some gold has been taken from the Mokelumne River in the district. Gold has also been recovered as a byproduct of copper mining, most of it coming from the Penn mine, in operation between 1899 and 1919. In 1937 the mine was dewatered, and copper was recovered from the mine water.[102] Gold was mined from the Penn during the 1940s, but after World War II the mine was closed.

The two-story sandstone and fieldstone buildings of the original Adams Express Company remain at this hamlet west of San Andreas. Some remnants of Chinatown can still be found.

Another camp named Campo Seco, or perhaps simply **Seco,** was located in Tuolumne County, one mile south of Jamestown.

Camp Salvado was a Tuolumne County camp immediately east of Chinese Camp. Early miners were Chinese who were driven out by white miners, who were, in turn, driven out by exhausted placers. The Chinese returned to re-mine the area, but in time they left, too.

Camptonville, southwest of Downieville along Highway 49, was named for Robert Campton, an early blacksmith. The placer and hydraulic mining town was founded in 1850 as a stop on the Nevada City–Downieville road. It became a gold boom town in 1852. Although Camptonville was moved twice to make room for hydraulic mining operations, and was almost destroyed by fire several times, it has survived.

Three monuments are situated on the western edge of town. One is in memory of Lester Pelton, inventor of the Pelton wheel used in electric power generation. Another marker is in memory of William "Bull" Meek, a stage driver, Wells Fargo agent, teamster, merchant, and mule skinner. The third monument is dedicated to Robert Campton, described by the sponsoring E. Clampus Vitus group as "the popular and sturdy blacksmith" for whom Camptonville is named.

An E. Clampus Vitus marker dedicated to Robert Campton, the "popular and sturdy blacksmith" for whom Camptonville was named.

A vintage Camptonville abode.

The Masons erected this marker in Camptonville in honor of Lester Allen Pelton, who invented the Pelton water wheel on this spot in 1878.

Whether "Ragged Ass" was a sobriquet or the actual initial name for **Canon City** is a mystery. The camp may have also been called **Jackass.** Nearby was **Mill Town** (Junction City), which, along with Canon City, was on Canon Creek.

The camp was in a primitive, hostile part of Trinity County northwest of Weaverville, which by 1894 had not even been surveyed.

Isaac Cox observed Canon City firsthand, and claims that the town was first settled by J. W. Statler in 1851. Cox wrote that the camp "was thrown open to this vale of pick-pocketing and humbug in the year of our Lord 1851, by one J. W. Statler, from Ohio; but no excitement, without which no mining locality is established, shook the canon's peace before the fall of 1852. During the hard and snowy winter of 1852 and 1853, extraordinary riches were discovered, and the miners flocked in in great numbers, and a scarcity of food ensued, and many starved."[103] After arguing with himself about whether his preceding statement was accurate, Cox continued with a highly artificial writing style that was considered derigueur by some writers. He thought the Canon City prices reasonable and gave examples, suggesting that the supposed food scarcity was overstated. He related this tale: "One company, consisting of four men, pronounced sentence of death, upon two feline companions to satisfy the demands of a super-supreme Higher Law, dogs can no more elude than Negro-worshippers and fire-eaters. What relation is there now between those prices for food and the dogs' meat story? On one hand there must have been some scarcity; however, the suffering cannot be credited, and as it is not charged that the two poor dogs did suffer the penalty of starving man or brute, the yarn has been spun off, as if any one might not anticipate the dread calamity a year hence by killing dog's meat today. Be this as it may, nominal money-value of necessaries as a measure of plenty and scarcity is extremely defective, and, with regard to starvation, the extreme of the same thing, even labor, the standard of all values, ceases to be so. From 1853, when the great rush was at Canon City, it has continued to improve; however, with some fluctuation in the population."[104]

The population of Canon City yoyoed. In 1855 it was estimated at about 400; in 1857, 200; in 1858, 300.

A fiery conflagration levelled most of the camp in August 1855, but the town managed to survive — for a while.

In his quaint writing style Isaac Cox criticized Canon City's communication. He quipped, "Facilities for intercommunication with the outside world might be supposed to be a first-rate arrangement, but surprise and regret will prevail when you are informed that it is of the meanest order. There is a trail to be sure, to the river, and they love to say that it connects Canon City and Weaverville, and so this trail does in the same way Shasta Butte is a connecting link between San Francisco and Salt Lake City, by way of Walker's kingdom, Nicaragua."[105]

Cantil, west of Randsburg, was a railroad town, but its post office served several El Paso Mountain mining camps.

Canton was near Coloma. During most of its brief existence, it appears to have been inhabited mostly by Chinese miners.

Canyon was an El Dorado County camp named for Big Canyon Creek.

Cariboo was a Plumas County mining camp on the North Fork of the Feather River.

Carlyle (Carlile) was a mining camp near Meadow Lake. It was probably named for prospector Thomas Carlyle.

A mining camp called **Carrier's Gulch** was established in the Hayfork area. Cox, in *Annals of Trinity County,* indicated that during the wet season the town afforded employment for "a considerable number of miners."[106]

Cox also reported that Carrier Gulch did not "conform to the rule of medium ground and good wages, as 'strikes' of unqualified riches [had] been brought to light."[107] Cox figured these "riches" at about ten to twelve dollars per day.

Cox reported that in 1858 the camp consisted of Hall's store and one butcher and one blacksmith shop.

Kellogg's Diggings was a couple of miles below Carrier's, but it may not have been a town.

Carrolton was a Placer County gold camp on the North Fork of the American River.

Carrville (Carrs, Carville), north of Trinity Center, was probably named for James E. Carr, an early settler who owned the Blythe, Upper and Lower Buckeye and Dave Hall, Nash, Abram, and Monroe mines. The dominant mine, however, was the Altoona quicksilver mine (a consolidation of the Trinity, Altoona, and Central mining claims) one dozen miles northeast of Carrville.[108] The mine was operated from 1875 to 1879, closed and reopened in 1894, and produced again until 1911. A mine fire in 1902 apparently destroyed part of the reduction plant. The mine was reopened in 1929 and closed and opened again in 1937. The mine has been operated spasmodically ever since.

Carson Hill was fathered by James H. Carson, who found gold in the area in August 1848. The story goes that the 180 ounces of gold panned by Carson in ten days were the first of more than $20 million worth to be taken from the Carson Hill mines, mostly from the Morgan.[109]

A good reason for Carson Hill to go down in history was the discovery on November 22, 1854 of the largest piece of gold ever reported in California, taken from the Morgan mine.[110] The 195-pound chunk of gold was valued at $43,534.[111]

Litigation over mining properties, racial strife, highgrading, and other sources of friction developed and festered and occasionally erupted into violence in and around Carson Hill.

Among those to briefly step upon the scene was nabob James G. Fair of Nevada Comstock Lode fame. While at Carson Hill, Fair married the former Tessie Rooney.[112]

Carson Flat, Albany, and **Frogtown** were among the obscure mining camps that briefly flourished in the Carson Hill area.

Carsons (Carson, Carsontown) came into being just west of Mariposa.

Cartago was conceived and nurtured at the southern end of Owens Lake.

It was a company town that housed workers from the lime, soda, and borax plant located in Cartago. When mining operations terminated, the settlement evolved into a railroad town.

Castle Crags, in the Dunsmuir area, may have been a railroad station at the mouth of Soda Creek. Had "Mountain Joe" Doblondy had his way, it would have been a mining camp.

Although Mountain Joe was the first alleged settler, Castle Crags is thought to have been founded in 1843 by Lansford Hastings, who had once camped on the site and built a "fort" of sorts named Hastings' Barracks. Mountain Joe reportedly liked the area, built a house or houses and a hotel there, served as a guide, and fought Indians. And he boasted about Castle Crags.

No evidence suggests that Mountain Joe ever saw a single nugget or flake, but nevertheless, reportedly in the spring of 1855, he convinced prospectors that gold could be found. When the theory proved false, the boomers left, but not before harvesting most of the timber and game in the area. In retaliation, Modoc Indians are thought to have burned the settlement, which pretty much sealed the fate of Castle Crags.

On the other side of the coin, a representative of the Shasta Historical Society writes of Castle Crags: "This is a geologic or natural feature, [and] was neither a mining camp nor a ghost town."[113]

So, it appears as if the mystery of shadowy Castle Crags remains.

Cat Camp was near Camanche in Calaveras County. It was named for Samuel Catts, who owned a trading post there. The gold camp's name was later changed to **Wallace.**

Cat Town was a Mariposa County mining camp, but nothing of its history could be unearthed.

Cave City was east of San Andreas. Gold was probably first found there in 1852.

Cecilville still exists. The Siskiyou County town was named for John Baker Sissel.

Cedar Grove sprouted up east of La Porte.

Centerville was a Butte County mining camp on Butte Creek. It was also the name of a mining camp southeast of Auburn in El Dorado County. Shasta County claims a town of the same name, as does Sierra County. There appears to have been a **Centreville** northwest of Auburn.

Cerro Gordo flourished overlooking Owens Valley near a dead sea called Owens Lake in the Inyo Range.

The first reported strikes in the area were made by Mexican prospectors in 1865 or 1868. Not until later did the "outside world" learn of the rich strikes of what was to become California's greatest producer of silver and lead.

The man responsible for much of the prosperity of Cerro Gordo was mining engineer

Mortimer W. Belshaw. Belshaw shrewdly bought into the Union mine[114] because it was the best source of the lead needed for area smelters. He built a smelter, a toll road, and a water system.

Beginning in 1868 rich ores were freighted from Cerro Gordo in the form of eighty-five-pound bars resembling large, long loaves of bread. Later a tram was built from the mine to the settlement of Keeler. By 1872, $1.5 million a year in bullion had been shipped from Cerro Gordo to Los Angeles. In *Helldorados, Ghosts and Camps of the Old Southwest,* Norman Weis claims that 120 bars of silver-lead amalgam were poured and shipped from the camp each day.

While people like Belshaw were at the height of the "social register" of Cerro Gordo, others resided at the bottom. One such person was "The Fenian," a tough, feared, morally loose woman who has been called the "reigning queen of Cerro Gordo."[115]

She didn't confine her carousing to Cerro Gordo, but even swaggered abroad to such places as Los Angeles. Among other things, she was accused by authorities of beating a man for calling her an Irish dog, and of breaking a boy's harp for his refusal to play a song for her. As a result, she was told to leave town by sundown — and she did. But she later returned to Cerro Gordo and continued her career of terrorizing man and beast.

Inevitably, Cerro Gordo ores gave out, and in 1876 the smelter was closed. The following year fire consumed much of the mining operation and part of the town. The last load of bullion was freighted out by mule team in October 1879. Other mining operations were attempted, but they failed.

Today Cerro Gordo is ghostly. Remains of the smelter still stand, along with the two-story American Hotel (or American House) built in 1871, and several residences and business establishments. But few see the remains locked behind fences of Cerro Gordo — a town that has to be reached via one of the most torturous roads leading to a western mining camp.

Remains of mining activity near Cerro Gordo.

Challenge is still a live, functioning town located east of Oroville, in Yuba County. It is a part of the Brownsville-Challenge-Dobbins mining district, where from 1880 through 1959, about 5,294,600 ounces of gold were taken — 4,387,100 ounces from placers and 907,500 ounces from lode mines.[116]

Chandlerville was northeast of La Porte. Its heyday was in the 1850s, its demise in the 1870s.

Chaparral House seems to have been a Butte County mining camp north of Inskip.

Cherokee, north of Oroville, was named for a band of Cherokee Indian gold miners who migrated to the area from Georgia in 1853. Gudde (page 68) claims that gold may have been discovered there as early as 1849. Wild tales indicate that the area was also rich in diamonds, sapphires, and platinum.

The hydraulic Spring Valley gold mine at Cherokee was fed by about 100 miles of ditches and pipelines built around 1870 to carry water from the Feather River to the mining site.

The operations on Table Mountain caused crop-killing sand to be spread over valley farmlands. When farmers fought the mining operators, the Anti-Debris Act of 1883 forbidding hydraulic mining was passed. By 1906 all mining ceased, and Cherokee became a ghost town. Scars left by the hydraulic giants can still be seen on Table Mountain.

There was also a camp called **Cherokee** in Nevada County, east of North San Juan, reportedly prospected by Cherokee Indians in 1850. Records indicate that a camp of the same name was near the Round Valley dam in Plumas County. An early gold camp called **Cherokee Camp** was a short distance north of Tuolumne.

Paradise, originally known as **Pair-O'-Dice,** is located nearby.

Cherokee in the 1870s — *Nevada County Historical Society.*

A view of Spring Valley and Cherokee Flat Mines —*Butte County Historical Society.*

Chile and its "mutations" were common names in California mining camp lore. There was a **Chili Bar** in El Dorado County in the Placerville area. The place has also been referred to as **Chile Bar, Chilean Bar, Chelalian,** and **Chillean.** There was a **Chili Camp** in Calaveras County; a **Chili Camp** in Tuolumne County; a **Chilie Camp** in Yuba County; and a **Chili** along Chili Gulch in Calaveras County.

A mining camp called **Chimney Hill** may have existed between Cherokee and North Columbia.

The Chinese influence on California mining history and lore was great. Some vestiges of these effects are left in place names. There were a number of **China Bars,** mostly river bars. However, a camp named **China Bar** was located on New River in Trinity County. A **China City** was an Amador County mining camp on the Mokelumne River. **China Flat (Chinese Flat)** grew up east of Downieville. There were at least three **China Towns** in Butte County, and two in Placer County.

Chinese Camp was inhabited by both Chinese and white miners. How the Chinese came to live in the town is a matter of debate. A rather intriguing theory is that the captain of a ship left his vessel in San Francisco Bay and took the Chinese crew to the mining camp.[117] More credence is given to the theory that the town was founded by a small group of Englishmen[118] who imported Chinese to work in the mines. Others claim that the camp was founded by an English ship's Chinese crew, who deserted when they heard the call of gold.[119] In any event, the Chinese population grew to the point that by 1850 — two years after the founding of Chinese Camp — the number of inhabitants may have reached 5,000. The Chinese must have accounted for about one-half the total population. Members of four Chinese companies, or tongs, lived in Chinese Camp. Two tongs "squared off" once, giving the mining town its notoriety.

The battle probably occurred at Six-Bit Gulch. The date: September 26, 1856. The players: 900 men from the Yan Woo Tong and 1,200 members of the Sam Yap (Tu) Tong. The reason for the battle: uncertain.

The conflict — perhaps the first tong war in California — was waged with pikes, shovels, pitchforks, daggers, clubs, a few muskets, and noise — including yelling, screaming, the popping of firecrackers, and the banging of gongs. For two hours the contestants battled. When the dust settled, four were dead and four were wounded. White lawmen rounded up and jailed 250 combatants.

Today, most of the buildings and the entire Chinese population are gone. But several stone buildings dating to early Chinese Camp days remain, including the Wells Fargo & Company's building, the post office, St. Francis Xavier church,[120] and Rosenbloom's store. Also to be seen are occasional "Trees of Heaven" (*Ailanthus*), mute testimony of the "Celestials" who planted and nurtured these hardy trees.

A picturesque Chinese Camp church.

Buildings dating to the 1850s in Chinese Camp. Photo taken in the 1930s — *Collection of Historical Photographs, Title Insurance and Trust Company, Los Angeles.*

The Chinese Camp elementary school.

Chips Flat (Chipsegs Flat) was a Sierra County mining camp located near Minnesota.

Chloride, or Chloride City, is located near the California–Nevada border, southwest of Rhyolite and Beatty, Nevada. It is nestled in a valley in the Funeral Mountain.

Chloride was spawned by the Tonopah–Goldfield mining excitement. Ruins of structures built for personnel of the Chloride Cliff mine are about all that remain in the town that probably expired in 1918.

Chrysopolis was an obscure Inyo County gold and silver mining camp whose post office existed for less than a year (May 1866 to March 1867).

Chub Gulch may have been a mining camp north of Oroville.

City of 76 (Seventy-Six) was named for a company of seventy-six men who mined in the area.

As the crow flies, **Claraville** is about forty miles east of Bakersfield, near the base of Piute Mountain. The camp was probably founded in 1866. Only crumbling ruins mark the townsite, although deserted mining shafts and ruins of a ditch can be found with diligent searching.

Another camp called Claraville was located in Placer County, north of Lake Tahoe. This gold and silver camp flared up, flickered, and died in the span of a few months.

Clinton was east of Jackson and for a short while was known as **Sarahville** or **Sarahsville.** Another camp of the same name was north of Cameron, in Mono County. It appears that the post office at Nevada County's Moores Flat was called Clinton for about three years in the 1850s.

Clio was originally known as **Wash.** The Mohawk Valley camp was a supply and trading center for area miners. The post office was established in 1875 and discontinued in 1904. The following year the camp's name was changed from Wash to Clio.

Relics of the past at Coarsegold.

Coarsegold (Coarse Gold) is south of Yosemite National Park. The town was founded by Texans in 1849 and may have been the first placer camp in Madera County. When the placers gave out, hard-rock mining was developed. The settlement still survives.

Coeur was a Trinity County town that served area miners in the 1880s and 1890s.

Cold Spring was an obscure Placer County camp. It apparently sprang into life and died in the 1850s. Perhaps there was a Sierra County camp called Cold Spring, plus a **Cold Springs** was northwest of Placerville in El Dorado County. The only physical legacy left at any of the camps is at Cold Springs, where a weed-infested graveyard remains.

Coleman City was named for Fred Coleman, a black who discovered gold near Julian. The camp was first known as **Emily City**.

Coleridge was above Sawyers Bar in Trinity County. Most mining in the area occurred just prior to and immediately following the turn of the century.

Colfax, primarily a railroad center, was also instrumental in the growth of area mining camps. It was here that goods were transferred to muleback for the journey to remote camps in the region. Several mines were located nearby, but none were rich.[121]

Initially called **Alden Grove** in 1849, the town was renamed **Illinoistown** in 1850, and finally Colfax around 1869 — in honor of Schuyler Colfax, vice-presidential running mate of Ulysses S. Grant in the election of 1868.

In 1850 a pioneer observer wrote that Colfax (at that time Illinoistown) had two hotels, and that the one kept by E. T. Mendonhall, previously of Iowa, was a place "where a man can always get the worth of his money." He observed, "The excellent landlady never fails to serve up the *eatables* in a palatable manner."[122]

The Morning Star mine, east of Colfax, produced $1,750,000 in ores until 1901, and total production in the district reached about $10 million. The Rising Sun mine, west of Colfax, produced about $2 million in gold.[123]

The facts and fictions of **Coloma,** recounted many times elsewhere, were addressed to some extent in the foreword to this book. Consequently, only a cursory glance will be given to this well-known California mining camp. However, an event that helped to revolutionize a nation and materially influence a large share of the world shouldn't be glossed over lightly — and Coloma was a central part of that saga.

On January 24, 1848, gold was discovered by James W. Marshall in the tailrace of a sawmill on the American River, forty miles from New Helvetia (Sacramento).[124] When owner John Sutter envisioned what might happen in the event of a gold rush, he tried to keep the discovery secret. But the word soon spread, and prospectors wildly rushed in.

The town that grew up near the discovery site became the first white settlement in the foothills of the Sierra Nevada mountains. By summer 1848 Coloma had a large hotel and perhaps as many as 300 frame buildings under construction — mostly made from lumber cut at John Sutter's sawmill. The population was about 2,000, but by 1849 it was 10,000.

Prices were high. Food costs were outrageous, and mining equipment was even higher. Shovels and picks sold for as much as fifty dollars, along with wool shirts and boots.

The town was once described as "a place of marked cards, loaded dice, and false weights."[125] Clearly, all the gold was not "mined" by conventional means. One woman supposedly took in washing at one dollar per load, while her husband worked in the mines. When he returned a month later, he had only half as much gold as she had salvaged from miners' clothing. Cases of merchants wetting thumb and forefinger and thereby getting a larger pinch of gold from a poke were not uncommon. Neither was the practice of growing long fingernails so that more than an average "pinch" of gold dust could be filched.

The story persists about a group of miners that "laid to rest" one of their own. The graveside rites were delivered by a former minister who happened to be long-winded. The restless miners began checking graveside dirt and found it full of gold. The alert minister caught on, dismissed the men, and switched from the Lord's work to his own — with a pan. It has been rumored that the deceased's body was moved to a site containing "just regular old dirt."

But the rich placers soon began to peter out, and the prospectors moved to other places in the Mother Lode country. In 1851 and 1852, so many pulled up stakes that the town began to die. In 1870 only 200 people remained.

The site of the Sutter mill is included in the Marshall gold discovery state historic park. The historical markers and a museum are frequently visited. The jail, the Robert Bell and Bekeart's stores, and the two Chinese stores survive, along with a bronze statue of James Marshall, which points to the site of the gold discovery. An operating reconstruction of Sutter's mill and the cabin of James Marshall round out the attractions of contemporary Coloma.

Gold discoverer James Marshall — *The Huntington Library.*

From an ambrotype entitled "Mining Gold at Coloma," made in 1850 or 1851 — *Society of California Pioneers.*

The reconstructed mill at Coloma.

A five-stamp mill on display at Coloma.

Colorado (Colorow?) was north of Mariposa.

Columbia was a boom town referred to by some as "Gem of the Southern Mines." It has also been called "the richest, noisiest, fastest growing, most spectacularly wicked camp in the Mother Lode."[126]

Probably Mexicans were the first to discover gold in the area. They arrived in 1850 after being driven from Sonora mines by white miners. A short time later a party of men led by Dr. Thaddeus Hildreth camped near the Mexicans. A heavy rain soaked the "gringos" belongings, and while waiting for their blankets to dry, they prospected. The results were encouraging. The party ousted the Mexican prospectors and established what became known as **Hildreth's Diggings.** Within two to four weeks the camp had swelled to six thousand, which portended the fifteen to thirty thousand that would soon reach the diggings. The town was renamed **American Camp;** later, Columbia. By 1853 the town had tried but failed to become the state capital.

Four particularly large gold nuggets valued at $8,500, $6,500, $5,265, and $5,000 were found in the area.[127] A total of $87 million[128] in gold may have been taken from Columbia-area mines — and more may still exist. It's rumored that St. Ann's Church, a red brick building, sits on gold-rich land, but the so-called profane miners stopped short of digging on the sacred church ground.

From 1853 through 1855, Columbia mines shipped about $100,000 in gold every week through the Wells Fargo and Company's facilities.

Water shortages continually plagued Columbia. It appears that the lack of water for drinking and bathing didn't particularly upset some, but its absence for mining was considered catastrophic. When miners tired of hauling their gravels to the meagre water supplies in nearby creeks, water was brought to the gravels by flume from neighboring Matelot Gulch, twenty miles away. But investors in the system, which had cost about $200,000,[129] worked themselves out of business by charging exorbitant rates. In 1855 the defiant miners lowered prices by forming a company and digging their own ditch.

On July 10, 1854 a $500,000 fire almost brought Columbia from the height of mining excitement to its knees. Another fire followed in 1857.[130] The rich deposits declined. In March 1867 the *Mining and Scientific Press* described the settlement as being in a state of "almost total desertion," where only a few graying gaffers remained.

The town still stands as perhaps the best example of early Mother Lode architecture, with such structures remaining as the St. Ann's Catholic Church, the Wells Fargo Express Office, the D. O. Mills Building, Stage Driver's Retreat, Fallon House, the Gold Nugget Saloon, the Springfield Brewery, Tun Sing Company Building, and the Masonic and Odd Fellows halls. The state administers the properties, and the site is a popular tourist attraction.

Another camp called Columbia was located north of Providence in San Bernardino County. The mining camp had a post office for only about one year.

Restored Columbia

The Wells Fargo office, Columbia, California, about 1872 — *Wells Fargo Bank History Room.*

Martinez was a camp just east of Columbia. It was founded in 1850 by Dona Josepha Martinez, a wealthy Mexican senora who wanted to get wealthier. The record isn't clear if her wish came true.

Italian Bar was northeast of Columbia; it was named for Joaquin de Lucca, an organ-grinder born in Nervi, Italy.

French Camp, east of Columbia, was founded by Charlie Maisson and five French companions. The founding year was probably 1851.

Springfield was built near Columbia and sprang to a population of perhaps 4,000 by 1851.

Columbia Bar was south of Jackson. Initial discoveries were apparently made by Mexicans, who were soon driven off by white miners.

Butte, El Dorado, and Tuolumne counties all claim gold mining camps called **Columbia Flat.** The Butte County camp was along the Middle Fork of the Feather River and was probably also known as **Columbiaville.** Its heyday was during the late 1850s. The El Dorado County camp was near Kelsey and may have also been known as **Lawrenceberg.** Tuolumne County's Columbia Flat was located near Columbia.

Confidence is said to have grown up between the Nevada state line and Bishop.[131] It served as a trading center for area mines and lumber operations and owed its name to the nearby Confidence mine, which produced about $4,250,000 in gold.

Although the camp called Confidence in the Bishop area could not be verified, Confidence in Tuolumne County could be. The camp was about twelve miles east of Columbia and was named for the nearby Confidence mine. The town apparently began in 1853. The Confidence mine may have produced in excess of $4 million in gold.

Contreras was situated a short distance southeast of Volcano. The camp seems to have been named for Pablo Contreras, one of several Mexicans who worked arrastres and mills in the area.

Cooks Bar was founded perhaps in 1849 west of Michigan Bar. The camp was named for Dennis Cook, who had a trading post there.

Cool was an early placer camp. Limestone has also been mined in the vicinity by the Cave Valley Lime Company, the California Rock and Gravel Company, and the Cragco Company.

Remains of quarries and kilns can be detected. Building foundations at Cool were made of the same material that was burned in the nearby limestone kilns.

Several modern business establishments mark this small town near Auburn.

Coolgardie was a johnny-come-lately on the California mining scene, having been established about 1900. Its site is about twenty miles north of Barstow. It was a short-lived camp.

Coon Creek was an early Placer County gold camp northwest of Ophir. Its life span covered four or five years.

Coon Hollow may have been a mining town southwest of Placerville. Although the mystery camp can't be proved to have existed, the rich diggings of the Coon Hollow mine (about $10 million) are not generally disputed.

Coopers Flat grew up adjacent to Jamestown.

One **Copper City** arrived on the mining scene in the 1880s, flourished during the next decade or so, fizzled, and died. It is located twenty-four miles east of Atolia, but because it lies within a naval ordnance test station area, it is closed to the public.

Another **Copper City** is a Shasta County copper mining town. The Bully Hill copper mine and smelter perches at the edge of Shasta Lake. The main settlement associated with Bully Hill is inundated by Shasta Lake.

Little else was ferreted out about this camp where W. L. Carter published the weekly newspaper, the *Pioneer,* from April 1864 to May 1866.

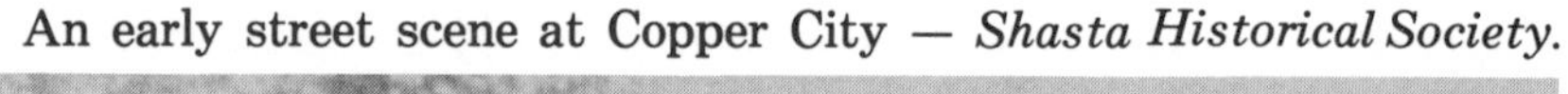

An early street scene at Copper City — *Shasta Historical Society.*

Bully Hill — *Shasta Historical Society.*

Copperopolis, a supply and transportation center, served as the fulcrum for the copper seesaw which alternately attracted and repelled many prospectors during the 1860s and 70s. Much of the town was built of brick hauled from Columbia when that settlement appeared to be falling into decay.

The peak population of Copperopolis may have reached 2,000 in 1868.

Although copper deposits were discovered in the Salt Springs Valley as early as 1852 by a man named McCarty, he was seeking gold and didn't want to be bothered with copper. He ultimately determined, however, that copper was better than nothing, so he returned in 1861 and helped found Copperopolis.

Between 1862 and 1865 Copperopolis was the principal copper-producing area in the nation.[132] In 1866 a drop in copper prices dealt a crippling blow to the town, and the next year a fierce fire levelled much of the settlement. A raise in copper prices in the early 1870s revived some mining activity, but by 1872 the mines were abandoned.

Some stories say that the biggest single gold shipment ever handled by Wells, Fargo & Company on a Mother Lode run was consigned to Copperopolis from Sonora. The shipment was supposedly valued at $190,000. A few miles from Copperopolis the coach hit a pothole in the road, and the 900-pound load of gold broke the coach frame, scattering the bullion on the trail.[133]

Poet-robber Black Bart (Charles Bolton) also figures into the warp and woof of Copperopolis lore. It was on November 3, 1883 that Black Bart concluded his "highwayman" career near Copperopolis. The Wells Fargo coach that was held up by Bolton contained $4,815 in gold[134] in a steel treasure box bolted to the floor. Not long after the robbery near Copperopolis, Black Bart was arrested in San Francisco and convicted. He was the last of the colorful highwaymen to hold up stagecoaches bringing treasures from the Mother Lode or Virginia City, Nevada, bonanzas.

A few original structures remain, including the Federal Armory, the warehouse and office of the Copper Consolidated Mining Company, and the brick Odd Fellows Hall.

Stagecoach robber Black Bart — *Wells Fargo Bank History Room.*

Copperopolis.

The Old Corner Saloon at Copperopolis.

Cordua Bar was northwest of Smartsville in Yuba County. It was named for Theodor Cordua, who ran a trading post there.

Cottonville was a Mariposa County placer camp named for G. T. Cotton, who mined the area in 1849.

Cottonwood came into existence as a miners' trade center near Redding.

At one time the community was located on the south bank of Cottonwood Creek, in what is now Tehama County, where it was a pack train stop.

Now the thriving farm community is located on the north bank of the Cottonwood.

The location of another **Cottonwood** is uncertain. The camp, southwest of Barstow, sported an ore mill. The place may once have been known as **Point of Timbers.**

Coulterville was first known as **Banderita** (Bandereta), either for the small red bandanas worn by the first Mexican settlers[135] or for the flag that hung in front of a store.[136] The town was later christened **Maxwellville** (of Maxwell Creek Diggings or Maxwell's Creek), but in 1872 the name was changed to Coulterville (or Coulter's Ville) for George W. Coulter, who set up a store at the site in 1850.[137] Coulter also built a hotel which is still standing today. Water for the hotel was pumped from a well by two dogs who powered a forty-foot wooden water wheel.[138]

During its prime, Coulterville probably contained 1,000 Chinese and 3,000 white inhabitants. Shirley Sargent, in *Mariposa County Guidebook,* puts the population at 5,000, including 1,000 Chinese and 1,500 Mexicans.

A quartz mill was built one mile below the town at a cost of $80,000. A contemporary observer wrote that "The Engine is from England, of eighty horse power, and works finely, and the prospect is that the Mill will be successful."[139] It apparently was, and its thundering stamps worked ores from several hardrock mines, mostly from the Mary Harrison.

Parallel with many mining camps, Coulterville suffered from the ravages of fires. Three struck the luckless settlement, the last, in 1899, being the most memorable, for it signalled what has been termed the village's last and perhaps the country's shortest "gold rush."[140] Remains of burned walls containing cached gold coins and dust were being used to fill potholes in Coulterville streets. When the first heavy rain exposed the hidden gold in the refilled street holes, a minor gold rush resulted as citizens took to the chuckholes to try their luck at finding instant riches. They found little or no gold, but their dug-up streets became impassable from their actions.

Although Coulterville once had a considerable Chinese population, the only real reminder of the Chinese influence is the Sun Sun Wo store, built in 1851 out of adobe. The Wells Fargo office (once run by Nelson Cody, brother of "Wild Bill"), the jail, the Wagoner store, and a hotel still stand as relics of "old" Coulterville.

Remains of a mill in the Coulterville-Mariposa area.

The Sun Sun Wo general merchandise store in Coulterville.

The combined Wells Fargo & Company express office and Pepper's Trading Post at Coulterville.

Cox Bar (or Cox's Bar) was a couple of miles west of Downieville along the North Fork of the Yuba River. Trinity County boasted a place of the same name on the Trinity River. That site is now at Big Bar.

Coyoteville (Kitaville, Kiota Diggins, Coyota City) is now part of Nevada City. The camp was probably named after the mining method of burrowing into the rich deposits. Other camps known as Coyoteville were in El Dorado County, between Bridgeport and Cedarville; and in Sierra County, west of Downieville. They still exist.

Crackerjack popped up on the mining scene southwest of Cave Springs, northwest of Baker. When it made its debut is undetermined. It appeared to have reached its zenith during 1907-08 and was deserted by 1918.

A few mouldering remains can be found, but the search is hardly worth it.

Craycroft appears to have been a camp located between Downieville and Goodyears Bar.

Crescent Mills was a mill town as well as a supply, trading, and transportation center for area mines.

Cromberg developed on the Middle Fork of the Feather River north of Johnsville. It was a supply center for hydraulic miners in the area.

Curtisville (Curtis) was a Sonora-area gold camp. The town had a post office for about three years, but has long since disappeared.

Cushenbury City (Cushionberry) was east of Holcomb Valley. It was named for John Cushenbury.

Cut-Eye Fosters Bar (Upper Fosters Bar?) was probably named for Cut-eye Foster, a horse thief who used a gang of Indians to steal for him.

Cuyamaca, south of Julian, was a mining camp probably founded around 1871. Very little of its background could be unearthed.

Daggett was a shipping point for the gold and silver ores extracted from area mines. It has also been classified as a silver mining camp. The town still exists east of Barstow.

The camp was named for John Daggett, California's lieutenant governor from 1883 to 1887. Daggett is credited with mapping the town and building its first house.

Three towns with the name of **Dale** appeared and then disappeared from the California mining scene in the Twenty-Nine Palms area.

Old Dale was established east of Twenty-Nine Palms early in the 1880s. It was kept alive until the early 1900s by ores from the Virginia Dale mine. At that time the mining excitement shifted southeast to New Dale. Yet another camp, Dale the Third, grew up near New Dale.

By the beginning of World War II, all three locations were virtually abandoned, although some work was carried on at New Dale in the 1930s. Dale the Third is the most visible of the trio, with a few old houses and walls still in evidence.

The tumbledown Stone Hotel at Daggett.

"Old Dinah," the steam tractor used to haul borax from the Calico Mountains to Daggett. This view was taken at Borate about 1895 — *U.S. Borax.*

The main street of Daggett about 1890 — *U.S. Borax.*

The locomotive "Francis" on the Borate and Daggett Railroad sometime after 1888 — *U.S. Borax.*

Damascus was a short distance southeast of Dutch Flat. It was first called **Strongs Diggings** for Dr. D. W. Strong when it was founded in 1852. In 1856 the name was changed to Damascus.

Dana (Dana Village) was a Mono County settlement in the Tioga district. It was named for its view of Mount Dana.

Dark Canyon was north of Oroville.

Darwin was named for Dr. Darwin French, who discovered silver and lead deposits while prospecting in the Coso Range, twelve miles south of what became Darwin. The town probably was established in 1874.

By 1875 Darwin had two smelters, 200 houses, and over 700 people. By the following year, the town contained five smelters and more than 1,000 citizens.

One of the smelters was closed in 1876. A couple of years later more of the population left for other rich strikes. In 1878 a fierce labor dispute broke out, further crippling the shrinking town.[141]

Darwin was revitalized in the late 1940s when the Anaconda Company mined lead on nearby Mount Ophir. Ruins of the Defiance smelter remain at Darwin, along with a deserted business section of town. Remains of a large company town above Darwin are truly ghostly.

Darwin.

Dawlytown was a Butte County camp along the Middle Fork of the Feather River. It was named for a storekeeper named Dawly.

Daylors (Daylors Ranch, Dayler's Ferry) was a Sacramento County settlement in the Jackson area.

The first prospecting in the **Deadwood** area was done by a man named Britton, who was seeking placer deposits. In 1872 George Klein, a placer miner, found the first quartz ledge, which he dubbed the Bismarck. Later he discovered the Montezuma quartz mine. He erected an arrastre in 1873, later he added another. The camp near the Trinity-Shasta County line seemed assured of a long, prosperous future.

Other area mines — including the Last Chance, Shafter, Monte Christo, Little Vein, McDonald, Brunswick, Celebrated Backbone, Barted, Enterprise, Dreadnought, Lappin, Niagara, and the Three Brothers group — were paled in comparison to the rich Brown Bear mine, mill, and camp discovered in 1875. The mine has grossed between $8 million and $10 million.

At its peak, Deadwood may have had between 400 and 500 people. It was on the daily stage route from Redding to Weaverville.

As the mines were worked out, Deadwood lost its post office in 1915. The Brown Bear mine, northeast of Lewiston, was active intermittently from 1875 to 1950.

Besides the Deadwood in Trinity County, Nevada, Placer, Plumas, Sierra, Siskiyou, and Yuba counties claimed camps of the same name. Nevada County's Deadwood was located a couple of miles from Nevada City. The Deadwood in Placer County was pretty much declining by 1855. It's open to debate whether the Deadwood in Plumas County, southeast of Spanish Peak, was a camp or only a mining area. Very little is known of the shadowy Sierra County Deadwood. Siskiyou County's Deadwood was about ten miles north of Fort Jones, where gold mining began in 1851.

Hauling timbers at the Brown Bear mine, Deadwood — *Trinity County Historical Society.*

The Deadwood mill — *Trinity County Historical Society.*

Miners pushing ore cars out of a lower tunnel at Deadwood — *Trinity County Historical Society.*

The Brown Bear mine — *Trinity County Historical Society.*

Deadwood Miner's Union Meeting — Independent Order of Clippers — *Trinity County Historical Society.*

Dedrick's history is elusive. The official Trinity County map of 1894 shows the settlement about one-half mile north of Canon City at the point where the Little East Fork branches from Canon Creek. The Bailey, Silver Gray, and Globe (or the Consolidated Globe) mines were major producers in the surrounding area.

Records indicate that Charles D. Bramlet, or Charlie or Bram, drove freight to the Globe mine at Dedrick in 1912, but little else could be found about this northern Trinity County camp. It was apparently almost inaccessible, as freight trains were limited to no more than two wagons and eight horses because of the narrow, poor road.

There may have been a camp named **Pennsylvania Bar** about one-half mile above Dedrick, or the two towns may have been one and the same.

Deer Creek Crossing is a Nevada County ghost camp near the junction of Deer Creek with the Yuba River.

The Shasta County gold mining town of **Delamar** was named for J. H. Delamar, an area mine owner.

Delta was the leading camp along Dog Creek, where several short-lived camps arose and died. Delta's post office survived for only five years; that of neighboring **Bayles** lasted only a few months.

There was probably an ephemeral camp known as **Diamond Creek Diggings** east of Washington, in Nevada County.

Del Loma, reportedly named for a band of French Canadian trappers, was established as a mining camp in the Junction City vicinity. At one time the town may have been referred to as **Taylor's Flat.**

Diamond Springs' early appearance and development were once described by a California gold mine guidebook writer: "Diamond Springs is a place that has sprung suddenly into existence, four miles west of Placerville [the location is about three miles south of Placerville rather than four miles west], on the road to Sacramento City. I passed over the ground about the first of August, 1850,[142] when no signs of a town were visible. No gold had then been discovered in this immediate neighborhood. But soon after, all the ravines and gulches near were found to contain deposits of the precious metal. Although they were not so productive as many, yet hundreds were soon attracted to the spot, the consequence of which was the erection of storehouses, hotels, mechanic shops, *gambling* houses, lawyers' and doctors' offices, hospitals, &c., &c., which, by the first of November formed a village of several hundred inhabitants."[143]

The camp was situated on the Carson Pass Emigrant Trail and flowered into a healthy supply center. Its peak population may have reached 1,500. A twenty-five-pound nugget, one of the largest found in El Dorado County, was discovered there in 1851.

The wooden I.O.O.F. Hall, built in 1852,[144] is one of the few original structures remaining in this lumber, lime, and agricultural center.

Near this stone building, an old general store, at Diamond Springs is the Tullis mine road.

Diamondville, northeast of Chico, was named for miner James Diamond.

Dicksburg was a Yuba County mining camp named for a man called Dick. The camp, dating to 1850, is sometimes referred to as **Vicksburgh.**

Dobbins (Dobbins Ranch) was settled in 1849 by Mark and William Dobbins. The nearby creek also was christened "Dobbins."

Doble sprouted up northeast of San Bernardino near the north shore of Baldwin Lake. The camp was established in 1900 and named for Budd Doble, son-in-law of Comstock entrepreneur Elias J. "Lucky" Baldwin. Baldwin was owner of the rich Gold Mountain (Doble) mine, which he operated from 1860 to 1900. The same mine was operated by Baldwin's successors until the 1940s.

Most of the settlement has passed into oblivion.

Dogtown, located south of Bridgeport, was the site of the first mining activity in Mono County. Founded in 1857 by Mormons, Dogtown's gold attracted hordes of prospectors mostly from the Mother Lode country.

One observer claimed that the settlement was named Dogtown (actually Dog Town) because "although there were only ten houses, there were sixteen fully developed dogs"[145] living at the camp. Others claim that the town derived its name from the common miners' term for camps that had little to offer.

By 1859 the tide had reversed, and most of Dogtown's population had flowed away to neighboring Monoville.

In time, Dogtown disappeared.

A marker near the Bodie turnoff along Highway 395 tells something of the history of this roisterous camp.

One source indicates that **Tailholt,** in Tulare County, was originally called Dogtown. A gold camp north of Amador City appears to have been called Dog Town (and New Philadelphia). Camps named Dogtown were also in Butte, Calaveras, El Dorado, and Mariposa counties. Butte County's Dogtown was first called **Mountain View.** The Calaveras County camp called Dogtown was north of Angels Camp; the El Dorado camp was southeast of Placerville. The Mariposa County Dogtown was east southeast of Coulterville.

Don Pedros Bar was a Tuolumne County camp named for Pierre ("Don Pedro") Sainsevain. The site is now under waters formed by a power dam.

There may have been a Nevada County camp called **Doodleburg,** but nothing of its history was found.

Dotans Bar (Dotans, Dotens, Datons, Daytons) was a Placer County mining camp now under the waters of Folsom Lake.

Double Springs (Two Springs) grew up from gold discoveries made in 1848 or 1849. The rapidly growing camp became Calaveras county seat in 1850, about one year before a post office was established. But by 1860 the post office closed and so did Double Springs; today a few structures remain.

Douglas City (Kanaka Bar)[146] mushroomed near the mouth of Reading's Creek, where Major Pierson Reading first discovered gold in 1848. Placer and hydraulic mining were carried out in the area for many years.

The miners worked hard, but didn't go without entertainment. In February 1863 the "Douglas City Rifles"[147] decided to host a military ball, dinner, and general celebration to which they invited friends from neighboring Weaverville. Before-dinner drinks were served and consumed, and numerous toasts were made. One participant observed, "After several patriotic toasts and speeches, it was observed that most of the boys, instead of sipping their wine at a toast, drank a whole tumblerful and as there were a great many toasts yet to come it was thought best to adjourn as we wished to make a good appearance at the Ball."[148] And what a ball it must have been, for "The dancing lasted from eight till four in the morning; supper eleven till two. As all the company could not sit down at once, it is reasonable to suppose that everybody got their fill of both."[149]

We are not told how the celebration ended for Douglas City revelers, but those who had visited from Weaverville concluded the festivities as follows: "After breakfast we marched out of town, cheered for everything and everybody and rode home. Made a grand entree [*sic*] into Weaverville, band playing 'Yankee Doodle' and 'John Brown.' None killed. None wounded. But several missing."[150]

Mining waned, although a flurry of activity occurred in the 1930s. Eventually the town reached its nadir, and all that remains of original Douglas City is a water tower located just above Major Reading's gold discovery site along the Trinity River.

Steiner's Flat appears to have been about two miles downriver from Douglas City.

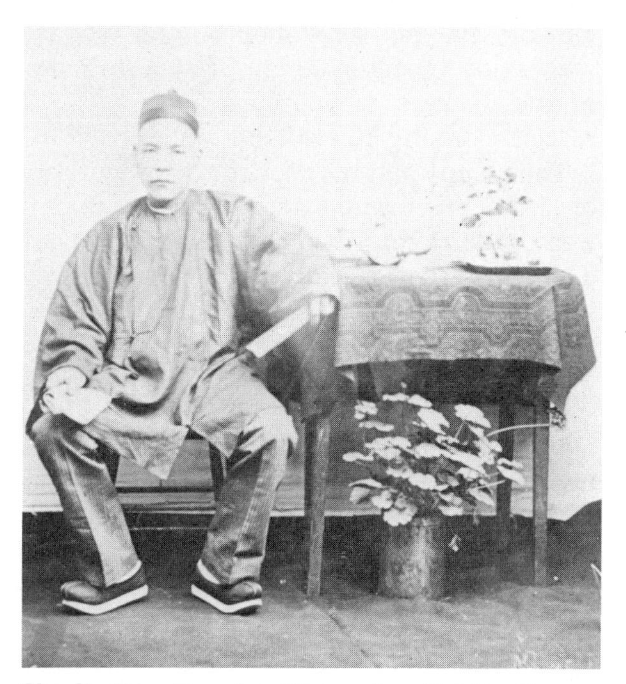

Charlie Kan, Douglas City cook — *Trinity County Historical Society.*

This tower at Douglas City has baled hay stored in it.

Douglas Flat, located between Murphys and Vallecito, was the scene of extensive hydraulic mining.

The only remnant of mining days is the Gilleado building, which once served as the town store and bank. A "shot gun" window can be found at the rear of the building. It was here that a guard protected the gold dust harbored in a large safe.

Downieville was founded at the junction of the north and east branches of the North Fork of the Yuba River. It was here that Frank Anderson[151] first panned gravels in September 1848. At that time the settlement was known as **The Forks.** However, it was changed to Downieville in honor of Major William Downie, an early settler who arrived at the site in November 1848 accompanied by a Kanaka named Jim Crow, an Irishman, an Indian, and ten black sailors. The group of men found rich placer deposits — so rich, in fact, that Downie ordered the band to build cabins and get on with the gold digging, even though the water was icy. When supplies began to run low, Downie sent nine of the men, including Jim Crow, back to "civilization" to buy food and supplies. The men didn't return. In the spring, however, Jim Crow reappeared, only to find

Downie and his three men on the verge of starvation. Accompanying Crow were scores of gold seekers, who fanned out in every direction claiming all available land.

The camp soon burgeoned to a population of 5,000. Hydraulic and hardrock mining were undertaken when the placers gave out. The Yuba River was diverted so that its rich bed could be mined.

Fires leveled the town in 1852 and 1858, but each time it was rebuilt.

One of the stories frequently told about Downieville is of Juanita, a Mexican dance hall girl. The specifics of the event are not very well known, but the story generally pieces together something like this. In 1851 a man named Cannon[152] became upset with Juanita and abused her in her cabin. According to most versions of the story, Cannon returned the next morning to apologize, but during an ensuing scuffle, Juanita knifed him to death.[153] A trial was hastily called, and Juanita was found guilty of murder. She was ordered to be hanged by the neck until dead. The woman may have been pregnant, although general agreement does not support this conclusion.[154] When the news spread that a woman had been lynched at Downieville, Californians reacted by not hanging another person for five years.

Reports of fabulous gold dust and nugget discoveries abound in accounts of Downieville. The "one-to-top-them-all" story concerns James Finney, who on August 21, 1856 reportedly found a 427-pound nugget near town. The nugget was supposedly worth $90,000, although Finney is said to have sold it for $87,000 to Philadelphia bankers, who later sent it to the Philadelphia mint. However, the superintendent of the Philadelphia mint finds no record of the nugget having been there, and Finney, in his biography published in the early 1860s, makes no mention of even finding such a nugget.[155]

One astute observer points out that Downieville was entering its waning years as early as 1865, when two events made "the fact hard and clear — the closing of a church for lack of members, and the coming of the Chinese."[156] In any event, the town declined.

Many reminders of bygone days remain in Downieville, including the Masonic building, churches, Major Downie's original cabin, a gallows, and several buildings dating to the 1860s that still cling to the mountainsides above the Yuba. A "twelve pounder"[157] cannon, brought to Downieville in 1862 and used to announce special occasions, perches atop a hill overlooking the town.

An overview of Downieville.

The "12-pounder" cannon near Downieville, used to shoot off on special occasions. It arrived in town in 1862. It is called a "12-pounder" because it used a 12-pound cannonball.

Dragoon Gulch (Dragoon Flat, Dragon) was a Tuolumne camp perhaps named for one or more dragoons who were in the area.

A mining camp called **Drummondsville** was near Michigan Bar.

Drunkards Bar may have been a Placer County town on the Middle Fork of the American River. The place may also have been known as **Drunkers Bar.**

A few shreds of evidence seem to indicate that a **Dry Bar** existed near Jacksonville.

Drytown, founded in 1848, is the oldest town in Amador County. It was probably named for neighboring Dry Creek. It was certainly not named for any propensity the settlers had for avoiding booze. As a matter of fact, the town supported twenty-six saloons during its heyday.

Two other mining camps grew up nearby — **New Chicago** and **New Philadelphia** — but by 1857 they had deteriorated.

Few vestiges of the past remain, for most of the original buildings were destroyed by a widespread fire in 1857.

Durgans Flat was originally south of Downieville but has now been absorbed by that town. The camp was first known as **Washingtonville** but was renamed for James Durgan, who built a sawmill there in 1850.

Dutch Flat was probably established by German (Dutch) miner Charles Dornbach, and perhaps Joseph Dornbach (also spelled Dorenback, Dornback, or Doranback) in 1851.[158]

Until the Central Pacific railroad laid its tracks to Cisco twenty miles away, Dutch Flat served as an important transportation center on the Donner and Henness Pass routes. In 1860 the town had the largest voting population in Placer County.

Although it has been rumored that a single boulder of quartz from the Polar Star mine of the 1870s yielded nearly $6,000 in gold, hydraulic mining is what kept the town alive.

Today Dutch Flat is one of the least commercial Northern Mines towns, still sporting a hotel, I.O.O.F. Hall, Masonic Hall, Methodist church, and Runckel Home.

A Chinatown housing 1,000 coolies existed near Dutch Flat during railroad construction days. Some scarred remains of the Dutch Flat hydraulic diggings can be detected in the vicinity.

Eagle City was near Georgetown. It was apparently located along the Middle Fork of the American River.

Eagleville was near the Yuba and Butte county lines. Settled in 1851, the camp died when miners hit borrasca.

The I.O.O.F. Hall at Dutch Flat. Originally, the first story was built as a store. The Olive Lodge was instituted on December 8, 1858.

The stately Dutch Flat Hotel, the first floor of which was built in 1852.

Dutch Flat in 1868 — *The Huntington Library.*

Eastwood was north of Julian. No evidence was found to indicate that the place ever existed except as a gleam in the eye of its planner, Joseph Stancliff.

Eclipse was south of Quincy. Area miners received and sent their mail through the post office there from 1897 to 1912.

Mud Springs was its first "monicker," inspired by the nearby watering hole that had been trampled into a muddy mess by immigrants' cattle traversing the Carson Branch of the California Overland Trail. In 1855, with the discovery of gold placers, the town's name was changed to **El Dorado.** Lumbering, cattle raising, and lime mining also nurtured the community.

A fire in 1923 destroyed much of the original business district. Many buildings were demolished in 1956, ruining much of the charm of this former mining camp located about four miles southwest of Placerville.

Another camp named El Dorado was planned south of Marysville, but little could be found of its history.

The Miner's Store at El Dorado.

Eldoradoville was a Los Angeles County mining camp along the East Fork of the San Gabriel River. Its heyday appears to have been from 1859 through 1861. A flood during January 1862 destroyed the settlement.

Election Camp isn't really a mining camp, but rather is remembered as the place where 300 miners of the New River country near the Trinity-Siskiyou county line voted during the presidential election of 1864.

Most of the miners involved, among the 1,500 or so working the gravels of Pony (Poney) Creek, called Lake City headquarters — until Indians burned the camp to the ground. The miners who were to have voted at Lake City were instructed to hike the six miles from Lake City to Election City, on top of the ridge dividing Trinity and Siskiyou counties.

The miners traipsed the distance on that November 8, 1864. It is not known how their votes were cast, but the county went heavily for Lincoln and Johnson.

A Forest Service sign marks the site of Election Camp, twenty-one miles by trail from the end of the road up the North Fork of the Trinity River in Trinity County's primitive area.

Eliza grew up as a supply and transportation center below Marysville. It was named for John Sutter's daughter, Anna Eliza.

Three **Elizabethtowns** appear in California mining lore. One was in Plumas County, northwest of Quincy. It was named for Elizabeth Stark and for a while was known as **Betsyburg.** A gold and silver mining camp called Elizabethtown blossomed and faded northwest of Kings Beach in Placer County. The camp's life must not have extended for more than a couple of years. A camp known as Elizabethtown or Elizabeth or Elizabeth Hill grew up on Iowa Hill Divide. This camp was probably named for mine owner Elizabeth Hill.

The *Historical Souvenir of El Dorado County, California* mentions an early mining settlement known as **Elizaville,** but no other details were found.

Elmer, northeast of Bakersfield, is now called **Granite Station.** It grew up near Granite. Quartz mines were located at both camps, as were post offices. Although the Granite post office existed for less than one year, the Elmer post office lived on for almost a quarter of a century.

Elsinore is a resort on the shores of Lake Elsinore. The town may have been named for Elsinore of Shakespeare's *Hamlet* . . . then again, perhaps it was not.

Elsinore occupies a niche in California mining lore for the eleven-pound nugget that was found nearby in Elsinore Valley.

Empire City still exists. It is the third California settlement to be called Empire City. The Stanislaus County town was predated by its namesake, which served as county seat for about fourteen months. By 1861 the camp was on the downslide, and a new town of the same name grew up nearby. A camp near the Empire mine southeast of Poker Flat in Sierra County died abornin'.

Enterprise was a supply center for miners in the area east of Bidwell Bar in Butte County. Its post office existed from 1878 to 1926. A mining camp named Enterprise briefly existed in Nevada County, near Meadow Lake.

Esmeralda grew up southeast of San Andreas as a supply center for area miners. The camp is frequently referred to as Esmerelda.

Esperanza (Esperance) was on Esperanza Creek in Calaveras County.

The history of **Etna** is outlined by the Siskiyou County Historical Society:[159] "Originally Etna was called Rough and Ready, while Etna Mills was the name of a community a mile on up the Salmon mountain road. In 1863 the post office was moved from Etna Mills to Rough and Ready, but the official name of the town was not changed to Etna until 1874. The first house was built in 1853. Now Etna is a town of many beautiful homes and a thriving business district which serves the surrounding farming area and the Salmon River mines."

Evans Bar was a mining camp on the Trinity River. Some claim that the first log cabin in Trinity County was built here in 1849.

Etna in the early 1900s — *Siskiyou County Historical Society.*

Evansville was probably first settled in 1850. The camp was southwest of Forbestown.

Little was found out about **Exchequer,** now under the waters of Lake McClure in Mariposa County.

El Dorado County's **Fair Play** began as a mining camp but later evolved primarily into an agricultural center.

A Sierra County camp of the same name appears to have been northwest of Downieville. Hydraulic mining occurred in the area.

Fenner still exists just off Interstate 40 west of Needles. It was a supply and transportation center for area miners.

Little is known of **Ferry Bar,** on the Trinity River, east of Douglas City in Trinity County. A camp of the same name grew up on the North Fork of the Yuba River in Yuba County. Some claim that Comstock king James C. Flood once mined in the area.

Fiddletown was settled by Missourians in 1849. Apparently older men in the discovery group accused the younger of "always fiddling."[160] The name stuck until 1878, when the state legislature changed the name to **Oleta.** The story goes that a Judge Purinton was very embarrassed when associates in Sacramento and San Francisco referred to him as "the man from Fiddletown," and so he had the town name changed. However, probably largely through the influence of Bret Harte's *An Episode of Fiddletown,* the name reverted to Fiddletown in 1932.

Quite a bit of the flavor of the 1850s remains of this former trading center for American, Loafer and French Flats, Lone Hill, and other mining camps.

Today Fiddletown is a typical, on-going Mother Lode town.

C. Schallhorn's blacksmith and wagon shop built in Fiddletown in 1870.

Detail of the rammed earth construction of the home, office, and store of Dr. Yee, a Chinese herb doctor in Fiddletown. Built in 1850, the structure is one of two rammed earth adobe buildings in California. The 2½-foot thick wall is made of solid earth, not adobe brick.

Sign at Fiddletown.

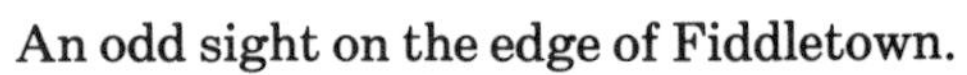

An odd sight on the edge of Fiddletown.

Fielding was established north of Redding. Its post office existed for six years.

There may or may not have been a **Fleatown** in El Dorado County's Kelsey township.

Flea Valley appears to have been a short-lived mining camp northeast of Magalia.

Folsom owes its beginnings to two black miners who sought gold along the American River in 1849. The camp was first called **Negro Bar.**

The land had initially been granted to William A. Leidesdorff in 1844. It was purchased by Captain Joseph Folsom in 1848 or later. In 1855 a town was surveyed, and in 1856 it became the temporary terminus of the Sacramento Valley Railroad, the first in the state. In 1857 construction gangs began to lay rails between Folsom and Marysville. In the era circa 1856-64, Folsom's prosperity was assured as the town became a jumping-off point for the mines. The settlement also served as a railroad center.

The settlement is often remembered as the place where Harry Roff, a fifteen-year-old boy, sped through on the initial run of the famed Pony Express. The date was April 4, 1860, and the run from Sacramento and Placerville took two hours and fifty-nine minutes. The distance was fifty-five miles.

Folsom was also the scene of gold dredging operations which began about 1899 with the first bucket-line dredge ever used in Sacramento County. Mining continued until recently,[161] but with ever-increasing sophisticated machinery and techniques.

Prairie City was located southwest of Folsom. Its site is buried under detritus left by dredging operations.

Forbestown (or **Tolls Old Diggings, Tolls Dry Diggings, Boles Dry Diggin's, Forbes' Diggings**), east of Oroville, was founded by B. F. Forbes in 1850. It was an expansive mining center for nearly one-half of a century. But in the late 1930s it was described as "deserted in its mountain cove, a ghost town of heaped debris, old foundations and crumbling structures with fallen roofs."[162]

Today Forbestown consists of dismal crumbling foundations and walls and scattered debris.

Forest City, originally called **Brownsville,**[163] became a mining camp when a group of sailors discovered gold in 1852. From the beginning, Brownsville was not the generally accepted name for the camp. One faction favored the name Yomana (or Yumama) — an Indian name for a nearby bluff. Others thought Forks of Oregon Creek to be more appropriate. A compromise was reached — the camp would be named for the first woman to live there. For some reason, the name of the *third* woman to reside in the town was applied; consequently, the raw camp became Forest City for the journalist Mrs. Forest Mooney.

Most of Forest City's population was siphoned off to Allegheny when mineral discoveries were made there. An old church and store stand as memorabilia scattered amidst the present-day town of Forest City east of Murphys.

Forest Hill (Foresthill) was established northeast of Auburn. Gold was found in the area before or during 1850. The richest mine was probably the Jenny Lind, discovered in 1852. It produced perhaps $1 million in gold, although total production in the area up to 1868 is estimated at more than $10 million.[164]

Forest Home grew up north of Ione. The camp seems to have grown around the nucleus of a saloon having the same name. Gold placering and hydraulic mining were undertaken. Later, copper was mined in the area.

At one time Butte County's **Forks of Butte** was a relatively large community west of Lovelock.

Forks of Salmon was spawned at the confluence of the North and South forks of the Salmon River. Gold discoveries were first made in June 1850 by a group of prospectors heading for the Salmon Mountains along the South Fork of the Salmon. From Forks of Salmon, the men fanned out along the North Fork and into Scott Valley, and the verdant banks of the river became the site of several camps.

Forks of Salmon, no date — *Siskiyou County Historical Society.*

The placers between Forks of Salmon and Sawyers Bar yielded about $25 million in gold, making the Salmon River District the most productive in Siskiyou County.

One of the most tenacious businesses in Forks of Salmon — the hotel — was forced to close its doors in 1947 following ninety years of continuous operation.

Forkville or **Forksville** was appropriately named, because it was located at the junction of the South and North Forks of the American River. Several hundred miners were there during the census of 1850.

There seems to be little hope of untangling the history of **Forlorn Hope** (or **Forlorn Hope Camp** or **Hopetown** or **Hopeton**) east of Bagby.

Foster's Bar prospered along the North Yuba River between the mouths of Willow and Mill creeks. The town was named in 1849 for William M. Foster, a miner who had travelled to the locality with the Donner party. However, when the insightful prospector realized that a larger and more steady income could be gleaned from operating a store, he changed professions.

The settlement grew to over 1,500 residents, and in 1850 a post office was established. However, by 1866 the post office had been transferred to Bullards Bar. At an undetermined date the town expired.

Fourth Crossing (Foreman's Ranch) was located between San Andreas and Altaville on San Antone (San Antonio) Creek, along the "golden highway" — Highway 49.[165] The settlement appears to have been primarily a stage stop, but some authorities believe that at least one man — Bret Harte — panned for gold at Fourth Crossing.

Francis came of age in northwestern Trinity County. The area supported limited gold placering until the turn of the century.

Fredonia was planned as a trading center for miners. The camp was laid out in 1850, south of Oroville, but little came of the proposed development.

Northwest of Yreka, **Freetown** enjoyed a brief existence. The story is that the ground under the town was mined away, and so the town disappeared.

A number of French Bars existed in California, but apparently they were just that — river bars. A mining camp named **French Bar** survived for a few years during the 1850s along the Scott River in Siskiyou County.

French Camps are listed as being in Amador, Calaveras, Mariposa, Nevada, Stanislaus, Trinity, and Tuolumne counties.

French Corral was appropriately named for a Frenchman who built a corral for his mules in 1849; or perhaps the name was derived from mapmakers who called the place Frenchmans Couill on their maps. The town is situated in a valley that lies on a tributary to the South Fork of the Yuba River. French Corral served as one terminus for a long distance telephone line[166] operated by the Ridge Telephone Company, apparently a subsidiary of the Milton Mining and Water Company. The line stretched for fifty-eight miles between French Corral, Birchville, Sweetland, North San Juan, Cherokee, North Columbia, North Bloomfield, and Bowman (French Lake), and its purpose was to link the French Corral headquarters with French Lake.

French Gulch was spawned by French miners in 1849 or 1850. By 1852 miners were destroying houses to reach gold deposits lying beneath them.

The Washington was the first quartz mine to be worked in Shasta County. It, along with the Brown Bear, Gladstone, Mad Mule, Milkmaid, Franklin, and the Niagara, produced at least $19 million from the French Gulch district.

Several sturdy brick structures remain from the gold era.

The French Gulch Hotel at French Gulch.

The hotel at French Gulch — *Shasta Historical Society.*

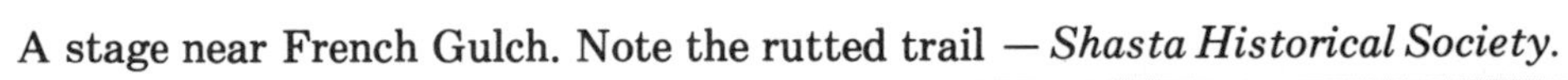

A stage near French Gulch. Note the rutted trail — *Shasta Historical Society.*

French Mills, located southwest of Coulterville, is known to have been a mining community; but when it began, lived, and died is uncertain. Foundations and walls are the only remnants of this mystery mining camp.

Frenchtown was a Butte County mining camp in the Yankee Hill area. Its post office was open for only about one year. Another camp named Frenchtown was on Humbug Creek in Siskiyou County. It was originally called **Mowrys Flat.** Yet another camp called Frenchtown grew up in Yuba County, west of North San Juan. It may have been named for Paul Vavasseur, who went there in 1854.

Frogtown, along with Albany Flat and Carson Flat, was an early-day gold camp whose remains are located near Highway 49. The town was situated between Angels Camp and Melones. Since the late 1930s, the annual Jumping Frog Jubilee has been held in Frogtown.

Frost Bar was a mining camp along the Salmon River in Siskiyou County.

Frytown was south of Ophir in Placer County. It was probably named for store owner Fry, of Fry & Bruce, in 1849.

Fulda Flat was southeast of Emigrant Gap. A stamp mill, a store, and a saloon apparently comprised the camp.

Furnace was an appropriately named Death Valley area copper camp located near Dante's View turnoff by the Amargosa Range.

Galena Hill's domain and terrain existed in the Camptonville area.

The now-gone camp may have numbered 1,000 during its brief boom years. Now, only hermit orchard trees mark the spot.

Amid giant sugar pines is the cemetery; four marble stones and one wooden marker dot the landscape. One stone marker tells of twenty-two-year-old Benjamin Ellis Garnett, "Killed in the Diggings, June 22, 1854."

Garden Valley debuted on the California mining scene north of Placerville. First known as **Johnstown** for a sailor who initially struck gold in the area, the settlement evolved into a farming center and consequently changed its name.

Gardiners Point was east of La Porte. Although noted for gold mining, at least one diamond was found in the area.

Garlock, at one time called **Cow Wells,** sprang up west of Randsburg in 1895 or 1896. Six mills, including the Garlock Pioneer Mill built by Eugene Garlock, for whom the camp was named, were erected in the area.[167]

By 1899 the camp had grown to several hundred people, and a few frame buildings lined the main street.

The town had at least two hotels — the Doty and the Lilard. The owners of the Lilard had three daughters who waited on tables, played the piano, and sang for guests. One source[168] claims that they were referred to as Tom, Dick, and Harry.

But the vicissitudes of mining hit Garlock, and by 1903 Juan Barsarto was the sole inhabitant of the town. Eventually even he left. In 1911 the settlement was temporarily inhabited by railroad track-laying crews who lived in the deserted, but still habitable, buildings.

Mining resumed in the area in the early 1920s, and parts of the town were again occupied. A post office was established, and Garlock again officially existed. But the facility was closed on June 30, 1926 for lack of patrons. Some mining continues to this day.

One of the more substantial structures at Garlock.

Ore hauling in Garlock, no date — *The Huntington Library.*

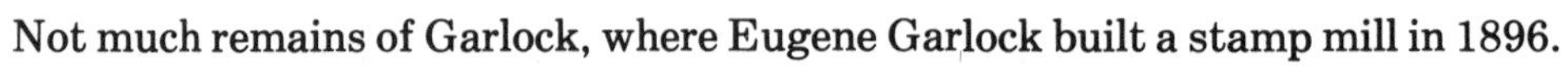

Not much remains of Garlock, where Eugene Garlock built a stamp mill in 1896.

Gasburg was an obscure Siskiyou County mining camp near French Flat.

Gas Point (Pinckney, Janesville) was east of Horsetown in Shasta County.

During its brief heyday, two mills and one arrastre were in operation at **Genesee (Geneseo)** east of Taylorsville. It was probably named for its counterpart in New York.

For a short while **Georgetown** was known as Growlersburg; why it was called such a name is uncertain.[169] George Phipps, or George Ehrenhaft, who led a group of gold-hungry sailors to the site, was the town's second namesake.[170] Georgetown was first settled in 1849, when a group of prospectors from Oregon discovered gold in the area. After placer mines petered out, lode mines became fairly steady producers.

The town was destroyed by a fire in 1856 but was rebuilt. Many of the reconstructed buildings remain, including the 1852 Masonic Hall, an armory built in 1862, the two-story brick I.O.O.F. Hall (formerly a hotel managed by Madame Balsar, or Widow Balsar or Balzar), and the Wells Fargo office.

Hotels in Georgetown.

There was a **George Town** north of Jamestown in Tuolumne County. At one time an attempt was made to form a camp named George Town from the northern part of Jamestown, but it failed. Early maps show separate camps, and the United States census of 1851 breaks the population down into two camps.

A **Georgia Slide** (perhaps **Georgia Flatts**) existed north of Georgetown. It's said that a goose egg-shaped gold nugget worth $1,000 was found there in 1850.

Gibsonville, northeast of La Porte, was probably founded in 1850. The camp was named for an early prospector who found gold along Little Slate Creek.

Gilta was in extreme southwestern Siskiyou County. It was home for many miners who toiled along Know-Nothing Creek.

Glen Aura is a Nevada County mining town now under Lake Spaulding. It was probably named by a member of the New York Volunteers, who mined the area in 1849.

It began as **Musquita Gulch** and continued to be called that until 1878, when it was renamed for the town in Scotland. The camp was northeast of Mok Hill.

A camp with the unusual name of **Glines Canyon** was founded about 1896 north of Green Lake in Mono County. The camp was probably named for prospector Charles Glines.

A number of places claim to be **God's Country**, but there truly is such a place in California. The camp was established northeast of Washington in Nevada County. The Baltic Lode mine seems to have been the major producer. It was located in God's Country Ravine.

Goffs is a ghost town located west of Needles between the Dead and Providence mountains. To the north are situated the mining camps of **Vanderbilt, Ivanpah, Hart, Barnwell,** and **Mescal.**

The town seems to have owed its early existence to being on the Santa Fe Railroad main line, where the Nevada Southern Railway branched to Manvel.

Visitors come to see the tiny Desert Lawn cemetery on the parched edge of town. Six markers — three of them wooden — call attention to this "bone orchard" where life ended for Goff residents. The cemetery is the best reminder of Goffs' early existence.

Goffs was apparently once called **Blake** (at least that was the name given the post office). The name "Blake" probably traces to Isaac Blake, builder of the Nevada Southern Railroad from Goffs to Manvel. Little other information could be ascertained about Goffs.

A joke? Maybe. However, it is possible that this sign near Goffs warns people to not cut Joshua trees, barely discernible in the background.

This barely readable sign marks the Desert Lawn Cemetery near Goffs. The cemetery is the site of six marked graves.

Remains of a structure near Goffs.

There are two places referred to as **Gold Bluff.** The Humboldt County camp was near present-day Orick (between Crescent City and Eureka). First gold discoveries occurred in 1850. The gold was in fine beach sand and was difficult to recover, although more than $1 million may have been mined from the area. There was a Gold Bluff above Downieville in Sierra County, but it may have been a geographic feature and not a camp.

Gold Camp was a Kern County gold camp west of Rosamond.

Two places called **Gold Canyon** exist. One is above Downieville; the other is southeast of Alleghany.

Gold Flat was immediately below Nevada City. It began in 1850, grew to a population of about 300 by 1851, was almost deserted by 1852, and was gone by 1853. Area mines later boomed, and the camp gained a second life.

A plethora of places called **Gold Hill** clutter California history. Residents of Gold Hill, northwest of Placerville, changed their town's name to **Granite Hill** to avoid confusion with other places of the same name. Still another mining camp changed its name *to* Gold Hill from **Orr City** (south of Ophir).

Gold Mountain was near Grass Valley. It was a gold quartz mining camp.

Gold Spring was immediately northwest of Columbia. It was first called **Gold Springs** (not to be confused with Gold Springs near Placerville). The camp began in 1850 and by 1855 had grown to 500 souls.

Goldstone, a Mojave Desert gold camp, was founded in late 1915 or early 1916 and flowered for only a few years. L. Burr Belden in the San Bernardino *Sun-Telegram* (October 6, 1957) seems to indicate that about 1912 was when gold was discovered.

Located near Goldstone Lake northeast of Barstow, the townsite now functions as a NASA tracking base. A few relics of miners' shacks mark the original settlement.

Gold Hill's oldest stone building.

Gold Run was an active mining camp during the 1860s and 1870s. Initially called **Mountain Springs** from 1854 to 1863, the settlement was founded by O. W. Hollenbeck in 1854.

The town's heyday began in 1859 and ended in 1884, when hydraulic mining was outlawed. A few remains mark the site, about eight miles northeast of Colfax.

The only thing resembling gold at contemporary Gold Run is this golden-colored railroad building.

Goldtown's existence was inextricably entwined with the Golden Queen mine.

An account of the settlement published in 1939 describes the Golden Queen as "extensive galvanized iron sheds, spidery loading shoots and great ore dumps" which "disfigure the slope of Soledad Mountain."[171]

The mine, located in 1935 by prospector George Holmes, was one of the latest developments in California mining history. Holmes supposedly sold the property for $3.5 million.[172]

Goler, one of the shortest-lived mining camps in California history, was founded in 1893 and deserted in 1895. Virtually nothing remains to mark the town's brief existence. The site of Goler can be found in Goler Canyon at the eastern end of the El Paso Mountains.

Goodyear's Bar was settled at the junction of Goodyear and Woodruff creeks and the North Fork of the Yuba River near Downieville. Miles and Andrew[173] Goodyear are generally credited with founding the town in 1849. The following year, Miles Goodyear was buried with a buffalo robe and a gold rocker.[174]

A high point in the camp's existence came in 1852, when a single wheelbarrow of placer dirt yielded $2,000.

A most bizarre event supposedly took place at Goodyear's Bar: a mule was tried and sentenced by Chinese miners for having refused to work for the men and for having kicked one of the miners to death.

Although the placers were extensive, the town began to die when a fire destroyed most of the settlement in 1864.

The Pioneer Hotel appears to be the only reminder of gold rush days.

Gopher Hill probably grew to a mining camp. The area northeast of Nevada City was difficult to mine because of the many large boulders. This may be relevant to the camp's naming.

Gorda, located west of Jolon, was a mining camp settled in 1887. Mining may have continued in the area until 1916. Gorda and Los Burros were apparently both fathered by the same quartz vein developments. The two camps comprised the Los Burros district, where by 1915 or 1916 about $150,000 worth of gold was produced. Mining has been sporadically undertaken since that time.

Gottville has been called **Klamath River** since 1934. The camp began as a trading and transportation center for miners along the Klamath River diggings northwest of Yreka. The camp was named for William Gott, a mine owner.

Gouge Eye was first seen on the California mining scene about 1855. It was located by a French company. Some people thought the name too gauche and called the place **Hunts Hill.**

East of Camptonville can be found the mining village of **Graniteville,** situated

5,000 feet above sea level on the San Juan Ridge. The town rests on the middle fork of the Yuba River in the Bowman Lake area.

The camp was originally called **Eureka** but was changed to Graniteville when the post office opened in August 1867.

A crowd gathered at the Golden State Hotel in Graniteville — *Nevada County Historical Society.*

Grass Valley has been termed the least ghostly of any Mother Lode town. It's a thriving place and is probably the most important gold mining settlement in California, vaunting the second and third largest gold mines in the world.

Grass Valley began as a small camp in Boston Ravine. Although 1849 is generally given as the year of discovery, evidence suggests that David Stump and two Oregonians had been mining in the area the previous year.

The town received its name from the verdant Grass Valley, where, in 1849, a company of immigrants found lush forage for their nearly starved cattle.

Hardrock ores — the state's first — were discovered by 1850, attracting men and capital to Grass Valley.[175] Soon the camp was booming. The first quartz mill in California was built at Grass Valley in 1851. Two years later the construction company went bankrupt. But improved techniques gave rise to greater mining and milling success, and by 1856 five quartz mills and seven mines were operating.

It was in Grass Valley that the first miners' discussion club of California was organized. Established in 1855, the club was to function as a forum for discussing ideas relating to lode mining. The information was important, for although the Grass Valley veins were rich, they were also narrow, and large quantities of rock had to be cut away to reach the ribbons of quartz. Consequently, extraction costs were very high. Grass Valley residents were up to the task, however, for as the *Mining and Scientific Press* of October 8, 1864, pointed out, Grass Valley [and Nevada County] "has the largest mining population, the largest gold yield, the most thorough system of ditches, the most profitable quartz and hydraulic mines, and within its borders many of the most important mining inventions were made or first applied in this State."

By the late 1860s, Grass Valley's quartz mines were producing $3.2 million per year, and the county's hydraulic and placer claims were yielding about $3.5 million.[177] Total production in Nevada County probably amounted to over $133.8 million by 1959,[178] and the Empire mine, discovered in 1850 (closed in 1956), may have produced up to $70 million.[179] The Golden Center, Idaho, Pennsylvania, Eureka, North Star, Empire, Spring Hill, Old Brunswick, and New Brunswick were among the other major producing mines. This frenetic mining activity modified the terrain in and under Grass Valley. According to Robert Ritchie, one observer wrote that it was a "tidy little community in the cup of surrounding hills [that] has been undercut in its every precinct by crisscrossing of shaft and stope in the viscera of earth below."[180]

A fire in September 1854[180] devastated most of the original Grass Valley. It consumed 300 buildings and was perhaps the worst conflagration to ever strike a Mother Lode town. The house associated with Lola Montez, although altered, may have escaped the flames.[181] The actress, dancer, mistress, lecturer, and author was known as "the Countess of Lansfelt" (also spelled Lansfeldt or Landsfeld). Maria Dolores Gilbert[182] took a number of detours before arriving in Grass Valley. This "creature of fire and fascination" first attracted the attention of King Ludwig of Bavaria while she was performing as an exotic Spanish dancer. The title of Countess of Lansfelt was bestowed upon Lola Montez while she was King Ludwig's mistress.

Lola left Bavaria, settled in Paris, and in 1851 came to America. She became famous

Main Street in Grass Valley in 1861 — *Nevada County Historical Society.*

for her "spider dance," in which she would fling artificial spiders off of herself. She went to San Francisco in 1853 and later to Sacramento. She settled in Grass Valley in the fall of 1853 surrounded by a husband, several dogs, horses, goats, sheep, hens, parrots, monkeys, one or two grizzly bears — and gentlemen. During the two years she lived at Grass Valley, Lola Montez was the source of incessant tongue wagging. It was here that she and her husband parted ways. He killed her bear, which had chased and bitten him. The fiery woman is said to have horsewhipped Grass Valley newspaper editor Henry J. Shipley, and in time is said to have had her welcome worn thin in the community. In 1855 she left for Australia. On January 17, 1861, she died — destitute — in New York.

Lola left a living legacy in Grass Valley in the form of Lotta (Charlotte) Crabtree. Lotta, who had been trained to perform by Lola, later became a famous — and rich — dancer.[183]

Lotta Crabtree — *Special Collections, University of Nevada, Reno.*

Greasertown was founded — by default — by Mexican miners forced by Americans to flee from San Andreas to the east.

Greenhorn was named for a tenderfoot, and the scene was immediately south of Yreka. The cast of characters included some "seasoned" prospectors who in the early 1850s had sought, and failed to find, gold. A greenhorn, so legend goes, approached the unsuccessful prospectors and asked where he might look for gold. The frustrated group suggested that the newcomer check out their abandoned claim. He did — and struck it rich. The settlement that grew up around the discovery site was called Greenhorn in the unknown man's honor.

Greenhorn was put on the map in 1855 when the so-called "Greenhorn War," which pitted Greenhorn men against the developers of the Yreka Flats Ditch Association, was waged. The company, which had diverted water from Greenhorn Creek for its own claims, ultimately won the battle.

Today, only a few frame buildings mark the spot where Greenhorn had once flourished.

One source lists **Green Mountain** as a mining camp in Little York Township of Nevada County. But little else was found about the place.

Green Springs was a camp located at what is now **Keystone.** The Tuolumne County camp had a post office from 1852 to 1869.

El Dorado and Placer counties had camps known as **Green Valley.** The El Dorado County camp was northwest of Shingle Springs; the Placer County location was southeast of Dutch Flat.

Records indicate that there were two camps named **Greenville.** The better-known was in Plumas County, north of Crescent Mills. The camp grew up around a Mrs. Green's hotel. A Yuba County Greenville may have instead been called **Oregon Hill.**

Greenwater, a Death Valley mining camp, grew up near a spring containing water of an unsavory green color. Whether the town was founded in 1905 or 1906 is a

Main Street of Greenwater, 1906 — *California State Library.*

matter of speculation. Russell Elliott (*Nevada's Twentieth-Century Mining Boom*) claims that the camp was originally located in 1884 as a gold and silver property. But little doubt existed in most people's minds — spurred in large part by promoter Patsy Clark[184] — that Greenwater would be a promising copper camp. By early 1907, 2,000 people temporarily called the town home.

For all the amenities to be found in Greenwater — a bank, two newspapers, even a magazine — the town lacked one critical resource — water. Most of the "liquid gold" was hauled from wells thirty miles away and was sold for as much as twelve cents per gallon. The tale persists that the office of the *Greenwater Miner,* one of the local newspapers, was allowed to burn to the ground in a fire. The reason: it was less expensive to rebuild the plant than to purchase water for extinguishing the fire.[185]

By autumn 1907 Greenwater and several other Death Valley camps had collapsed.

Greenwood (Greenwood Valley) prospered west of Georgetown from gold discoveries made in 1848, 1849, or 1850. The town was named for the Greenwood Valley,[186] which, in turn, was probably named for trapper Caleb Greenwood or one of his sons, John, who discovered gold and built a cabin at the site in 1848 or 1849. The Greenwoods later gave up mining and turned to supplying venison to prospectors.

In the following years Greenwood became a trading center, the site of several wineries, a supply center, and continued as a placer region, as well as becoming a hydraulic mining center. During its heyday the town contained four hotels, fourteen stores, a brewery, and four saloons.

An unusual grave marker in the Greenwood cemetery.

Grizzly Flats was an El Dorado County mining camp perhaps named in 1850 by prospectors who killed a grizzly bear in the area. It appears that the camp was called a number of names, including **Grizzly Flat, Chickamasee, Grizzle Flat,** and perhaps **Grisly.**

About twenty miles north of Trinity the placer camp of **Grizzly Fork** romped on the mining scene like a newborn calf, stumbled, and died.

Grizzly Gulch was a short-lived Yuba County camp between Camptonville and North San Juan.

Grizzly Hill was an Amador County camp near Volcano. Another place of the same name was located in Nevada County below North Columbia. Another spot called Grizzly Hill was north of Downieville, but it may not have been a camp.

Ground Hog Glory was on the North Fork of the Middle Fork of the American River in Placer County.

Groveland was initially called First Garrote[187] by French miners for the hanging that had befallen a Mexican horse thief in 1850.[188] By 1875 the name had converted to Groveland.

Several relics of gold rush days remain, including the Wells Fargo Office (the Iron Door) and a former grocery store. But gone is F. S. Stachler's 1853 "Garrote Brewery," a popular "watering hole" for travelers on the Big Flat road into Yosemite Valley.

Guadalupe was below Agua Fria. It was a quartz mining camp.

Hacketville was a Nevada County mining settlement near Spenceville.

Hamburg flourished briefly as a Klamath River mining camp. When it began is uncertain, but the original town died in 1863 when a flood washed it away. Part of the town was rebuilt, but today Hamburg is just a small settlement with several reminders of its mining heyday.[189]

Reminders of mining activity abound at Hamburg.

Hamburg Bar on the Klamath River — *Siskiyou County Historical Society.*

Hamilton was a short-lived mining camp located about fifteen miles south of Oroville along the Feather River.

The town was probably named for William S. Hamilton, son of Alexander Hamilton, who had at one time mined along the Trinity River. The place may also have been named for a nephew of Alexander Hamilton.

Hamilton became the Butte County seat in 1850, but in 1853 the county seat was moved to Bidwell's Bar. This action apparently doomed Hamilton.

Hammonton was first known as **Dredgertown** or **Dredgerville.** It was located northeast of Marysville on the Yuba River as headquarters for dredging activities along the Yuba. It was established in 1904.

Hansonville (Rackerby) was a short distance southwest of Forbestown in Yuba County. It was named for James Hanson, who settled there in 1851. Peak years were mostly in the 1850s and 1860s, and then the camp began a steady decline. The post office was closed in 1892, when another post office was established named Rackerby.

Happy Camp, an isolated community situated along the Klamath River, was a mining camp that prospered in the 1850s. Exactly when the town was founded is not known, but 1851 is the most likely candidate. Part of the founding date confusion stems from the fact that early-day Happy Camp may have been called **Murderers Bar.**

Because a road was not built to Happy Camp until 1866,[190] the area was more isolated than other California mining communities.

Although the town died as a mining camp shortly after the 1850s, it survives today as a center for hunting and steelhead fishing. Some original Happy Camp stone buildings with iron doors grace the site.

Hardisons Camp, near Mariposa, was named for W. Hardison.

Hardscrabble was probably established by New Hampshire miners. The camp was southeast of La Porte in Sierra County. Another camp of the same name was situated east of Columbia.

Happy Camp in 1899 — *Siskiyou County Historical Society.*

Harrison Gulch, no date — *Shasta Historical Society.*

Hardscrabble Gulch, above Fort Jones in Siskiyou County, was named by miners from Hardscrabble, Wisconsin. First mining may have occurred in 1854.

Harrisburg may owe its existence to gold discoveries made in 1905 or 1906 by either Nevada gold-finder Shorty Harris, or Pete Aguerreberry, or both, or neither. In any event, this Death Valley camp probably never grew beyond 300 residents.

Little remains of this site located near Emigrant Pass in the Panamint Mountains.

Harrisons was southwest of La Porte. The camp, established in the mid-1850s, lasted less than two years.

Hart sprouted up in the Ivanpah area, just west of the Nevada border in the Castle Mountains. The camp is generally considered to be contemporary with Tonopah and Goldfield, with gold discoveries dating to 1907. The town was probably named for one of its discoverers, Jim Hart.

Hart was one of the few "dry" California mining camps, apparently because liquor licenses were difficult to obtain. Private booze supplies were "augmented" by water, which sold for as high as eight dollars a barrel.[191]

A few mouldering ruins mark the spot.

Manvel (Barnwell), west of Hart, was founded in 1893 as a transportation center. By 1915 its demise was clear and the post office was closed . . . the same year Hart's post office was closed.

Harts Bar, a couple of miles south of Jacksonville, was probably established in 1850.

Havilah, located near Kernville, served as the Kern county seat from 1866 to 1872.

Little of the original settlement remains, but graves of its early settlers dot the pioneer cemetery.

Hawk Eye was northwest of Angels Camp. It lasted such a brief time that little else is known of this shadowy Calaveras County camp.

Picturesque wooden grave markers can still be found in the Havilah cemetery.

The marker of the three Canty daughters in the Havilah cemetery. Margaret, born November 26, 1877, died the following April, less than five months of age. Mary was born December 13, 1874, and Catherine was born July 3, 1876. They died about two weeks apart; Catherine on April 6, 1879, Mary on April 21.

Hawkins Bar was a Trinity County gold and platinum camp. Most mining ceased by about 1909. Another camp of the same name was below Jacksonville. It was settled in 1849 and named for a man named Hawkins, who ran a store. The camp began to falter in 1858, was a ghost town six years later, and completely vanished by 1870. The waters of Don Pedro reservoir now cover the site.

Remains of **Hawkinsville** can be found along Yreka Creek immediately north of Yreka. The town, which consisted of a string of miners' cabins, was named for Jacob Hawkins, a leading citizen. Founded in the early 1850s,[192] the settlement still retains some of its original structures, including a remodeled Catholic church dating to 1858.

Hayden Hill was a mining camp established south of Adin. Unlike many California mining camps, Hayden Hill's gold and silver mines were good producers from the middle of the nineteenth century well into the twentieth century.

The camp was named for J. W. Hayden, who located several mining claims in the area, some as early as 1869.

The camp, on the stageline to Susanville, was also known as **Providence City** and **Mount Hope.**

Hayfork was first called **Kingsberry,** then **Hay Town,** and then **Hay Fork.** It began as a farming and ranching community and has prospered ever since. It has added the lumber industry to help assure stability.

However, there was some mining in the area as early as 1852 when D. M. Kellogg was one of the largest mining operators.

It's hardly a ghost town, with a current population of about 1,000.

The Carter House at Hayfork in 1897 — *Trinity County Historical Society.*

Helena, west of Weaverville on Highway 299, began as a mining camp in 1849. The richest strike was made by a French-Canadian named Gross. The location was four miles above present-day Helena, along the north fork of the Trinity River. The camp was first known as **North Fork,** but also was nicknamed **Bagdad** and **The Cove.**

By 1852 North Fork was large enough to support a hotel and boardinghouse run by Lee[193] and Weed. Later, another was built.

By 1858 the population was about fifty. The town is still "alive and kicking," but the town now known as Helena is about one and one-half miles up the Trinity River from old Helena, or North Fork.

Brick building in Helena.

The H. Schlomer feed store and stable at Helena.

Hells Delight was a Placer County camp, but its location along or near the Middle Fork of the American River is uncertain, as is virtually everything dealing with this evanescent place.

Helltown was established along Butte Creek, northeast of Chico. Hydraulic mining in the area continued until about World War II.

Henley was located north of Yreka. The mining camp of **Cottonwood** was situated near the mouth of Cottonwood Creek, northeast of Henley. Gudde does not agree with this, hinting that the camps were one and the same. He states on page 84: "When the post office was established January 3, 1856, it was called Henley, but the name Cottonwood prevailed among the people." When a stage road was built to Henley, about 1854, Cottonwood was bypassed, causing its downfall.

When the railroad was built in 1887, most of Henley's population was attracted to Hornbrook, and Henley also joined the list of ghost towns.

There appears to have been an ephemeral camp in the Nelson Point area of Plumas County named **Henpeck Camp** or **Henpeck City.**

Herbertville was an Amador County camp south of Amador City. Area mines were not very rich, and the camp died relatively early.

Hermitage was located in Butte County above Oroville.

Hicks was a short distance northwest of Copperopolis. It was founded about 1848.

High Grade was founded near Fort Bidwell, in extreme northeastern California.

The town probably began in 1905 and grew steadily until about 1910.

A few tattered remains can still be found.

Hoboken is a mystery-shrouded Trinity County camp. Its other names may have been **Hoboken Bar, Grand Slide,** or **Grant's Slide.**

Henley — *Siskiyou County Historical Society.*

A man named Holmes may have fathered two camps called **Holmes Camp.** One was along Weber Creek in El Dorado County; the other was somewhere in Shasta County.

Honcut's is a murky history indeed. The camp was apparently at different sites and had different names in Yuba and Butte counties. The camp appears to have been known as Honcut and **Bryden** at Yuba County locations; and as Honcut and **Moores Station** in Butte County.

The post office at **Honolulu,** on the Klamath River near Gottville in Siskiyou County, apparently served area placer and hydraulic miners. The camp probably only lasted about four years.

A few gaunt structures remain at **Hooperville,** west of Fort Jones. The Siskiyou County camp, named for Frank Hooper, an early prospector, probably began about 1853.

Hopkinsville was a transitory mining camp near Hopkins Creek. It may have been founded as a placer camp in 1850, and later became a hydraulic mining camp.

Hopland still exists in Mendocino County, along Highway 101, west of Lakeport. Gold and platinum were mined near the town.

Hornitos was initially settled in 1850 by Mexicans who had been driven from Quartzburg by white miners. The town's name was taken from early Mexican tombs, which were shaped like square bake ovens (hornitos: Spanish for "little ovens").[194]

The town was built around a Mexican-style plaza and was supposedly a favorite haunt for outlaw Joaquin Murieta.[195]

Hornitos was a rough-and-tumble town, variously called a place "of evil fame"[196] and, according to Bret Harte, a place "where everything that loathes the law found congenial soil and flourished." As late as 1857, a man who visited Hornitos said that he felt as though he were "outside the pale of civilization."[197]

One tale relates that because the men of Hornitos didn't like to exert themselves, they placed the jail in the center of town, where most of the action occurred. The cemetery was located near the jail for the same reason.[198] The jail, built in 1851 from stone quarried by Chinese, with an iron door and one small window near the ceiling, was the scene of tragedy. A Chinese man who was being harassed by a white adult (or a group of white boys) was driven to the point of shooting his tormentor(s). When the Chinese was jailed, Hornitos residents attempted to break in and hang the man. The plan failed, but an alternate scheme was devised. While one man handed the Chinaman some tobacco, drinks, or drugs (depending on which sources are believed), several miners seized the Chinese man's hand, pulled him against the window, fastened a rope around him, and tore him to pieces.[199]

The Ruth Pierce mine was located near Hornitos, but little has been reported about it. The Washington, or Jenny Lind, mine was one of the best producers in the Hornitos district. It was here that the first milling machinery of any note in the district was installed in 1851. A stamp mill at the mine was reputed to have crushed $1,000 in gold per day.[200] The Mount Gaines mine, northeast of Hornitos, was also a good gold producer.

The peak population of Hornitos may have reached 15,000 — a seemingly high figure.[201] Today, several adobe-stone structures remain as mementos of gold rush days. The old Wells Fargo building still stands,[202] along with the Masonic Hall and the ruins of the D. Ghirardelli store.[203]

A number of businesses have come and gone as evidenced by this false front on a building in Hornitos.

The Hornitos Lodge F & AM.

Hornitos, featuring an arched doorway of Chinese adobe.

The "one-cell jail" at Hornitos — *Collection of Historical Photographs, Title Insurance and Trust Company, Los Angeles.*

The D. Ghiradelli and Company store in Hornitos. It dates to 1858.

Two places called **Horseshoe Bar** were located on the American River. The "upper" bar was on the Middle Fork, the "lower" one on the North Fork. The fortunes of both camps varied from borrasca to bonanza, but in the end, as John Letts (*California Illustrated; Including a Description of the Panama and Nicaragua Routes,* New York, 1852) put it, neither bar paid for the labor "bestowed upon them."

Horseshoe Bend was along the Merced River southwest of Coulterville. The Mariposa County placer camp may have peaked at a population of 400. The site is now under waters forming Lake McClure.

Hotaling and **Clipper Gap** grew up near Auburn. The Hotaling iron mine was located in the area in 1857, but no ore was shipped from it until 1869. A blast furnace that was built on the property operated between 1880 and 1885, using charcoal made at the mine and limestone mined from nearby. The facility produced from thirty to thirty-five tons of pig iron daily.[204]

Records indicate that red and yellow ocher were shipped from the vicinity in the late 1920s for mineral paint, but apparently no attempts have been made to extract lower-grade ores from their iron content since about 1900.

Howland Flat was a Sierra County mining camp founded in 1850. The camp was in Gold Canyon, north of Downieville.

Many places in California were dubbed **Humbug.** However, the only place officially called Humbug was in Siskiyou County. The camp, probably founded in 1851, was short-lived.

Hunter's Valley grew up about seven miles northeast of Hornitos. A July 1870 report indicated that the town was resplendent with live oak and buckeye, but today the setting finds redbud and buckeye competing with gnarled fig trees planted by Italian homesteaders. But the camp is known primarily as a mining camp where the major gold producers were the Iron Duke, Oakes, Reese, and Schoolhouse mines. The La Victoria was the leading copper mine.

A few mines still pock the area. A few people live at Hunter's Valley, but it is ghostly.

Hurleton (Hurlton), east of Oroville, had a checkered career first as a mining camp, then as a resort ultimately named for ranch and hotel owner Smith Hurles.

Hyampom is west southwest of Weaverville on the Hayfork River. The camp may have been known at one time as **Hyampum.** Some gold mining was carried on near the town, plus the camp was a trading center for area mines.

Igo and **Ono** are now twin farming communities in the Redding area. However, the Eagle Creek, Chicago, and other mines were worked in the area.

An interesting tale surrounds the naming of the settlements. A man named McPherson, who had been one of the first to build a house in the area, had a small son who, when his father left for the mines, would say "I go." His father would counter, "Oh, no." When one camp was dubbed Igo, the other was called Ono.

Yet another version of the naming of the settlements involves a Chinese man and two whites. The Caucasians supposedly came upon the Chinese and found him working rich ground. When they suggested he move on, he replied, "Oh, no." But when the request was punctuated with a pointed, loaded pistol, the Chinese declared, "I go!" One white man named his claim for the Chinese's first response, the other man for the second response.[205]

Strangely, little information is recorded about the area. One source claims that gravels along Clear Creek near Igo were worked in the early days, but they are only briefly mentioned in the literature, and no published account of their discovery, development, and early production are found.[206]

In 1933 placer mining was again undertaken in the Igo district. Over 113,000 ounces of gold were mined until 1942, when operations were sharply curtailed. From 1942 on, perhaps no more than two thousand ounces of gold were recorded from the district, mostly from placer mining.

The nearby mining settlement of **Piety Hill** is gone.

Illinoistown is an extant Placer County town near Colfax. It was probably established in 1850 and by 1853 had a post office which was moved to Colfax in 1866.

Two places called **Independence** figure into California mining history. A camp in Plumas County was located near Nelson Point in 1850. For several years, mining was controlled by a British company. The other camp called Independence was in Sierra County, east of Downieville. It lasted about twenty years. The record is not clear, but there may have been a transitory mining camp called Independence located along Independence Creek near Railroad Flat.

Indiana Ranch was a Yuba County mining camp named by the Page brothers, who discovered gold there in 1851. The overpromoted and underdeveloped camp soon died.

Indian Bar had germinated in the Rich Bar area by 1851. As one observer noted, "across from Rich Bar was Poverty Bar, and below, opposite Indian Bar, was Peasoup Bar."[207]

The camp must have vanished a short time after its founding, for a contemporary observer described the town as being pretty much deserted by 1852. During October 1851 the settlement was considered to be "so small, that it seems impossible that the tents and cabins scattered over it can amount to a dozen; there are, however, twenty in all, including those formed of calico shirts and pine boughs."[208] The townsite must have been a mess, for it was "so completely covered with excavations and tenements, that it is utterly impossible to promenade upon it at all."[209]

The first — and for a while, the only — hotel in town was the Humboldt, described as "A large rag shanty, roofed, however, with a rude kind of shingles, over the entrance of which is painted in red capi-

Piety Hill, no date — *Shasta Historical Society.*

The former home of popular Mary Austin in Independence.

tals . . . the name of the great *Humboldt,* spelt [*sic*] without the d."[210] The Humboldt was the scene of a wild Christmas evening-through-New Year's Day celebration, called a "Saturnalia," which took place in 1851-52. On the fourth day of the celebration, men "got past dancing, and, lying in drunken heaps about the bar-room, commenced a most unearthly howling — some barked like dogs, some roared like bulls, and others hissed like serpents and geese. Many were too far gone to imitate anything but their own animalized selves."[211]

Besides this camp in Plumas County, another town called Indian Bar was located in Tuolumne County, below Jacksonville. The site has been covered by waters of the Don Pedro reservoir.

Indian Creek (Indian Creek Town), a mining and ranching community, was about three miles southeast of Douglas City, in east-central Trinity County.

Much of what is known of the camp comes from a journal of the minutes of the Franklin Literary Debating Society of Indian Creek. The society was formed on November 7, 1857.

Apparently not enough hot air was generated by the debating group, and one of its first orders of business was to purchase a thirty-dollar stove and ten dollars worth of firewood.

But by February 1858 the society decided to permanently adjourn the group, after having debated such topics as: "Which has been the most benefit to the world, iron or gold?" "Which exerts the greater influence over men, money or women?" and "Which deserves the greatest applause, Columbus for discovering America, or Washington for defending it?"[212]

Indian Diggins was an El Dorado County mining camp dating to 1849 or 1850. When the post office was established in 1853, the camp was called **Indian Diggings,** which was changed to **Mendon** in 1869 and to Indian Diggins in 1888; although some claim that **Whorehouse Gulch** was the town's unofficial monicker.

Ingot still clings to life northeast of Redding on Highway 299. The town was probably formed to satisfy the needs of workers at the Afterthought Mining Company, which built a copper smelter in the area about 1922. The 1,650-acre mining complex consisted of company houses, a million-dollar plant, and a tramway system. However, the plant was unable to successfully handle the ores from the Copper Hill lode, and the holdings were abandoned.

In 1925 the California Zinc Company began operating a flotation plant and reverberatory smelter but had troubles processing both the copper and zinc. The company later used an 8½-mile-long tramway to transport ore to its Bully Hill smelter. The operation failed.

Gaunt reminders of unsuccessful mining operations still clutter the Ingot landscape.

Little is physically left of early-day **Inskips** in Butte County near the Plumas County line. First gold discoveries are generally credited to a German named Eenskip, for whom the camp was named. The post office was closed in 1915, and the town has slowly mouldered.

Ione was probably named, either by design or accident, for the heroine of *The Last Days of Pompeii.* In any event, the name appears to have been a better one than its predecessors — **Bedbug, Freezeout, Hardscrabble, Rickeyville,** and **Woosterville.**

Although not a mining town, Ione was still a part of the gold rush saga. The town served as a stage stop, rail center, clay and sand producer, and as a cattle and agricultural center.

Iowa Flat was situated at the upper base of Jackson Butte in Amador County, southeast of Jackson.

Between $10 million and $20 million have been wrenched from **Iowa Hill** mines since the town's founding in 1853.[213] Its post office was called **Iowa City** from 1854 to 1901. The ores were mined mostly from the ridge on which the town sits. Several hydraulic giants have all but washed away the town.

Fires struck Iowa Hill on several occasions. The first, in 1857, took all of the original town except one brick building and a few frame houses. The last fire occurred in 1922.

The pioneer cemetery on Banjo Hill is one of the few original remains of old Iowa Hill.

The flotation plant at Ingot — *Shasta Historical Society.*

Iowaville had a short existence southeast of Placerville. Little is known of this camp once located along Weber Creek.

Irish Hill was northwest of Ione. It was literally washed away by hydraulic mining.

Very little information was located about **Iron Mountain**, a copper and silver camp described as being "some sixteen miles from Redding."[214]

Irvine was a Calaveras County mill town that developed near the end of the last century.

Isabella grew up as a mining camp near Kernville and was contemporary with Kernville, Bodfish, and Havilah.

It still exists on Highway 178, in "recreation country" — the recreation including fishing, boating, and camping.

The camp was probably named in honor of Queen Isabella, patron of Christopher Columbus.

Island Bar was probably on the Big Bend of the North Fork of the Feather River.

Ivanpah was established near Interstate 15, just west of the Nevada border. Three prospectors struck silver north of Mountain Pass in 1869, on the east slope of Clark Mountain. But what happened between then and 1872, when Pat Palen made a new silver strike, isn't clear. It appears that for several years silver ore was freighted from Ivanpah to San Pedro and thence via steamers to San Francisco smelters.

Between 1872 and 1885 about $4 million was mined from the area, some by Indian labor. Nevertheless, Ivanpah died in 1872, short of ore and capital.

In a way, Ivanpah was resurrected, for in 1901 the California Eastern Railroad built a branch line to the Ivanpah Valley and called its terminus there Ivanpah. One dozen years later, however, when the spur line was discontinued, Ivanpah died its second death. The remains of two mills (one of which was apparently built in the early 1870s), a smelter, and several rock and adobe buildings still stand.

Jackass Hill was probably named after the jackasses that were tethered at the site by packers on their way to or from the mines. But when gold was found on Jackass Hill, the donkeys were evicted to make room for the miners. In a short time, at least 3,000 prospect holes dotted the hill.[215]

Mark Twain stayed at Jackass Hill for three months during 1864–65. It was here, on February 25, 1865, that Clemens saw his first snowstorm as he walked between Angel's Camp and Jackass Hill.[216]

Clemens had just departed San Francisco, either because his debtors were after him, or because he had overly criticized the corruption of the San Francisco police while writing for the *San Francisco Morning Call.*[217] Clemens' departure from the city also involved an incident with Steve Gillis, a printer who had left the Washoe country with Clemens and accompanied him to San Francisco. When Gillis severely wounded a man in a brawl, both he and Clemens deemed it prudent to leave town. Gillis went to Virginia City, Nevada. Mark Twain, accompanied by Steve's brother, Jim Gillis (who was in San Francisco visiting at the time), headed for the family cabin at Jackass Hill. While visiting the camp, Twain "pocket hunted" for gold.

Some of Twain's writings may have been conceived at the Gillis cabin. A replica of the cabin has been built at Jackass Hill, incorporating the original chimney and fireplace. William Gillis[218] was at one time caretaker of the site. Bret Harte may have also visited the Jim Gillis cabin.[219]

Jackson was founded as a way station on the branch of the Carson Pass Emigrant Trail where roads met from Sacramento and Stockton. The town was a slow grower — by 1849 its population was only sixty.[220] Although the town lacked many citizens, there were plenty of hard-drinking visitors. The town was so strewn with liquor bottles that it was first called Bottileas, or Botellas, or Botilleas.[221] But when rich diggings were discovered along nearby Jackson Creek, the town began to bustle. By 1850 the camp had grown to 1,500 and its name was changed to Jackson, for Colonel Aldan Jackson.

The town had a reputation for being "tough." A great oak tree on Main Street was used to hang ten or fifteen persons (depending on whose estimates one believes).

Claim jumping was common, especially on land claimed by "foreigners." One tale persists that a group of Frenchmen holding valid claims near town had their claims jumped by a group using a rather unusual rationale for their action. They accused the Frenchmen of flying a tricolor flag rather than that of the United States, and to avenge this "insult," they drove away the French and claimed the property.[222]

Even though Jackson was situated on a major transportation route, supplies apparently were not always ample. At one time, a slice of bread at the Brandy and Sugar Hotel reportedly cost one dollar, and it cost two dollars if you wanted it buttered.[223]

The settlement was ravaged by fire in 1862 and flooded in 1878 but managed to survive mostly because of the rich hardrock mines in the area.

The two richest mines in the region were the Kennedy (referred to in the section on Jackson Gate) and the Argonaut. The Kennedy, which operated from 1856 to 1942, may have produced $34,280,000; the Argonaut, from 1859[224] to 1942,[225] $25,179,160.[226]

Jackson, county seat of Amador County,[227] still boasts the 1854 courthouse. Also of interest are the I.O.O.F. Hall, the National Hotel (Louisiana House), St. Sava's Serbian Orthodox Church, the Wells Fargo office, and a museum housed in an 1858 building.

Stagecoach at the National Hotel, Jackson, California, about 1893 — *Wells Fargo Bank History Room.*

Jackson in May 1851 — *Society of California Pioneers.*

The Butte Store near Jackson.

Clinton grew up east of Jackson as a placer mining community during the 1850s. Quartz was mined there as late as the 1880s.

Jackson Gate was founded immediately north of Jackson perhaps as early as 1850.

Large wheels used to help raise tailings from the ground level of the Kennedy mine to the summit of a ridge (beyond which lies the tailings disposal dump) are nearby attractions. The wheels, assembled in either 1902[228] or 1912,[229] once had a circle of 176 buckets, were sixty-eight feet[230] in diameter, and raised the tailings a vertical distance of forty-eight feet with electric motors. Sheet metal buildings which once housed each wheel were removed many years ago.

Jacksonville was named for Colonel Aldan Jackson, who discovered gold in the area in June 1849 (Jackson in Amador County was named for the same man). Jacksonville served as a supply and "fun" center for miners toiling along Moccasin and Woods creeks.

A visitor to Jacksonville on April 2, 1849, described the settlement: "the houses are of every possible variety, according to the taste and means of the miner. Most of these, even in winter, are tents. Some throw up logs a few feet high, filling up with clay between the logs. When a large company are to be accommodated with room, or a trading depot is to be erected, a large frame is made, and canvas is spread over this. Those who have more regard to their own comfort or health, erect log or stone houses, covering them with thatch or shingles."[231]

The Eagle-Shawmut was Jacksonville's best producing mine. It was located northwest of Jacksonville at the foot of Shawmut grade. Most of the riches recovered from the Eagle-Shawmut were found after the turn of the century. Total production is usually given as $7.5 million.[232] The mine was forced to close November 1, 1947.

Another gold camp named Jacksonville was located in Del Norte County.

James Bar (Lower Bar) was northwest of Double Springs. The site is inundated by Pardee reservoir.

Jamestown was named for San Francisco attorney Colonel George F. James, who prospected in the area in 1848. The miners and prospectors may have referred to the settlement as "Jimtown," although another version of the town's naming has it that a group of settlers following a man named George settled on one side of a creek. That settlement was known as George's Town. Followers of a man named Jim settled on the opposite creek bank in a community known as Jim's Town. As one writer[233] recounts it: "George's popularity soon dwindled, and his followers moved across the stream to Jim's Town — Jamestown today."

A plethora of mines existed on nearby Table Mountain, including the Humbug, which may have yielded $4 million.[234]

The Jamestown of today still harbors much of the gold rush look, including covered balcony architecture.

Jamison City (Jamieson) is above Johnsville, on Jamison Creek. The Jamison mine seems to have been the richest, producing more than $1.5 million in gold.

Jamestown.

The Emporium in Jamestown.

Jayhawk, west of Placerville, was named for J. Hawk, an early prospector. The camp was sometimes referred to as Jay Hawk.

Jefferson City's life span was less than one year. The camp was a mile south of Washington. The camp had a tent or two in the middle of 1850 but was deserted by December.

Jenny Lind may have been named for the "Swedish Nightingale."[235]

A high percentage of Jenny Lind's 400 or so population by 1850 was Mexican and Chinese.

The nearby Mokelumne River exhibits rapacious evidence of dredging by both draglines and dredges, in use from the mid-1930s until 1951. Placer mining also occurred in the area.

Not much of original Jenny Lind remains except the I.O.O.F. Hall and a few frame houses.

Jerseydale began during early gold rush days and has been an on-again off-again mining camp for many years.

Jersey Flat was immediately east of Downieville. When discovered in 1849, the place was called **Murraysville.** When the Jersey Company acquired the place, it was renamed Jersey Flat.

Jesus Maria was a Calaveras County camp perhaps named for a Mexican who sold vegetables to miners in the area during the early 1850s.

Jillsonville was a Shasta County camp that began in the 1860s but didn't flourish until I. O. Gillson bought the Gladstone mine and made it a profitable producer. Gillson had the company town of Jillsonville built in 1912. It is now very ghostly.

Johannesburg, more commonly known as Joburg, grew up in the shadow of Randsburg.

Johannesburg suffered from several fires during its mining days.

The center of social activities was a thirty-five-room hotel. The town also had several saloons, but no church. A ten-stamp mill was located at the site, but when it was built is not clear. The settlement was served by a railroad until the early 1930s, when the tracks were removed.

Little of the "golden era" remains in present-day Johannesburg, although miners still toil in the area.

Part of the vacant St. Charles Hotel at Johannesburg.

Slowly, but surely, the desert is claiming this remnant of man's efforts at Johannesburg.

Johnsville was built in the 1870s by a company of British capitalists who had invested in the area's land. At one time the town was known as **Jamison** and/or **Johnstown.**

The nearby Plumas Eureka mine began operation in 1851 and proved a good producer — yielding about $8 million in gold — until about 1925.[236] Mining in the Johnsville District has been sporadic since that time.

The L & C Livery in Johnsville.

The 1908 firehouse in Johnsville.

One of the more imposing buildings in Johnsville.

Johntown was a camp north of Coloma, on Johntown Creek. The camp was probably named in 1848 for a prospector named John, who, with others, had come to the area from Coloma.

Jordan (Jordon) was southwest of Bodie. It was home for a large quartz mill. Most mining activities seem to have occurred during the 1890s and early 1900s.

Josephine was an El Dorado County camp above Volcanoville.

Judsonville was a coal-mining town near Mount Diablo in Contra Costa County. The settlement existed from the mid-1850s to the mid-1880s, but little is known of the now extinct town.

Julian was established by the Bailey brothers and their cousins, the Julian brothers. They travelled to the region in 1869 shortly after gold was discovered near the soon-to-be-settled town of Julian.[237] The camp was probably named for Mike Julian.

The initial gold discovery seems to have been made on Tuesday, February 22, 1869 — George Washington's birthday. Naturally, the gold mine was dubbed the George Washington.

The town grew rapidly and supported two stamp mills and a number of houses. By 1890 four mills were thudding and clanking, while a fifth was under construction. By 1896, 1,000 people lived in and around Julian. Total gold production may have reached $15 million.

By the turn of the century, however, the entire district had become moribund. A flurry of mining activity was reported in the late 1930s and early 1940s, when perhaps 1,500 ounces were produced. No activity has been recorded since that time.

Julian found new life as an agricultural and stock-raising center.

Junction City (nee **Milltown**) grew up as a trading center for ranchers and miners.

It was at Junction City that a mining company laid 5,700 feet of siphon pipe to carry water down a 280-foot-deep canyon and up the other side. This was one of the few inverted siphons known to have been used in California mining.[238]

Julian in the early 1870s — *California State Library.*

Kanaka Bar was a Butte County mining camp that existed for several years. It was north of Bidwell Bar.

Southwest of Garden Valley, the El Dorado County mining camp of **Kanaka Diggings (Kanaka Town)** grew up. Its history may span about thirty years.

Kanaka Flat was east of Downieville.

Katesville was located near Michigan Bar in Sacramento County. The mining camp existed for less than ten years.

Keane Wonder was named for mine discoverer Jack Keane. The Inyo County mining camp on the west slope of the Funeral Range was a gold and silver camp.

Kearsarge may have been established in 1864. Apparently, Southern sympathizers in Owens Valley called their mine the Alabama, after a warship. After the *U.S.S. Kearsarge* sank the *Alabama*, several Union sympathizers named their mine the Kearsarge, in honor of the sea victory. The camp that arose near the mine inherited the name.

The town grew and supported a forty-stamp mill . . . or vice versa.

On March 1, 1867, a giant snowslide smothered most of Kearsarge. That night the entire population vacated their mountain homes and slipped down to Owens Valley, and that night, Kearsarge died.

Keeler, home of the Sierra Talc Company, is also the jumping off point for the torturous mountain trail to Cerro Gordo. The camp was named for mining superintendent Julius Keeler.

The narrow gauge rails of the Carson and Colorado Railroad stretched to Keeler from Mound House (east of Carson City), Nevada.[239] The place reached by the rails in 1883 is indicated by a marker in Keeler. Borax was hauled from the Keeler end of the line. As mines at Cerro Gordo and other places began to peter out, plans for extending the rail line from Keeler to Mojave were abandoned, leaving Keeler as "end of the line."

The little settlement snuggled near the northeastern edge of Owens Lake, in the shadow of Mount Whitney, still survives.

Cadaverous twin buildings at Keeler. Note the standing wall to the right.

A Keeler church.

A Keeler saloon.

Kelsey was initially known as **Kelsey's Diggings** and was founded six miles north of Placerville in 1851. James Marshall died at Kelsey's Union Hotel in 1885. Tom Allan's saloon — where Marshall sometimes bellied up to the bar — still stands. The saloon was one of twenty-four in the town.

Kennebec Bar popped onto the mining scene in 1849 and was abandoned the next spring. The camp was on the Yuba River in Yuba County.

Kennett, established in 1896, was a copper-mining town north of Redding. The town was not incorporated until 1911, with a population of 1,700.

The town site is now under water.

Kentucky Hill Diggings was a short-lived Sierra County camp.

Kenworthy was established in 1897 in Garner Valley, Riverside County. It was named for English investor Eugene Kenworthy, who lost all the money he had when the mines petered out in 1899.

The old hotel and post office at Kennett. The corner of Maguire's Drug Store is pictured at the right — *Shasta Historical Society.*

Kennett, looking west toward the Kennett Smelter, 1914 — *Shasta Historical Society.*

Kernville was first christened **Whiskey Flat**, from founding in 1860 until 1864. The camp's first "building" was opened by Adam Hamilton, who laid a plank across two whiskey barrels and declared his saloon open for business. The name of the camp was changed, probably at the insistence of the town's more "sensitive" citizens.

Placers were worked in the area as early as 1851. Gold-bearing quartz veins were discovered in 1860, and Kernville grew from the subsequent boom.

The Big Blue mine, owned by Kern Mines, Inc., was the richest of them all. It is credited with producing $1,746,910 in gold, much of which was crushed through an eighty-stamp mill.

In 1883 most of the workings were destroyed by fire. The Big Blue remained inactive until 1907, when the first of several attempts to reopen it failed.

The camp was swallowed by the backwaters created by the building of a dam to form Lake Isabella.

Keswick was northwest of Redding. Mining in the area was spawned by copper, but some gold was mined.

Keyesville grew up around the Keyes mine, discovered in 1854. The camp was named for pioneer prospector Richard Keyes. For many years the cacophony of stamp mills punctuated the air around this town west of Isabella.

A trench and breastworks of a fort built to protect citizens against Indian attack still remain at the site.

Kimshew probably straddled Butte Creek, northeast of Stirling City in Butte County. The name may be derived from an Indian name meaning "little water."

Kinsley (Kingsley) was east of Coulterville in Mariposa County. Mining has been carried out in the area spasmodically since the 1860s.

Klamath was on the Klamath River south of Happy Camp.

Klamath City was founded and surveyed by Hermann Ehrenberg in 1850. But by the next year the camp at the mouth of the Klamath River was vacant.

Klau, located in an area rich in quicksilver deposits, dates to the 1870s. It was founded between Cambria and Paso Robles in San Luis Obispo County.

Knight's Ferry was named for William Knight, who in 1848 or 1849 built the first ferry to straddle the Stanislaus River on the road between Stockton and Sonora. Knight's Ferry was also the center of placer mining along the lower Stanislaus, as well as being Stanislaus county seat from 1862 until 1872.

In 1856 an unsuccessful attempt was made to name the town Dentville, in honor of the brothers-in-law of Ulysses S. Grant — Lewis and John Dent. Grant, married to Julia Dent, travelled to Knight's Ferry in 1854 and stayed at the Dent House, which still stands. While visiting, Grant designed a bridge that was later constructed across the Stanislaus at Knight's Ferry. Although the bridge was washed away in 1862, it was replaced by a covered bridge two years later. The new bridge was very similar to the Grant design, but its floor was eight feet higher. The covered toll bridge was bought by the county in 1884. It still stands as a popular attraction.

Knob was a Shasta County village that served area miners.

Knoxville was one of several camps hastily established north of Lake Tahoe when mining excitement hit the area.

Kongsberg was founded about 1860 by Norwegian miners, who named the camp in honor of the Norwegian mining town. The Alpine County town burgeoned to a population of around 3,000 about one year after its founding. In 1863 when the post office was established, the place was called **Konigsberg.** Two years later it was renamed **Silver Mountain.**

The mines petered out, and by 1886 the town expired.

Kramer, west of Barstow, served as the home of the main plant of the Pacific Coast Borax Works.

Borax was not discovered in California

until 1856. The deposits near Kramer were located in 1912 by a homesteader drilling for water.

The camp was a supply center and a railroad center for area mines. In 1926 a spurt of gold mining activity caused some turbulent times, but not for long.

Kunkle (Kunkles) was located above Cherokee. Some mining was carried on in the area.

La Commodedad, in Tuolumne County, consisted mostly of Mexican (possibly Spanish) and French miners. It apparently was not a rich camp.

La Grange,[240] west of Coulterville, was founded as a mining camp in 1852. The town was settled by French miners who first dubbed it **French Bar.**

It has been speculated that Bret Harte taught school at La Grange and that the town is a likely setting for some of his writings.

The town grew to about 5,000 and from 1855 to 1862 served as Stanislaus county seat.

Tailing piles along the banks of the Tuolumne River attest to mining activity. The wooden I.O.O.F. Hall still remains from forty-niner days.

The mansion at the La Grange mine, June or July 1917 — *Trinity County Historical Society.*

A "piper" riding a hydraulic giant at the La Grange diggings — *Trinity County Historical Society.*

Lake City was immediately west of North Bloomfield. It was a rich hydraulic mining center, founded probably in 1858.

Lancha Plana was an Amador County camp settled by Mexicans in 1848. The camp located on the Mokelumne River is now blanketed by waters of the Camanche reservoir.

La Porte served as a hydraulic mining center during the 1850s and 1860s. Until 1857 or 1862[241] the town was apparently known as **Rabbit Creek.** With the passage of the debris control laws, which ended hydraulic mining, miners undertook drift mining.

All mining operations near La Porte were apparently difficult. The main channel of the Yuba River is about 500 feet wide, and most of the gold was situated at bedrock level or in the lower two feet of the gravel. Yet, $93 million in bullion is credited to area mines.

The Union Hotel and the decaying Wells Fargo building are about all that physically remain of early mining days, when the settlement sported three hotels, six stores, and fourteen saloons.

Last Chance was appropriately named in 1850 for a group of prospectors who almost starved at the camp. Feeling it was the last chance for survival, one of the men was sent in search of wild game. He shot and killed a large deer, saving the men and the camp.

By 1852 Last Chance had become a boom town, and by 1858 it housed three lodge halls. However, along with so many other camps, Last Chance declined. Today it is only a shadow of what it once was.

The gravemarker of Allen Grosch remains in the Last Chance cemetery.[242] Grosch and his brother Hosea are credited by some authorities as being the original discoverers of the Comstock Lode in Nevada.

Another camp known as Last Chance flourished briefly in Butte County, north of Oroville.

Latimers was northwest of San Andreas. The camp was named for store and boardinghouse owner David Latimer.

Lake City in 1880. Water for hydraulic mining was stored here — *Nevada County Historical Society.*

Leadfield was situated on the top of Titus Canyon, west of Rhyolite, Nevada.

The person generally credited with "fathering" the town is C. C. Julian, who promoted the camp as being in the midst of a mineral-rich district.

In March 1926, about 1,000 or more Los Angeles investors came by train and car to Leadfield. The camp grew to the point where a post office was established, but, overpromoted and undercapitalized, Leadfield lost the post office the following year.

Foundations, walls, and detritus mark the spot.

Lee is a ghost town that barely resides within the California boundary. Located near the Nevada state line, the town is virtually inaccessible, and its history is obscure.

The camp was probably founded in 1906 but officially not platted until 1907. The town very likely straddled the state line, but most buildings appear to have been on the California side.

A gold strike in 1852 led to the founding of **Leevining** (also spelled Lee Vining). The town was named for nearby Leevining Canyon, which, in turn, was named for Lee (Leroy) Vining — the man who led a party of prospectors to the gold field.

Lewis (or **Lewisville, Louisville,** or **Lewis Ferry**) was founded about 1850 by Daniel Lewis in Tuolumne County.

Lewiston was located east of Weaverville during gold rush days. The town was named for B. F. Lewis, who settled there in 1854.

One of the town's vintage buildings is the schoolhouse, erected on October 18, 1862 as the meeting hall for the Sons of Temperance lodge. On July 9, 1865 the structure reverted to the school system. The schoolhouse was repaired and improved about 1896 when the "tasty and convenient"[243] Lewiston Congregational Church was built near it.

One of the more stately structures in the camp was the Lewiston Hotel, where guests were charged two bits a meal — the same for a bed.

Goetze's Butcher Shop at Lewiston about 1894. Butcher L. Schall is on the left, H. W. Goetze, owner, on the right — *Trinity County Historical Society.*

Paulson's store at Lewiston — *Trinity County Historical Society.*

A sizeable Chinese population came to Lewiston, perhaps up to 1,000.[244] Chinatown was located about one-half mile from Lewiston proper. The joss house was much like the one in Weaverville.

Lewiston (the site was actually about three miles upriver) is remembered as being near where construction was begun on the first dredge built on the Trinity River. The wood-burning steam dredge was built in 1887 but didn't go into operation until 1889. One of its builders described its initial startup as sounding "like a four-horse gravel wagon on a rocky bar."[245] But flood waters washed the dredge away that spring, and dredging wasn't resumed until about 1913. The dredge (built by the Trinity Dredging Company) was shut down in 1940 and dismantled, although some of the hull and framework can still be seen. For a time the Madrona Dredging Company operated another dredge near Lewiston.

Liberty Hill was a Nevada County mining settlement in Little York Township.

It's not absolutely clear if there was a camp called **Lincoln.** If so, it would have been in Placer County, about fifteen miles west of Auburn. The camp was situated in copper and gold-mining regions.

Linda was on the Yuba River above Marysville. It was named for the steamer *Linda,* brought up the Feather River in 1849 by the Linda Company. It was the first steamboat to enter the Yuba River.

Lindsays Bar was located above Oroville. Its brief existence as a Butte County gold camp left very little for the record.

Linns Valley was named for an early prospector named William Lynn. The Kern County camp was on Poso Creek.

Little Grizzley was above Downieville. It's said that a gold nugget worth $2,000 was located there in 1869.

Little Kimshew was situated east of Inskip. It must have been fairly close to Big Kimshew, another short-lived Butte County mining camp.

Little Prairie was south of Big Bar along Trinity County's Trinity River.

Little Rock was a mining camp near Bear River. Its neighbors, **You Bet** and **Red Dog**, were both short-lived mining camps in the Grass Valley area.

Little York was southwest of Dutch Flat. The town was organized in 1852 and received its post office in 1855. After placer mines gave out, hardrock mining followed, and it, in turn, gave way to hydraulic mining. After the prohibition of hydraulic mining in 1884, the camp began a gradual, but definite, decline.

Live Oak was a Sacramento County mining camp that began prior to 1854. But by 1860 or so the camp was "on the skids." Chinese miners breathed some life into the declining camp about 1880, but its demise clearly was near at hand by that time.

Loganville was established west of Sierra City. The Sierra County mining camp was probably founded in 1851. Although not particularly robust, the old camp exists to this day.

Logtown's site is marked by ruins of a stamp mill that crushed ores from area mines, probably including the rich Montezuma.

The town was located in Logtown Ravine, between Plymouth and El Dorado.

Ruins of an arrastre have been found near Logtown. When the machinery was in service is not known, although the first quartz mills probably began operation in 1856.

Another camp known as Logtown was once located near Mariposa.

The town of **Long Bar** once stood on the banks of the Yuba River. The camp was probably established in the late 1840s.[246] It may have been named for brothers John and Willis Long.

By 1864 the post office was closed, and three years later the site was buried by gravel from hydraulic mining operations upstream.

One observer and participant in the gold rush wrote about setting up a store and boardinghouse for miners at Long Bar.[247]

Six other geographic features or mining camps of the same name were located in the state. **Longs Bar** was on the Feather River near Oroville.

Apparently there were three camps known as **Long Gulch**; in Siskiyou, Tuolumne, and Calaveras counties.

The silver camp of **Lookout** was perched above the Modoc and Minnietta mines on Lookout Mountain west of Death Valley National Monument. Several intact structures and some ruins remain.

Los Burros was founded on the western slopes of the Santa Lucia Range west of Jolon.

The discovery of the Last Chance mine on Alder Creek in 1887 kept Los Burros area mining activity alive until about World War I.

Los Muertos was near Altaville and was probably also known as **Campo de los Muertos.** It was here, in 1851, that several hundred Americans totally destroyed the camp of about 3,000 Mexicans.

Lost City was probably founded by French miners. It was established north of Copperopolis but abandoned when the gold gave out. Some physical remains still exist of the approximately twenty that at one time comprised the settlement, also perhaps known as **Stone City** or **Stone Creek Settlement.**

Lotus was first known as **Marshall,** in honor of gold discoverer James Marshall. Its name was then changed to **Uniontown,** and finally to Lotus.

The community flowered to 2,000, but when the placers were exhausted, the town dwindled to a few diehards.

Gold associated with roscoelite, a rare mineral found in only a few places in the United States, was discovered in the Stuckslager mine, making the Lotus mining area rather unique.

The brick Adam Lohry store and house, built in 1859, still stand. The Uniontown pioneer cemetery holds the graves of many early Lotus settlers.

Louisville was first called **Spanish Flat.** The abandoned camp north of Kelsey dates to about 1850. The Alhambra and Lost Ledge mines are nearby.

Lovelock was above Magalia, in Butte County. Mills were built here, but it is possible that only one other building existed in the town — a store.

Some gold was panned in the area of **Lowden Ranch (Loudens)** southeast of Weaverville. The camp had a post office from 1874 to 1908.

Ludlow area lode mines produced over $6 million in gold, more than half the total recorded gold production for San Bernardino County. The Bagdad-Chase mine, discovered in 1903, produced $4.5 million in gold in seven years.[248] The same mine also produced copper and silver.

For almost one quarter of a century the post office at Ludlow was called **Stagg.** The settlement east of Barstow is on the Santa Fe Railroad.

A reminder of more halcyon days at Ludlow.

The Ludlow Mercantile Company building, dating to 1908.

Bagdad mine in the Ludlow area — *Collection of Historical Photographs, Title Insurance and Trust Company, Los Angeles.*

Lundy grew up as a lumber camp to help satiate the housing and mining needs of people in Bodie, twenty miles to the east.

The town swelled to 3,000 people, with a main street four blocks in length. Lundy was located on the western end of Lundy Lake, in Mill Creek Canyon. The town was a part of the Homer Mining District, organized in 1879[249] shortly after William D. Wasson had discovered gold. The town was named for William Lundy or his daughter.

The May Lundy was the most prolific mine. It has been credited with a total production of $1.5 million or more.[250] Mines on Copper Mountain were a part of the Jordan Mining District, northeast of Lundy. These operations generally spanned the period from 1894 to 1902, although some sources place the May Lundy as being a major producer until 1911, and as operating on a limited scale until the 1930s. A forty-stamp mill, run by water diverted from Lundy Lake, was erected in the area in 1896.

A number of other mines were worked in the area, but frequent slides washed them into Lundy Lake.

During Lundy's early days, an English company which owned local properties decided to establish a newspaper to tell of the "glorious" happenings at Lundy. They hired J. W. E. Townsend as editor. It has been suggested that in coastal circles the man was known as "Lying Jim Townsend."[251] He published the *Homer Mining Index,* which may or may not have told the truth in any given issue. The *Index* fabricated items about celebrations, timetables, and entertainment events.[252]

With the closing of the May Lundy mine in 1898, the town began to die, and, as one observer noted, "There is now only good fishing at this shadow town."[253]

Lynchburg was launched southeast of Oroville. Named for store owner George Lynch, the camp was once robust but began to atrophy by the mid-1850s.

In addition to the Butte County Lynchburg, another place of the same name may have existed in Placer County in the Ralston Divide area.

McDowell Hill (McDowellsville) was an El Dorado County mining camp on the South Fork of the American River. The gold camp may have reached a population of 100, but by 1883 it was a ghost town.

McKinneys (McKinneys Humbug, McKinneys Secret Diggings) was east of San Andreas, in Calaveras County. It's known that a ten-stamp, water-driven mill operated there and that the camp's peak population may have reached 1,000.

Magalia (also known as **Dogtown, Mountain View,** and **Butte Mills**), north of Oroville in north-central Butte County, is situated in the Magalia Mining District.

Gravels of the Magalia stream were mined in early placer days, but the Perschbaker hardrock mine produced most of the gold in the district.

A logging team at Magalia — *Paradise Fact and Folklore, publishers of "Tales of the Paradise Ridge."*

Mammoth City was founded near Mammoth Lake. A. J. Wren and John Briggs may have made the first mining discovery in the area in 1875.[254] A prospecting party led by James A. Parker discovered the Alpha claim on June 20, 1877, near what was to become Mammoth City. Wren and Briggs later located the Mammoth mine on July 30, 1877.

In the spring of 1878 the boom began, and twenty cabins were soon under construction. The camp had a population of 125. By 1879, six hotels and twenty-two saloons signalled that Mammoth City was the scene of yet another California bonanza. One thousand people flooded the settlement. A contemporary newspaper account described the town as having "three physicians, three police, jail, school superintendent."[255]

Two other virile mining camps —**Pine City** and **Mineral Park** — originated in the area, but Mammoth City outstripped both of them.

Mammoth City even boasted a hot spring five miles below town. One could cook a potato in seventeen minutes in the spring's boiling water.[256]

Five claims that were consolidated into the "Mammoth group" were purchased by General George S. Dodge, Union Pacific railroad builder. When the $30,000 purchase was made in 1878, the Mammoth Mining Company was formed, and a forty-stamp mill, run by water power from Lake Mary, was constructed. By 1880 the company had spent about $185,000 more than it had taken in — although a newspaper reported that the mill was closed down from a lack of quicksilver and chemicals. Whatever the truth, people left in droves, and by spring the camp was deserted. The *Mammoth City Times* commented about their departure: "Twenty pairs of snowshoes, each with a man on top, left this morning." The Mammoth Company came to an end with a sheriff's auction in September 1881.

Mariposa[257] is the site of the oldest courthouse in California, built in 1854 and fastened together with wooden pegs. The courthouse opened for business in February 1855.

Explorer-soldier John C. Fremont enters into the history of the founding of the settlement. When he learned about the gold discovery at Coloma in 1848, Fremont "floated" his 44,000-acre Mexican land

The 1858 jail at Mariposa.

grant, Rancho Las Mariposas, to the east, just in case the area might contain gold. Sure enough, in the summer of 1849 gold veins were discovered at his ranch on the southern extreme of the Mother Lode. Fremont hired Mexican miners and began operating a quartz mill in 1850. The town that grew up around the operations was Mariposa, named for the mine. The boiler for the steam engine used in the mill may have come from a ship that had run aground near San Francisco.[258]

The Mariposa mine thrived between 1900 and 1915, with its peak production year being 1901. By 1955 total production was almost $2.5 million. The Black Drift, the Princeton, the Josephine, and the Pine Tree were other leading mines in the area.

Although some of Mariposa's early buildings still stand, the settlement could hardly be classified as a ghost town. Located on the busy route to Yosemite National Park, Mariposa serves as a tourist center, plus retains its status as a farming community.

Markleeville, located on Highway 4 east of Placerville, near the Nevada border, was also on an early immigrant route. Settled in the 1850s, the town was a supply point for timber used in the Comstock Lode mines of Nevada.

Martell, northwest of Jackson, was supported primarily by the Oneida mine, which produced over $2.5 million in gold. Operations ceased in 1913,[259] and today only the mine dumps mark the location of this once-rich bonanza.

The camp was probably named for Canadian Louis Martell.

Martinez (Martinas) was a camp of Mexicans southeast of Columbia. It may have been named for a Mexican woman who used a number of peons to work for her.

Martins was east of Marysville. The camp was originally a gold camp, then later became a stage stop. As it faded and died, it was superseded by **Marigold,** a headquarters town for gold dredging operations in the Yuba River area.

Marysville sprouted up in 1842 at the confluence of the Feather and Yuba rivers as a way station on the Oregon–California Trail. The townsite was platted in 1848–49 and named for Mary Murphy Covillaud, a survivor of the ill-fated Donner party and wife of a townsite owner.[260]

Marysville's growth was phenomenal. Within two years it had become the third largest city in the state, boasting a population of 5,000. By 1855 the town peaked at 8,000. The impressively large amount of local mule traffic could also serve as a measure of Marysville's hustle and bustle: an estimated 1,000 braying, brawling mules a day left Marysville for area mines.[261]

Placer, hardrock, dredging, and hydraulic operations were all carried on in the area. As early as 1850 a small river steamer named the *Phoenix* was outfitted as a dredge to mine the bottom of the Yuba River about nine miles above Marysville. It was apparently a failure. Hydraulic operations had so changed the lay of the land around Marysville that the Yuba River bottom had been raised seventy feet or more. Although the original Marysville had perched above the river, the riverbed now rests above the city streets behind large dikes.

Unfortunately for Marysville, both fire and flood ravaged the town. Fires struck in 1851, 1854, and 1856, and floods swept through in 1852, 1853, 1861, 1862, 1866, and 1875, destroying most of the original buildings. By 1880 the town's population had dwindled to 4,300.

A near-flood also threatened the community in 1907, when it rained for the entire month of February. An observer said, "it rained day and night the entire month and was so foggy that large flocks of ducks and geese feeding on the sprouting winter wheat would be come [*sic*] so confused they would fly into electric-light-and-power lines."[262]

Brown's Valley, east of Marysville,[263] was in Bonanza ore — $25 million of it.

Masonic was a mining town that may have been founded in the 1860s.

Located in Masonic Gulch northeast of Bridgeport, Masonic was actually composed of three closely grouped towns: Upper Town, Middle Town, and Lower Town.

A view from the west side of the plaza at Marysville — *Society of California Pioneers.*

The town had three grocery stores, two hotels, and a post office. Peak population may have reached 600.

Early mining activities in the area were sporadic. More extensive operations were begun when the Pittsburgh-Liberty mine was opened in 1902. Five years later a ten-stamp mill and cyanide plant were built. The Chemung mine was discovered in 1909 and was operated until the 1940s.

Some mining and prospecting have occurred in the vicinity in recent years.

The silver camp of **Clinton** grew, fizzled, and died in Ferris Canyon, northwest of Masonic.

Massachusetts Flat was an El Dorado County mining camp near the confluence of the North and South forks of the American River. First references to the camp were in 1854, and the following year it was considered a thriving town, composed mostly of Portuguese and blacks.

Matildaville was located in Nevada County (northeast of Nevada City) and was probably named in honor of the camp's first female resident.

Meadow Lake (also known as **Summit City**) is now a shadowy ghost town in Nevada County.

The 160-acre settlement[264] was established in 1865[265] and incorporated the following year. It has been estimated that 3,000 people visited the town in its early days and that perhaps 200 stayed during the summer of 1865 when 75 to 150 buildings were erected.

Apparently no mining activity of any significance occurred during 1866, and as winter approached, most people left Meadow Lake. However, as the next mining season drew near, between 4,000 and 10,000 men began to crowd the town. When it was discovered that gold in the area could not be successfully treated, residents once again departed, and the town began to die.

The town's newspaper, the *Meadow Lake Morning Sun,* began as a daily, but the next issue appeared as a weekly. By November 1867, the publication had completely ceased. Only one person remained in Meadow Lake by 1872, although ten men, two women, two cats, one mule, and a dying dog were reported in 1880. However, the town was completely deserted by the winter of 1892–93.

During its heyday, Meadow Lake was hardly recognized as a culinary capital. One observer assayed Meadow Lake hash to be composed of the following percentages: "Hair-7; Gum boots-3; Potatoes-60; Flies-2; Yellow jackets-1; Pork, very old-15; Beef-10; False teeth-2."

Camps located near Meadow Lake included **Richport, Wrightman's Camp, Baltimore City, Lakeville, Hudsonville, Excelsior, Ossaville, Enterprise City, Rocklin, Carlisle, Paris, Mendoza, Atlanta,** and perhaps **Petroliaville** and **Kerosene City.**

Meadow Valley Camp grew up on the route between Oroville and Quincy. The camp was nearly stillborn, surviving only from 1852 to 1855. Little is known about this ephemeral place.

Melones was founded by Mexican miners in 1848 and probably was named for the coarse gold in the shape of melon seeds that had been discovered at a nearby camp.[267] Melones had first been called **Slumgullion,** then **Roaring Camp,** and finally **Robinson's Ferry,** for a man who ferried travelers across the Stanislaus River. Robinson foolishly sold his ferry at a low price in 1856 to Harvey Wood, who operated it for half a century and made an enormous profit.[268]

Much of the town's mining history went up in flames during a fire in 1942 that destroyed the large 100-stamp mill and other buildings.

Mendoza was a Nevada County camp near Enterprise. The dim record seems to indicate that it was alive in 1866 and dead by 1880.

Merrimac was probably on the Butte-Plumas County line. It was named for the Civil War Confederate iron-covered battleship. Its post office's lifespan was from 1883 to 1934.

Mescal, a silver camp founded in 1887, can be found today near Interstate 15 just west of Mountain Pass.

The camp may have once been called **Nantan,** because the local post office carried that name for about three years.

Messerville was in the Weaverville area in Trinity County. Its post office, established in 1860, was in operation for slightly over one year.

Mexican Flat was west of Jamestown. The obscure camp was apparently on the east slope of Whiskey Hill.

Michigan Bar is the monicker for two camps — one in Sacramento County, one in El Dorado. The former probably peaked at a population of 1,000, while population figures for the latter weren't located. The El Dorado camp is the center of controversy, because some authorities believe that it, and not Michigan Bluff, was where financial wizard Leland Stanford owned a store.

Michigan Bluff (Michigan City) perches on a ridge 2,000 feet above the Middle Fork of the American River. Leland Stanford[269] managed a store at Michigan Bluff from 1853 to 1855, according to some reports. An old house reportedly once occupied by Stanford has been a landmark for years.[270] Others argue if the store and cottage were Stanford's.

Today little of the original settlement remains.

Middle Bar was located near Mokelumne Hill. A bridge was built in 1851 across the Mokelumne River — the first to span that river. The site is sometimes inundated by the waters of Pardee reservoir, depending on the ebb and flow.

Middletown was in the Shasta City area. Its post office survived for less than two years in the 1850s; the camp was deserted in the 1860s.

Mill City was a mining camp situated near Mammoth City.

The town is now deserted. The ruins of the

Mammoth Mining Company's forty-stamp mill can be detected. Scattered foundations also remain to mark the spot where yet another California mining camp arose, grew, and died. Rest in Peace.

Millertown (Millerton?) was near Ophir in Placer County. Nothing of its history was unearthed.

Millspaugh was a camp concurrent with the Tonopah–Goldfield saga. It lies within the U.S. Naval Ordnance Test Station, so travel to it is prohibited.

California had two places named **Milton,** both on or near county lines. The Calaveras County transportation and trading center was on the Calaveras-Stanislaus line between Copperopolis and Stockton; the Sierra County camp was a transportation center near the Sierra and Nevada County lines.

Mineral King was established in 1873 by three spiritualists who staked a silver claim named White Chief Lode, in honor of the Indian spirit which, they said, had guided them to the riches.

A toll road was built to the site, but since the silver couldn't be profitably mined, most people left the area. A snowslide in 1888 further discouraged settlement.

Today the town serves as a site for summer homes development.

Minersville (Diggerville or **Diggersville)** was located at the confluence of Digger Creek and the East Fork of Stuart's Fork of the Trinity River in the early 1850s by a Reverend Morris, a Methodist minister, and a man named Cameron.

The tangled skein of its early days may be somewhat clarified in this account from a publication of the Trinity County Historical Society which states: "Minersville Post Office was established in 1858 at Bates and Van Matre Ranch. It was moved to Old Minersville in 1859, and was soon moved to the Unity Mine three miles north. In 1902 it was returned to Minersville or the Van Matre Ranch after the Unity Mine ceased operations."[271]

The settlement had the reputation of being a place famous for pretty girls and "fast" young men.[272] A newspaper[273] in the autumn of 1857 indicated of the bustling village: "The carpenter's hammer and blacksmith's anvil are keeping time to the song of hope for the future."

The 1885 county directory only listed one woman and thirty-nine men (twenty-five of them miners) living in Minersville.

Old tales don't seem to die, or fade away, or change much over the years. One which persistently circulates in the area is of a couple who built a cabin near Old Minersville, near Granite Peak. When the wife died, the husband buried her on a ridge over Digger Creek. The property changed hands and because the new owner didn't want a grave close to the cabin, she ordered the body exhumed and re-interred at Weaverville. When the woman's body was dug up, it was found she had turned to stone. Some say there's "something in the ground" in the Minersville area that makes such things happen.

The camp was destroyed by the formation of Trinity Lake.

Ridgeville was a town of about 700 located on the ridge between Minersville and Mule Creek. At one time it was known as **Golden City.** Men named Allen and Wasson probably first settled the camp in 1855. By 1858 the population had shrunk to 150, and a few years later the town was abandoned.

Sebastopol was on the East Fork of Stuarts Fork, near Minersville. It was fathered by J. F. Chellis in 1853. Chellis had a woodworking factory where he made armchairs, beds, window sashes, door casings, and cabinets. He also ran a planing mill and a grist mill. He later became lieutenant governor of California.

Minnesota was a Sierra County camp probably settled in 1851 by a man, or men, from Minnesota. A couple of very large nuggets of gold were found here in the 1850s.

Mississippi Bar seems to have been a transitory settlement along the American River near Folsom. Another place on the North Fork of the Yuba River in Yuba County of the same name may have been a camp or simply a geographic feature.

Missouri Bar was a popular name in California mining history. Of places so named, most were river bars (in Butte, El Dorado, Nevada, and Plumas counties), and two were perhaps mining camps (in Trinity and Yuba counties). The Trinity County camp was located on the river of the same name. It prospered during the 1850s. The Yuba County mining camp was probably on the North Fork of the Yuba River, also having its prosperous years in the 1850s. Another place called Missouri Bar may have been on the main Yuba River between the North and South forks.

Moccasin Creek (Mocosin, Mocassin) was a mining camp southeast of Jacksonville. Some say the place was named for water snakes in the area, mistakenly thought to be moccasin snakes.

Modock was in the Modoc (?) mining district east of Darwin, in the Argus Mountains. The post office opened in 1890 but was closed in 1903.

Mogul was near Markleeville in Alpine County. Gold, silver, and copper were mined in the area during the 1860s and 1870s.

Mohawk was named for Mohawk Valley, New York. The Mohawk Valley trading center served miners and prospectors working gold and copper mines in the area. The Plumas County camp is along Highway 89.

Mojave, located on Highways 6 and 466 near Edwards Air Force Base, is an unusual mining town. It was here that J. W. S. Perry built wagons to haul borax from Death Valley. From 1883 until 1888, twenty-mule-team wagons hauled borax to Mojave, which in later years became an agricultural center.

A Mojave Desert stamp mill — *Collection of Historical Photographs, Title Insurance and Trust Company, Los Angeles.*

Mokelumne Hill was established in 1848; by 1849 it was a thriving community. The town, frequently called "Mok Hill" or "The Hill," was county seat of Calaveras County from 1852 to 1866, despite the rumor that one man had been killed every weekend for seventeen weeks and five had been killed in just one week.

The I.O.O.F. building is unique. The structure was erected in 1854 with two stories housing the Adams Express Company. A third story was added in 1861 by the I.O.O.F., making the hall the first three-story building in the Mother Lode.

Mokelumne Hill was the scene of two "wars": the "Chilean" and the "French." In 1849 a man named Dr. Concha was working claims with Chilean labor. The claims were registered in the names of several of Concha's laborers, but Concha took the profits. The war itself was precipitated when Concha's men drove some Americans off rich placer ground. The men entered "The Hill" in December 1849, killing two men and capturing thirteen. The prisoners, in turn, seized Concha's men, brought them to town,

The I.O.O.F. Hall at Mok Hill.

The Calaveras County courthouse and Leger Hotel in Mok Hill.

The L. Mayer & Son building in Mok Hill, dating to 1854.

Ledbetter's at "Mok" Hill.

hanged three of them, and punished the others. Thus ended the Chilean War.

The "French War" occurred in 1851 when American miners tried to seize properties being worked by French miners. The French had planted a Tricolor at the location called French Hill. The Americans quarreled that the French were defying Old Glory, stormed the hill, took a fortune in gold, and appropriated French claims.

No Chinese "War" is chronicled, although Mokelumne Hill had a large number of Chinese. One source[274] even claims that Mok Hill's Chinatown had a slave market, where female servants were bought, sold, and exchanged.

Despite debilitating fires in 1854, 1864, and 1874, remains of the Hemminghoffen-Suesdorf Brewery, the I.O.O.F. Hall, the Congregational Church, and the Leger Hotel still stand to remind visitors of Mok Hill's colorful past.[275]

Monitor (also called **Loope**) was located in the Markleeville area.

The settlement boomed during the 1860s and 1870s and even supported a weekly newspaper, the *Alpine Miner.*

Silver, copper, and gold were mined in the region, but little else is known of this mystery camp near Monitor Pass.

Mono Mills was founded in 1872 but didn't build up much steam until 1881, when it evolved into a lumber and cordwood center for southern Nevada mining camps such as Tonopah and Goldfield. The town was located on the Bodie Railway and Lumber Company line.

The railroad and mills kept many Chinese and Paiute Indians occupied in the summer, but the workers deserted the camp for the remainder of the year.[276]

Monoville is gone, but the site is remembered as being the focus of activity surrounding the searches for the lost "cement mines," where three German brothers allegedly found "lumps of gold set like raisins in a pudding." The winter weather drove the men from their fortune, killing two and leaving one insane. The treasure has never been found.

A miner from Dogtown supposedly found gold in 1859 at what later became Monoville. The prospector told fellow Dogtown residents of his find, and the *Inyo Register*[277] reported that when people visited Dogtown the following month, they found only four men remaining. In almost one day Monoville bloomed into existence.

Men from several other camps scampered to Monoville, and soon the town held 700 residents. That winter the camp's population shrivelled to about 150. When the severe winter sealed the camp with snow, starvation threatened. But provisions were finally scrounged and the miners survived. Mark Twain may have been correct when he speculated that the Monoville area had only two seasons: the breaking up of one winter and the beginning of the next.

In the spring of 1860 a ditch brought water for hydraulic mining. Sawmills whined, buzzed, sputtered, and spat out lumber for buildings. But when news of other discoveries came to Monoville, most of the town's population departed. Evidence of early hydraulic operations at Sinnamon Cut are about all that mark the site of the former mining camp that "lasted soon," as the saying used to be.

Monte Cristo was a Sierra County mining camp that grew up northwest of Downieville during the 1850s. Another camp of the same name existed briefly in Mono County, southeast of Star City. Its founding seems to date to the 1880s.

Montezuma was situated below Jamestown. Mining in the area may have begun as early as 1849. The settlement was apparently initially known as **Oak Spring,** but in 1854 the name was changed to Montezuma; however, by 1887 the post office was closed.

Moore's Flat was founded southwest of Graniteville in 1851 or 1852 by H. M. Moore. When the post office was established in 1853 the camp was known as **Clinton,** but it was changed to Moore's Flat in 1857. The town was apparently moved from place to place as hydraulic mining consumed the community and its sister camps such as **Orleans Flat, Illinois Flat** (or **Illinois Ravine** or **Illinois Bar**), **Blue Diggin's,** and **Chinee Flat.**[278] The camp may have reached a peak population of 5,000. What hydraulic washings did not flush away, fire did, and Moore's Flat died.

Mooretown was in Butte County, between the Middle and South forks of the Feather River. Area miners were supplied by Mooretown businessmen and by the town's post office, which lasted from 1888 to 1913.

The exact location of **Mooreville** could not be determined; but it probably was in southeastern Butte County. It was the scene of unsuccessful hydraulic mining.

Mormon Bar was located southeast of Mariposa in the southernmost part of the Mother Lode. Little remains of the town founded in 1848 or 1849 by Mormon miners on the bank of Mariposa Creek.

The Mormons were searching for farms, not mines. The camp grew from the efforts of Chinese miners, who cleaned the creek bed of gold and established a settlement.

Part of the Mariposa County fairgrounds rest on the site of old Mormon Bar.

Mormon Island (Lower Mines, Mormon Diggings) is now submerged beneath Folsom Lake. Gudde (page 225) claims that it was the first "regular" gold camp in the state, following closely the discovery of gold at Sutter's mill. Gold was discovered here on March 2, 1848 by two Mormons. Gudde (pages 225-26) further claims that the findings at Mormon Island actually started the California gold rush.

Morris Bar (Morris Ravine, Morrisons Ravine) was a Table Mountain camp above Oroville. It may have been named for Morris, Illinois, home of the Armstrong brothers, butchers at neighboring Longs Bar. The camp was probably founded following gold discoveries during May 1848. Mining continued sporadically for many years.

Morristown was northwest of Downieville. The camp along Canyon Creek served as headquarters for drift and hydraulic miners.

Mosquito Gulch was northeast of Mok Hill. It was sometimes spelled Musquito. Germans, Mexicans, and Italians pocket mined the area. The post office was established in 1858 and closed in 1878.

Mosquito (Mosquito Valley) was northeast of Placerville. Gold discoveries were first made in 1849. When placers gave out, men turned to quartz mining and finally to agriculture.

A tent was pitched in 1849 at **Mountain House** to serve miners en route to the goldfields. The town grew up near Altamont Pass near Livermore, east of San Leandro.

In addition to this Alameda County camp, others of the same name grew up in Butte, Plumas, Shasta, and Sierra counties. They were all gold camps.

Mountain Ranch (originally called **El Dorado**) was the site of an old sawmill used to provide lumber for area mines and miners. The still-extant settlement can be found northeast of San Andreas on Flat Road.

Sender's Market, Domenghini's General Store, and ruins of other structures remain.

The diminutive nine- by six-foot post office may have set a record as being the smallest in California.[279]

Mount Bullion, established in 1850, is located on Highway 49 northwest of Mariposa. The town was originally called **La Mineta**, then **Princeton**, but was renamed after a nearby mountain which, in turn, had been named for Senator Thomas Hart Benton.[280] Benton had been dubbed "Old Bullion" from his many political battles to maintain hard currency.

The camp's population may have peaked at 2,000. The Princeton mine, named for its co-discoverer Prince Steptoe, produced at least $4 million. Opened in 1852, the mine was worked until 1915.

Mount Hope, east of Forbestown, was located near the Yuba-Butte county line. Both placer and hardrock mining were carried on here, but only for a short time.

Only a few stone ruins remain to mark the site of **Mount Ophir**, located on the old highway that parallels the present Highway 49 north of Mount Bullion. Louis Trabucco's roofless schist store is the most imposing ruin.

The rumor that Mount Ophir was the site of California's first mint has not, however, disappeared along with the town. Contrary to popular opinion, it was the Pacific Company in San Francisco that produced the first gold coins in 1849.[281] However, when the first United States Mint was opened in California, several private firms were approved by federal inspectors to produce the gold coins. The Mount Ophir Mint was one of the chosen concerns. By 1851[282] John L. Moffatt and Company was coining hexagon-

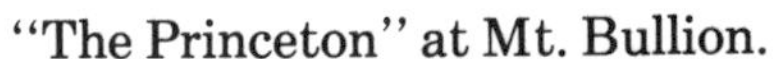
"The Princeton" at Mt. Bullion.

shaped fifty-dollar gold slugs at Mount Ophir, although the mint may have gone into operation in late 1850.

Mugginsvilles appeared in Placer, Sierra, and Siskiyou counties, and maybe in Plumas and Calaveras counties. The Sierra County camp was probably near Gold Hill, near Auburn. It appears to have begun with Gold Hill in the early 1850s and to have died a short time later. The Siskiyou County camp was on Mill Creek in Quartz Valley. Remnants of a stamp mill still mark the spot.

Muletown was on Mule Creek, above Ione, in Amador County. Here, at one time, admission to a dance hall was: single man, six dollars; with one lady, three dollars; with two ladies, free. Another Muletown (originally known as **One Mule Town**) was located in Shasta County, southwest of Redding.

Murderers Bar, along the Middle Fork of the American River in El Dorado County, was probably named for five Oregonians who were killed by Indians at the site.

Places of the same name were also in Siskiyou and Yuba counties.

Murphys[283] (also spelled Murphy's) was founded by brothers John and Daniel Murphy, who struck gold on Angel's Creek in July 1848. The camp reached its peak in 1855, and during the following year, J. Sperry and J. Perry constructed the Mitchler's Hotel,[284] now known as the Murphy's. The hotel still survives, along with the guest book, which reveals such names as Mark Twain, U. S. Grant, Henry Ward Beecher, J. Pierpont Morgan, Horatio Alger, Jr., outlaw Black Bart, and others.

Area mines eventually produced about $2 million in gold.

On August 20, 1859, fire leveled most of the business district. The hotel, a bakery, two stores dating to 1855, and a Wells Fargo express office still remain, along with an 1860 schoolhouse.

A mile east of Murphys was the mining camp of **Brownsville,** named for Alfred Brown, former ranch owner.

Placer mining at Murphys — *Society of California Pioneers.*

The Valente building at Murphys. Built about 1891 by James Valente, a custom bootmaker and dealer in hats, the building is made of local lava rock.

Murphy's Hotel.

Nashville (Quartzville, Quartzburg) was probably named for the Tennessee city. At one time as many as 100 arrastres were at work in the area, on the North Fork of the Cosumnes River.

Natoma (Notoma) began as a mining center in 1880. Dredging operations allowed the town to retain its status as a rich gold producer. Production totals probably exceeded $40 million. The Natomas Company headquarters at Natoma, near Folsom, is no longer on postal or highway maps. The company had an office building, a retort house, and a machine shop.

Natchez was located along the Natchez Fork of Honcut Creek. Born in 1850, the camp died a few years later.

Neals Diggings was on Butte Creek near Chinese Camp. It was probably named for rancher Sam Neal.

Nebraska Diggings (Nebraska City, Nebraska Flat) was southeast of Downieville. At times the place has been referred to as **Cornish House.**

Negro Bar was on the American River below Folsom. It was probably named for blacks.

Negro Hill was near Mormon Island on the South Fork of the American River. Dewitt Stanford (brother of Leland Stanford) opened a store there.

Negro Slide was above Camptonville in Sierra County. Another camp of the same name was along the North Fork of the Yuba River north of Camptonville, but in Yuba County.

Nelighs Camp was near Placerville. It was named for businessman Robert Neligh.

Nelson Point was a Plumas County mining camp. The diggings were rich but were rapidly exhausted. The post office serving the area was apparently first located at nearby Nelson Creek but was soon transferred to Nelson Point.

James Marshall, who discovered gold at Coloma, located colors at Deer Creek in the summer of 1848, but he moved on for what he hoped would be better diggings. The first town to grow up in the area was initially known as **Deer Creek Dry Diggin's** or perhaps **Beer Creek Diggin's** or **Caldwell's Upper Store.** At one time the settlement was also known as **Coyoteville,** named for the method of tunneling used in the area. River deposits were mined with small "coyote" holes, which led to the use of the term "coyoting." The community was later named **Nevada City.**[285]

Deer Creek was the site of initial gold discovery in the Nevada City area. It also was the scene of near disaster four years later. The winter of 1852 had been troublesome, with floodwaters taking a heavy toll. That year Dr. Robinson's Dramatic Hall, built on stilts over the roily creek, was washed downstream with an audience in it.[286]

By 1850 the town boasted more than 400 buildings and 8,000 to 10,000 people. The town was virtually burned to the ground upwards of seven times,[287] but was rebuilt each time. In the early 1850s mining declined, and so did Nevada City. Hydraulic mining initiated in 1856 caused a revival, and by 1880 the population was just over 4,000. Deep quartz mines helped sustain the city in its later periods.

Much of the past remains at Nevada City — the town that has been sometimes termed the best preserved mining camp in northern California. A mahogany bar, hauled around Cape Horn by ship, is still an attraction at the National Hotel.

Nevada City in 1852 — *Nevada County Historical Society.*

Cinnabar ore was long used by Indians prior to the arrival of white men to the area that became **New Almaden.**

In 1824 a Mexican citizen, Antonio Sonol[288] (possibly Sorol), searched for gold and silver in the area but didn't find it. Andreas Castillero, a Mexican army officer, is generally credited with proving that cinnabar ore contained mercury, or quicksilver. In 1845 he, Secundino and Leodero Robles, and Jose Castro obtained the mine named for the world's greatest mercury producer in Spain. By 1848, with the help of English capital, limited mercury production had been undertaken. By 1852 six big furnaces were in use.

As the California gold boom spread, the demand rose sharply for New Almaden mercury, which was used in the amalgamation process to extract gold from ore. In 1850 the mine produced over 7,000 flasks.[289] By 1881, 54,378,418 pounds had been manufactured. The New Almaden mine produced more than $70 million in quicksilver, which probably made it the most valuable single producing mine in the state.

The twenty-room Casa Grande of the mine superintendent was one of the grandest mansions of its day. It still stands, along with a number of other relics of New Almaden's mining heyday.

Newark was along Little Slate Creek near the Plumas–Sierra county line. It was formerly known as **Whiskey Diggings.** There also seems to have been a Newark on the North Fork of the American River in Placer County.

Newcastle is now an agricultural and transportation center, but in the 1870s and 1880s it was a placer camp. Several mining camps were located at the head of Secret Ravine, but Newcastle was the only one to survive. Orchards and vineyards have grown up around the town, softening the ugly scars left by quartz mining operations.

The 1,500-foot level of the New Almaden quicksilver mines (Randol Shaft) — *California State Library.*

New Chicago was an Amador County mining camp north of Amador City.

New Indria, located southeast of Hollister, was a quicksilver mining town named for the Indria quicksilver district of Austria. The New Indria mine was second only in production to the state's largest producer — the New Almaden.

New Mexican Camp was located in Bear Valley. Mexicans discovered gold here in 1851, but soon the camp was deserted.

New Philadelphia was north of Amador City. It was also known as **Dog Town.**

Newton (New Town, Newtown) was southwest of Nevada City. Perhaps the place was discovered by sailors and first known as **Sailors Flat.** A **Newtown** was southeast of Placerville along Weber Creek. A gold camp called **New Town** was between Auburn and Marysville.

A **New York Point** and a **New York House** existed in Yuba County. New York Point was east of Forbestown. It was a short-lived mining camp. New York House may have only been a hotel — the Union — east of Brownsville.

Nimshew was northwest of Magalia in Butte County. Some say that the word is Maidu Indian for "big water."

Nolton was a Siskiyou County trading center for placer miners. It was located above Happy Camp.

North Bloomfield was once called **Humbug** for a lying, hard-drinking miner who lured compatriots to the area by bragging of nonexistent gold. It may have also been named for the creek on which the camp was located. Founded in 1851 about ten miles northwest of Yreka, the town was defined by Joaquin Miller as "a savage Eden, with many Adams walking up and down and plucking of every tree."

Hydraulic mining sustained the settlement for much of its life. The Malakoff hydraulic pit west of North Bloomfield graphically shows the rapacious hydraulic mining scars. An account of 1948 stated, "The immensity of the North Bloomfield pits must be seen to be believed. Although excavated entirely by powerful jets of water, the pits compare favorably in size with many of the open pit copper and iron mines of other states which have been excavated by modern mechanical means. The Malakoff pit west of North Bloomfield resembles a miniature Bryce Canyon."[290] The hydraulic mining scene around North Bloomfield must have been impressive. Two large reservoirs high in the Sierras at about 6,000 feet above sea level — 3,000 feet above town — provided water for the hydraulic giants through about one hundred miles of canals and flumes.

Between 1855 and 1884 the town was the largest hydraulic mining center in California.[291]

Gold was reduced to bars at the Malakoff mine properties.[292] From there the bars were transferred to the San Francisco mint. One report states that the largest bar, weighing 500 pounds, was valued at $114,000[293] and was the largest bar to be shipped from Nevada County.

North Bloomfield is one of the more charming, relatively unspoiled California mining camps left from the past.

North Branch was established near the confluence of the North and South forks of the Calaveras River in Calaveras County. The camp is gone, but its pioneer cemetery is a historic landmark.

A jet vapor trail adds a dimension to this view of the old schoolhouse near North Columbia.

North Columbia was founded near North Bloomfield in 1853 and was contemporary with that settlement.

Placer, lode, and hydraulic mining have been carried on in the vicinity for many years, and the total gold yield is between $3 million and $4 million.

North San Juan was probably founded in 1853 when Christian Kientz, or Keintz, a Mexican War veteran, saw a similarity between the topography of San Juan de Ulloa, at the entrance of Mexico's Santa Cruz harbor, and the hill on which he discovered gold. This presumably makes the town's name a Yankee-Spanish hybrid. But as one saying goes, "Hybridization seldom produces pleasing results. The offspring of a bulldog sire and a dachshund bitch is an example."[294]

The hydraulic diggings on San Juan Ridge were the great attractions. It has been purported that the ridge was the site of the main office of the first long distance line in the West, a sixty-mile line connecting Milton and French Corral, thus connecting hydraulic mining centers.[295]

Peak population estimates vary from 1,000[296] to 10,000.[297]

Several original structures remain in this quaint, relaxed Mother Lode town.

The crumbling garage at North San Juan.

North San Juan in 1876 — *Nevada County Historical Society.*

Norton Diggings was named for the Norton Company, a water company that built a water race to the Trinity County mining camp. Some claim that it was the richest mining camp in Trinity County during 1858.

Nortonville was a coal-mining town on the northeast approach to Mount Diablo. The camp began with a roar in the mid-1850s and died with hardly a whimper about one quarter of a century later.

Six of Nortonville's miners died in an explosion at the Black Diamond mine on July 24, 1876, accounting for one half of the coal miners killed in the entire state.[298]

Oahu was northwest of Downieville. It was named after the Hawaiian island because the camp's diggings were first worked by men from that island.

Oak Bar was above Hamburg in Siskiyou County. It was a trading center for miners.

Oakland was north of Marysville and established as a trading center for miners. Its life was short.

Oak Spring had a post office for about three years before it was transferred to nearby Montezuma. The camp south of Jamestown left few traces.

Oak Valley, northwest of Camptonville, was populated mostly by Frenchmen.

Ogilby, in extreme southeastern Imperial County, was a mining center near the Cargo Muchacho mining district. White explorers and Mexicans visited the area, but little actual mining occurred until about 1879.

Total production in the district probably exceeded $4 million from both placer and lode deposits.

Ohio Bar was a short-lived camp north of Oroville.

Ohio Diggings was north of Soulsbyville.

Olancha was a trading center for area miners south of Owens Lake. The Inyo County camp's name is derived from a Shoshone word.

Old Coso was the site of a gold discovery in 1860. The area was situated between Little Lake and Darwin in the Coso Range. The camp was never large and probably didn't surpass several hundred people.

The site rests within the northern part of the United States Naval Ordnance Test Station; therefore, it is off-limits to the curious ghost towner.

Almost inaccessible **Old Denny** was founded as **New River City** in 1883 in extreme northwestern Trinity County. At its height the camp probably had one store, a butcher shop, a blacksmith shop, a hotel, three or four saloons, and several sawmills.

Sometime after 1894 the town was renamed Denny, in honor of a Mr. Denny, who was co-owner of a store in town.

A wagon train north connected Denny with the camps of Marysville and White Rock.

An early view of the store at Old Denny — *Trinity County Historical Society.*

Marysville was named for Mary Larcine, daughter of Frenchman Peter Larcine, the hotel owner.

White Rock was above Marysville. The camp was perhaps also known as either **Couer**[299] or **Coeur**[300] for a man who ran the A. Brizards store and post office there.

The three camps combined may have had a population of about 500. But by 1913 they were deserted. The better known mines were the Mountain Boomer, the Hard Tack, the Tough Nut, the Ridgeway, and the Sherwood.

Only ruins remain.

New River City — *Trinity County Historical Society.*

Ophir (Opher, Ophirville), located west of Auburn, was first known as **Spanish Corral.** In 1852 the settlement was the largest in Placer County.

Placers in the Ophir mining district were worked from 1850 to 1880. First known production from area quartz mines occurred in 1867. Dredges began working the area in the late 1930s.

Orchards and vineyards have overgrown the scattered remains of quartz mining as Ophir has metamorphosed from a mining to a fruit-growing settlement. A marker describes the old town.

Oregon Gulch sprouted up near the La Grange mine, a short distance west of Weaverville. The camp was founded in 1850 by miners from Oregon; hence, its name. A small Catholic church satisfied the spiritual needs of the 1,200 or so people who lived there, while four saloons slaked the thirst of the hard-drinking miners. Pioneer Trinity County observer "Jake" Jackson wrote about what he termed a quaint custom concerning the purchasing of drinks on the house. In *Tales from the Mountaineer* (Rotary Club of Weaverville, 1964), he states: "If one of the miners passed a saloon and did not stop in and purchase a drink, it was charged to him nevertheless. At the end of the month, a bill was sent to him for drinks. Actually consumed drinks and passed up drinks were charged for alike. If necessary, and sometimes it was, force was used in collecting the account."

But in 1893 the camp was washed away by the hydraulic mining operations of the monstrous La Grande mine. The only survivor was the church, which was removed to Junction City. The town site is covered by an estimated 300 to 500 feet of mining debris.

Oregon Hill was situated along Oregon Creek in Yuba County. It appears to have been called **Greenville** when the post office was established in 1857.

Oregon House may have been simply a house with a post office that was established in 1854. Placer mining in the area covered one-half century.

Orleans Bar is on the Klamath River near its junction with the Salmon River. The Humboldt County mining camp was originally called **New Orleans Bar** when mining began there in 1850.

Orleans Flat was northeast of North Bloomfield. The camp began in 1851 and grew to a population of several hundred. By 1867 white miners had abandoned all claims, and Mexican and Chinese miners toiled over the leftovers.

Oro City was a Placer County camp that squatted in Auburn Ravine. Miners formerly from Gold Hill founded the town.

Oro Fino was a Scott Valley gold mining camp southwest of Yreka. When the mines petered out, the camp was absorbed by other valley towns.

Oro Fino is known as the site of the "first white grave stone," which marks the grave of the first white man buried in the area. The marker simply reads: "Died June 10 1839 Jno B Smith."

Oro Grande (Halleck), founded in 1878, became a boom town in the 1880s. The rich gold deposits drew hoardes of prospectors, and the population soon soared to 2,000. However, the community along the Mojave River soon faded as a mining camp of significance. It was no longer even classified as a mining town after 1928, when the last of the mines were closed.

Oroleva (Orolewa, Oroliva, Oroleeve) was in Strawberry Valley, east of Forbestown. It was a short-lived company town.

Oroville was first dubbed **Ophir City** when gold was discovered in the area in October 1849. During the winter of 1850–51, the settlement contained one dozen houses.[301] Two years later most of the people had left for other "bonanzas," but they were attracted back to Oroville when a canal brought water to the dry diggings in 1856, two years after the town was named Oroville.

In 1856 the town of 4,000 became county seat of Butte County. In 1872 Oroville's Chinatown was the largest in the state. Peak population may have stretched to 10,000.

The point where the Feather River enters the Sacramento Valley at Oroville was ideally suited for dredging, which began in March 1898. The first successful bucket elevator dredge in the state was used here. Success begat more success, until the area was teeming with perhaps forty-four dredges,[302] all operating at one time. The Oroville area probably has floated more dredges and seen more dredging companies than any other region in the state.[303] The Oroville mining district became the largest producer in Butte County, with production totals reaching about two million[304] ounces.

A view of Oroville about 1856 when it was the most populated mining town in California — *Butte County Historical Society.*

As mining dropped in importance, area residents began to grow semitropical fruits, and the town thrived with its new financial base. The 1863 Chinese Temple, a popular place for modern visitors, is a reminder of the sizeable Chinese population that once resided in Oroville.

Oroville didn't become a ghost town, and today several thousand people comprise the community.

Miners in Oroville — *Butte County Historical Society.*

The United States Hotel in flames in Oroville, 1892 — *Butte County Historical Society.*

Ossaville (Osoville) was located near Meadow Lake. The gold was not free milling, so mining soon ceased, and so did Ossaville.

Owensville sprang up as a mining camp near Laws, probably in 1863.

Only crumbling foundations and walls mark the site.

Paloma (Fosteria) began in 1849 as a placer mining camp near Mokelumne Hill, at Lower Rich Gulch. J. Alexander discovered quartz deposits there in its early years. The area's richest mine was probably the Gwin mine, owned by William M. Gwin, California's first United States senator.

Panamint City's remains can be found in Panamint (also spelled "Panomint") Valley at the head of Surprise Canyon, on the west side of the Panamint Range. William Alvord and his party of seventeen are generally credited with discovering the site. He visited the area three times, but during the third trip, Alvord's berserk partner — Jackson — killed him. In 1861 prospectors led by S. C. George came to Surprise Canyon (north of Wildrose Canyon) and discovered antimony and silver. They were killed by Panamint Indians who rightfully resented the intrusion.

The area remained undisturbed until December 1872, when Richard C. Jacobs, W. L. Kennedy, and Robert Stewart blustered into Surprise Canyon.[305] They built a furnace to test the content of the rock and found rich copper-silver deposits valued at $2,000[306] to $3,000[307] per ton. By October 1874, 400 men populated Panamint City, which Wells Fargo's superintendent John Valentine dubbed a suburb of hell. By the winter of 1874–75, the town had a population of 5,000, a street one mile long, 200 houses, and the Hotel de Bum.[308] But the mines hit borrasca, and in the spring of 1876 the mill was shut down. Finally, on July 24, 1876, a cloudburst sent floodwaters cascading down the valley into town, swirling it away. As one writer remarked, "When the storm had ended, the town had been demolished, the buildings nothing but flotsam and jetsam, ending up, along with the bodies of 15 miners, on the desert floor below."[309] By May 1877, the last mines had been closed.

Lurking among the macerated remains of Panamint City is a tale of Panamint Pete — the saturnine prospector who was so lazy that during searing Death Valley summers he would not have the gumption to crawl

An old arrastre at the site of Panamint — *Society of California Pioneers.*

into a cooling shadow. Pete supposedly spent the winters trying to recover from midsummer shade temperatures of up to 130 degrees. The settlement may have been named for Pete, who would aver that one day he'd get his slothful body up in the surrounding hills and "Pan-a-mint" of gold. When he died at age eighty-six, he still had not quite gotten around to doing that.

A stack, foundations of a mill, walls, and graves[310] are about all that now remain of Panamint City.

Paradise was in the Placerville area. It seems to have been in a spectacularly rich gold mining area; however, when the gold gave out the population gave up, and the camp expired.

Paris was along Indian Creek, north of Tehachapi in Kern County. The camp began in 1902, received its post office the following year, and lost it in 1912; that same year the camp was renamed **Loraine.**

Another camp of the same name seems to have been located near Washington in Nevada County.

Parks Bar was a Yuba County mining camp first known as **Marsh Diggings.** During discovery year — 1848 — the camp was renamed for store owner David Parks. In the late 1860s the camp was literally smothered by detritus brought to the site from hydraulic mining operations along the Yuba River.

Partzwick was near Benton in Mono County. The settlement was founded in the late 1860s and was named for Julius Partz.

Paso del Pino was situated north of Columbia. It has been variously referred to as **Passo El-Pino, Pine Crossing, Pine Log, Passo-del-Pin,** and **Paso La Pine.**

Patterson was east of North San Juan. It served as the post office for Cherokee.

The word **Paxton** pops up every once in a while in California lore and history. There is a shadowy hint that it may have been a placer mining camp that grew up near and may have been contemporary with Rich Bar. The camp may have been originally called **Soda Bar** because of its mineral springs. Then comes the man J. A. Paxton, who built a hotel on the Virginia Ranch in Yuba County. Lastly comes Paxton in Plumas County, located on Highway 70 just west of the intersection with Highway 89. Paxton was a johnny-come-lately railroad town on the Western Pacific Feather River Route, completed in 1910.

Peavine Flat was a short-lived Sierra County camp. Its "business district" consisted of one saloon.

Perris was platted in 1885–86 but not incorporated until 1911. The town, formerly known as **Pinecate (Pinacate),** is located in the still extant Pinecate mining district.

The principal mine in the area is the Good Hope, originally worked by Mexicans who extracted about $2 million in gold.

Production in the district's dozen mines gradually declined. In the mid-1930s, largely unsuccessful rehabilitation efforts were undertaken on the Good Hope and several other mines. But from 1943 to 1959, only three ounces of mined gold were reported from the district.[311]

Peru (Peru Bar) was north of Kelsey, in El Dorado County.

Petersburg was a Calaveras County mining camp west of San Andreas. The camp, founded by Germans, is now under the waters of Hogan reservoir. Another **Petersburg** was located between the Kern River and Poso Creek in the Greenhorn Mountains. The Kern County mining camp may have sometimes been referred to as **Greenhorn.** Still another **Petersburg** rested on the South Fork of the Salmon River in Siskiyou County. The camp's name may have been spelled **Petersburgh;** at least that's the official name of the post office which existed there from 1869 to 1876.

Petticoat Slide may have been named for a demimonde who fell on a slippery place on the edge of town and slid into camp.

There may have been a mining camp called **Philadelphia Diggings** northeast of Columbia in Tuolumne County. For some unknown reason, the post office there was named

Jupiter when established in 1901.

Picacho was founded about 1897 north of Yuma. Discoveries were probably first made by Mexican miners as early as 1857, or possibly 1862. When placer operations gave way to hardrock mining, the Americans bullied in. Frank Love, in *Mining Camps and Ghost Towns,* claims that the town plat was recorded at the Imperial county seat in April 1897.

A railroad was built from the Picacho mine (the largest producer) to one of the mills in anticipation of rich mining activity.

A rock house has withstood the numerous floods which have all but wiped away the old camp. Some of the camp is in a watery grave formed by backwaters from Laguna dam.

Pike City was a Sierra County mining camp. Hydraulic mining has been carried on in the area until recently.

Pilot Hill was a camp that never really made it. John C. Fremont and his men may have visited the area in 1844, but apparently no mining was undertaken until 1849.

The settlement became more of a transportation center than a mining center. But in some respects it even lost out along that line. Alonzo Bailey (Bayley) built a hotel to house and feed people brought in by the Central Pacific Railroad. However, the railroad wasn't routed to Pilot Hill, and the three-storied, porticoed brick hotel was little used. The structure that became known as "Bailey's Folly" still stands, but it leans to one side ever so slightly.

The Pilot Hill cemetery, resting in a field, is one of the few tattered remnants of historic Pilot Hill.

Pinchemtight is shrouded in mystery. Its location was probably near Weber Creek in El Dorado County. The place was perhaps also known as **Pinchem Gut, Pinch Gut Ravine,** and **Pinchgut.**

Pine City was situated along the shores of Mary Lake in Mono County. It was a part of the late 1870s Mammoth Lake gold rush scenario.

Pine Grove was south of Sutter Creek in Amador County. The camp was probably named for "Pine Grove," as the home of Albert and Caroline Leonard was called.

Another mining camp of the same name was near the Sierra–Yuba county line. The camp seems to have sprung into existence in 1852.

A Placer County gold camp dating to about 1850 may have also been called Pine Grove. The site was in Secret Ravine. However, when the post office was established, its name was **Pino.**

Placerville was first called **Dry Diggings** when three men discovered gold in the region in the summer of 1848. The name was later changed to **Old Dry Diggings,** and still later to **Ravine City.** The camp subsequently was known as **Hangtown** because of its violent ways. One story relates that the town was named for the hanging of three men who had attempted to rob an old miner of $6,000 in gold dust.[312] Another story says that in January 1849 five men robbed Mexican gambler[313] Lopez and were tried and sentenced to receive thirty-nine lashes each. Three of the five men were then tried for robbery and attempted murder that they had supposedly committed in another mining camp a few months previous. They were found guilty and summarily hanged.[314]

The settlement's main street may have extended for over one mile, but apparently the thoroughfare wasn't the best. J. D. Borthwick arrived in town in 1851 and found the street knee-deep in mud and "plentifully strewed with old boots, hats, and shirts, old sardine-boxes, empty tins of preserved oysters, empty bottles, worn-out pots and kettles, old ham-bones, broken picks and shovels, and other rubbish too various to particularize."[315] Borthwick also wrote of the street's multifunctional aspect. He commented, "Here and there, in the middle of the street, was a square hole about six feet deep, in which one miner was digging, while another was baling [*sic*] the water out with a bucket, and a third, sitting alongside the heap of dirt which had been dug up, was washing it with a rocker."[316]

Not only was the main street in deplorable shape, so too was the road leading to Placerville. One observer described it as being "cut up by heavy teams, a foot deep with dust, and abounding in holes and pitfalls big enough to swallow a thousand stages and six thousand horses without inconvenience to itself."[317]

Another observer called the town a squalid queen beside one of the creeks of the American River.[318]

By April 1850 both the Methodists and the Catholics had established religious organizations. The town soon became the most prosperous and populous mining community in El Dorado County.[319] Population was probably about 2,000.

The town grew rapidly and was incorporated in 1854, the year it apparently was first called Placerville. Its population came close to rivaling that of San Francisco and Sacramento. The mines were rich. The Pacific quartz mine alone produced $1,486,000,[320] and the entire Placerville mining district generated more than $25 million in gold.[321] Not only was Placerville a mining center, it was also a trade, transportation, and communication center. Because it was situated on the California Overland Trail, Placerville served as an important station for the Central Overland Mail and Stage line,[322] the overland telegraph, and the Pony Express. When the Comstock boomed in Nevada, Placerville became the main stop on the way to the new strikes.

For a while several well-known people lived in Placerville. John Studebaker of automobile fame was once a wheelbarrow builder in the community. Mark Hopkins, who later became a railroad magnate, once sold groceries there; and Philip Armour of meat-packing renown once ran a butcher shop in Placerville. Horace Greeley was a visitor to the town.

As the Nevada mines boomed, so did Placerville. But as the mining bubble burst, so, too, did Placerville. The town still survives, but many of its older buildings have been so changed that they cannot be recognized.

Pleasant Hill seems to have been near Mud Springs in El Dorado County. Its residents were mostly miners. Little else was discovered about this camp.

Pleasant Springs was on Alabama Gulch in Calaveras County. The camp probably began in 1849. By 1855 there was a post office, but it was closed in 1857.

Plumas was a transitory camp that briefly bloomed a few miles down Feather River from Marysville. Although the camp was on the main route to California's northern mines, it never flourished. It was promoted by real estate men when founded in 1850, but by the following year the only surviving structures were "the battered remains of an ungainly frame hotel and a few rough shacks, already falling apart."[323]

Gold discoveries were made in the 1850s near **Plymouth,** first known as **Pokerville.**[324] Between Plymouth and an area about twelve miles south of the town, the Mother Lode has produced more than $160 million in gold, making the region the second richest section in Mother Lode country. Plymouth is exceeded only by the Grass Valley district of Nevada County.[325] The Plymouth Consolidated Mines — located within the city limits of Plymouth — produced about $15 million in gold.[326]

Spasmodic mining has occurred in the area since boom days, but little gold has been produced since World War II.

Lingering evidence of mining at Plymouth.

Poker Flat led a fiery existence north of Downieville. The mining camp burned down and was rebuilt several times. It has no known connection with Bret Harte's story, "The Outcasts of Poker Flat."

Pony Creek was located on Pony Creek, a tributary of the East Fork of the New River in Trinity County. The mining area was rich but was soon worked out; the camp subsequently died.

Port Wine is southeast of La Porte in Sierra County. The place may have been so named when someone found a keg of port wine nearby.

Poverty Bar was south of Ione. The post office was established in 1854 and closed ten years later. The site is now under Camanche reservoir.

A camp of the same name is also listed as being in Placer County on the North Fork of the American River. It is covered by waters created by the North Fork dam.

Places of the same name were in El Dorado, Plumas, Trinity, Tuolumne, and Yuba counties, but they were apparently river bars, not towns.

Powelltown was north of Magalia. The Butte County camp was settled in 1853 by R. P. Powell.

Prairie City was south of Folsom. The camp dates from 1853 and by the following year had more than 1,000 people. The place is now a historic landmark.

Prairie Diggings was northwest of Browns Valley in Yuba County. The camp began in 1854 and was dead one decade later.

Priest's Station (or **Priests**) grew up on the Mother Lode as a supply point for gold miners near Big Oak Flat. It was named for a Mr. Priest. The old Priest Hotel was a popular social center. Not only did the hotel boast a view of seven counties, but it was also known for its excellent food. Fire consumed it many years ago, and today little remains to remind visitors of the settlement sometimes referred to in the early 1850s as **Kirkwood's**, or **Rattlesnake House.**

Priest Valley was founded near the top of the Coast Range in the Visalia area in 1849 by trapper Ben Williams.

The story persists that two men named William Galman and Captain Walker found a priest and a group of Indians resting on the site after a horse roundup; hence, the name Priest Valley.

For years the tale has lingered that Joaquin Murieta was killed near the settlement in 1853.

Providence sprang up in the Providence Mountains, located in the eastern part of the Mojave Desert. It was a company town, headquarters for miners who worked the Bonanza King mine. The apogee of the Bonanza mine seems to have occurred during the 1870s and 1880s, when, according to one report, the mine produced nearly $1 million in a single eighteen-month period.

Remains of an old stamp mill and several other buildings mark the spot of this relatively well-preserved desert camp, first called **Hicorum** for an Indian named Hicorum.

Pulga, situated at the mouth of Flee Valley, was a mining camp called **Big Bar** until renamed by a railroad. The town was a satellite of Oroville.

Purdy was a copper and gold camp located along the Goffs-to-Ivanpah-connecting California Eastern Railroad near the Nevada state line in San Bernardino County. It was named for Purdy Blake, daughter of the man who built the Nevada Southern Railroad from Goffs to his mines in the New York Mountains.

Quartz (Quartz Hill, Quartz Mountain) was established south of Jamestown. Its early existence was closely tied to the fortunes of the App mine, discovered by John App in 1856. App had married Leanna Donner, one of the six Donner girls orphaned by the Donner Pass tragedy of 1847.[327]

The town's original structures burned in a 1927 fire, and what buildings remain in the town date to that time. Placer and hardrock mining operations were developed, with the App, Dutch, Sweeney, Heslep, Jumper, New

Era, and Golden Rule claims being the most profitable in the area. Total production probably reached $7 million.

Quartzburg[328] was initially known as **Nashville.** Miners were in the vicinity in 1849. In November 1849 Thomas Thorne (or Thorn) located a rich quartz ledge and in gratitude freed his slaves and gave them each a claim. Soon Quartzburg was thriving, and by 1850 it came within a few votes of becoming Mariposa county seat.

Thorne died in 1854, and the graves of he and his wife are at the cemetery, the only lasting memorial to a once-virile camp.

Queen City was southwest of Rough and Ready near the Nevada–Yuba county line. It was spawned by the spurt of copper excitement during 1862–63 but died as quickly as it was born.

Another place named Queen City was northeast of Port Wine, in Sierra County near the Plumas county line.

Quincy is alive and thriving — hardly to be called a ghost town. But the community's roots grew in mining history. H. J. Bradley was one of three commissioners responsible for organizing Plumas County. He placed the seat of government at the hotel[329] located on his property known as American Ranch. The town of Quincy grew up around the ranch beginning in 1854 and was named for Bradley's hometown in Illinois.

Elizabethtown grew up a couple of miles north of Quincy, in the Tate's Ravine area. The original camp was probably settled by Alex and Frank Tate, but by the autumn of discovery year (1852) the name became Elizabethtown in honor of the daughter of Lewis Stark, who found a rich mine in the vicinity.

Rackerby, not far from Quincy, was an old mining camp near South Honcut Creek. Little is known of the town's early mining history.

Railroad Flat grew up east of Jackson as a placer and quartz mining center. The camp was named for wooden track laid by a miner who wanted to carry ore in a mule-powered car.

The best-producing mine in the area was probably the Petticoat — so named because it was discovered by a woman.

The old post office of Railroad Flat can be found in the back part of a grocery store that dates back to the town's early days.

Nearby was the ephemeral camp called **Bummerville.**

Another camp called **Railroad Hill (Diggings, Gulch)** may have also been named for railroad tracks used to convey ore and mine waste. This Yuba County mining camp was located northeast of Camptonville.

Ramms Ranch (Dutchmans Ranch) was northwest of Camptonville in Yuba County. It was a mining camp, but also known as a grape-growing settlement.

Randolph Flat was immediately northeast of Rough and Ready in Nevada County. The place was named for Randolph County, Missouri.

Randsburg is a mining camp named for the Rand gold mining district in South Africa.

Gold was first found in the area about ten miles northwest of what became Randsburg. During the winter of 1893–94, placer de-

Hard Cash mine in Randsburg, 1927 — *Collection of Historical Photographs, Title Insurance and Trust Company, Los Angeles.*

posits were found at Goler Wash. In 1895 the lode deposits of the rich Yellow Aster mine were developed. The mine produced about $6 million in gold. However, 1895 was not a "big" year for Randsburg, for the town consisted of only thirteen buildings.[330] But when the St. Elmo mine was discovered east of the Rand by Si Drouillard in 1896, the boom began.

The town grew to 2,500 people and 300 buildings[331] and sported a brass band, a volunteer fire department, a theatre, and other marks of "refinement."

But gold mining became less profitable. Law suits, labor strikes, and other troubles plagued the Yellow Aster and other mines. The Yellow Aster was once closed by a labor strike that lasted for sixteen years. By 1918 the situation looked hopeless.

However, a silver strike at nearby Red Mountain brought a second breath of life to the area. The bonanza didn't last long, though, and little mining occurred in the area during the World War II era.

Several buildings mark the present town of Randsburg, and mining still continues to this day.

A five-stamp mill at Randsburg.

Desert miner at home near Randsburg — *Collection of Historical Photographs, Title Insurance and Trust Company, Los Angeles.*

Randsburg, no date — *Collection of Historical Photographs, Title Insurance and Trust Company, Los Angeles.*

Randsburg in the winter, about 1900 — *Collection of Historical Photographs, Title Insurance and Trust Company, Los Angeles.*

The Yellow Aster Saloon in Randsburg, no date — *The Huntington Library.*

The Last Outpost, where Randsburg miners gambled at "low ball" (poker).

An interior view of the ore house at Randsburg — *Collection of Historical Photographs, Title Insurance and Trust Company, Los Angeles.*

Purington's Desert Shop at Randsburg, also housing Jake's Junquery.

Ratsburg was a Los Angeles County mining camp at the junction of Bouquet Canyon and San Francisquito Canyon roads.

Rattlesnake Bar was above Whiskey Bar in Placer County. It was named for nearby Rattlesnake Bar on the North Fork of the American River.

Rattlesnake Creek was near Moccasin Creek in Tuolumne County. It was probably founded in late 1849. Lack of water for mining spelled the doom of this gold camp.

Rattlesnake Gulch was above Trinity. The Trinity County gold camp was never large, probably sporting no more than three business establishments.

Ravenna was northeast of Los Angeles near Acton. It was first called **Soledad,** perhaps for the Soledad Mining Company. The camp was officially dubbed Ravenna in 1868 when the post office was established. By 1877 the camp was deserted.

Rawhide (Rawhide Ranch), northwest of Jamestown, was fathered by the Rawhide quartz mine, which produced about $6 million in gold during its productive life. The mine appears to have been active until 1867, idle until 1891, then productive again until 1905.[332] Since that time pocket mining has been sporadically carried on in the old mine workings.

Raymond is east of Merced, north of Madera in Madera County. The Knowles granite quarry and the Green Mountain copper smelter are landmarks. Two graves rest near the old smelter — one of a mine worker and the other of Frank Ault, a young boy who fell on a syrup can, cut his throat, and bled to death on July 4, 1874.

Pierson B. Reading fathered two towns named **Readings Bar.** In the spring of 1848 Reading found gold on Clear Creek, east of Igo in Shasta County.

In July of that same year, Reading found gold on the Trinity River, in the Douglas City area of Trinity County. Reading used Indian laborers to take out about $80,000 in gold before white prospectors objected to Indian labor, at which time Reading ordered his men to quit digging.

A "bungalo" near Redding — *Shasta Historical Society.*

Red Bar was below Douglas City on the Trinity River in Trinity County. The first gold strikes were probably in 1850, and by 1856 the camp was booming.

Red Diamond was northeast of Quaker Hill in Nevada County.

Red Dog was established in the Grass Valley vicinity. Two thousand miners toiled for gold at Red Dog, Little Rock, and You Bet in the 1870s.

Panning for gold at Red Dog — *Nevada County Historical Society.*

Two theories have been forwarded to explain how the camp was named. One story relates that when the miners met to decide a name for their new "city," the original discoverer of a nugget in the area was consulted. The man believed that because his red collie had walked to California from Independence, Missouri, the dog should be memorialized. Thus, the settlement was dubbed "Red Dog."[333]

The other theory is that the camp was named for a drunken miner with long, russet-colored hair.

The elusive, murky history of the community also seems to indicate that at one time an attempt was made to change the camp's name to Brooklyn — but the attempt failed.

Red Hill was a shadowy Trinity County mining camp.

It's known that Frank Lorenz, Martin Sharp, and Louis F. Rabb owned a miners' store there, that Henry Lorenz bought out Sharp's interest, and that he bought from his brother, Frank, a one-third interest in a trading post, nineteen mules, a ferry, and a small boat on the Trinity River, for $2,600 in gold coin.

Another bit of information about Red Hill was that in 1856 a bucket of gravel yielded twelve dollars. But little other information was gleaned about this obscure camp, except that the state mineralogist in 1890 reported that a mining elevator at the Red Hill mine wasn't functioning satisfactorily. Apparently Henry Lorenz had something to do with making it or other mining equipment work better.[334]

A camp called **Red Hills** also grew up in Trinity County. It was located between Weaverville and Junction City.

Red Mountain[335] was a silver camp founded as a result of discoveries made by prospector Hank Williams. The story goes that Williams had apparently sought shelter from a snowstorm in a prospect hole dug years earlier by another "pilgrim." While waiting in the hole, he picked up some samples that were rich in horn silver.

Williams staked his claim, which was a part of the Big Kelly mine, later known as the Rand silver mine. The mine may have produced more than $7 million in its first four years of operation.

The Red Hills hydraulic mine in 1891 — *Trinity County Historical Society.*

Red Mountain's still-functioning Silver Dollar Saloon.

One of several defunct businesses at Red Mountain.

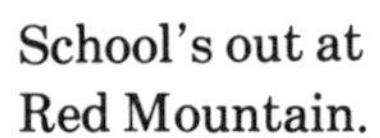

School's out at Red Mountain.

Mobil products were once sold at this building in Red Mountain.

Relief Hill was southeast of North Bloomfield. The camp was established in 1853.

Remington Hill was probably named for the owner of a cement mill at a nearby camp. Nuggets worth $2,400 and $3,500 were found at the site.

Reward came into being north of Lone Pine in Inyo County. It was probably named for the Reward mine.

Rices Crossing was on the main Yuba River near its confluence with the South Fork. It went by various names, including **Lousy Level, Liars Flat,** and **Liases Flat.**

There were a number of places in California known as **Rich Bar.** The best known was a camp on the East Branch of the North Fork of the Feather River between Belden and Virgilia in Plumas County.

Rich Bar was opulent: over $3 million in gold dust was wrenched from its gravels. Pans of dirt were estimated at yielding from $100 to $1,500 in gold each.[336] One tale even relates that two German prospectors came to the area in 1850 and removed $2,900 in their first two pans; also, that the two men panned over $30,000 before others crowded them out.[337] Another story tells that in 1850 a party of Americans and a group of Frenchmen arrived at Rich Bar simultaneously. They decided to arrange a fight, and to the victor would go the spoils of all the claims in the area. Each side selected its strongest fighter, and a three-hour slug-fest ensued. The Frenchman finally lost, but he and his countrymen moved a short way upstream and found even richer deposits at French Gulch.[338]

A visitor to Rich Bar during March 1851 reported that the town had only six cabins and one canvas house.[339] Eight or nine months later another visitor remarked that the camp then had about forty "tenements:" among which "figure round tents, square tents, plank hovels, log cabins &c., — the residences, varying in elegance and convenience from the palatial splendor of 'The Empire,' [hotel] down to a 'local habitation,' formed of pine boughs, and covered with old calico shirts."[340]

But Rich Bar was doomed to desertion, for although the deposits were rich, they were shallow. The camp's mining history spanned only six years.

A second Rich Bar was on the Middle Fork

Rich Bar, nestled along the Feather River, no date — *The Huntington Library.*

of the Feather River near its confluence with Onion Valley Creek. It probably was discovered a short time before the other camp. It is not always clear what records refer to which camp.

Rich Gulch was a Butte County camp that began in 1851. The town was soon depopulated when the rush developed to nearby Yankee Hill.

Two camps known as Rich Gulch flourished briefly in Calaveras County. One site was west of Mok Hill; the other northeast of Mok Hill.

There was a Rich Gulch north of Weaverville in Trinity County, as well as another Trinity County gold camp on the East Fork of the North Fork of the Trinity River.

Riderville was founded east of Walker in Siskiyou County. The settlement began in 1851 and was called **Plugtown** for a doctor who wore a plug hat. Later it was changed to Riderville for W. G. Rider, a local miner. By 1866 the camp had vanished.

Riggs came into being north of Baker. The Riggs gold mine helped sustain the town. It was also nurtured by the Tonopah and Tidewater Railroad, on which Riggs was a station.

Roaches Camp was a Tuolumne County mining camp between Sonora and the Tuolumne River. Its peak population may have been 3,000.

Rock Creek was north of Oroville. Actually, there may have been two camps in the area — **Big Rock Creek** and **Little Rock Creek.**

Rollin was south of Sawyers Bar in Siskiyou County. It was apparently named for Rollin Fergundes, who discovered rich gold deposits there.

Rosamond, located south of Mojave, began as a supply center for ranchers and miners. The local hotel was long an attraction because it was built of quartz and had a fireplace studded with gold ore.

Rosemine (Rose Mine) was a company town east of Baldwin in San Bernardino County. It was probably named for the rose-colored, iron-oxide ore found in the area.

Roses Bar grew up in the Smartsville area of Yuba County. It was named for store owner John Rose, who had come to the area from Deer Creek, southwest of Nevada City. Some say that John Rose's trading post was the first traceable settlement in Nevada County; therefore, he is a part of the history of two counties.

Ross Corner was the center of mining activity for the old Picacho mines. One legend relates that an Indian found gold in the region in 1860. However, the town wasn't established until 1880, when Mexican prospectors found deposits in the area.

A stamp mill and a railroad were built. The mill seems to have produced only miners' false hopes of rich ores. By the early twentieth century, mining had ceased, and the town near the Yuma Indian Reservation, in extreme southeastern California, declined.

Rough and Ready was named for General Zachary Taylor, old "Rough and Ready" of Mexican War fame. The group that founded the town in 1849 was led by Captain A. A. "Cappy" Townsend, who had served under Taylor. The group had painted "Rough and Ready" on the sides of the dozen wagons used to make the trip west from Wisconsin. Since the men called themselves the "Rough and Ready Company," so would the camp be called.

One story tells that the Wisconsin men didn't care for the New Englanders who later came to the camp. At a meeting called by E. F. Brundage in 1850, it was decided to organize the independent state of Rough and Ready, adopt a constitution, and secede from the Union, so that "they would have more freedom to deal with New Englanders as they felt they should be dealt with."[341] The men established an independent government known as "The Great Republic of Rough and Ready."[342] It has been speculated that their real objective was to retaliate against a federal tax on miners. The republic existed from April to July 4.[343]

The growth of the settlement must have been phenomenal. Franklin Street wrote of

Rough and Ready, "When I first saw the place, about the middle of August [1850], the only signs of a town, visible, were some ten or twelve canvas houses, and the timber for a few frame buildings which were then being prepared for erection. Two months afterwards, I passed through the town, along a street nearly three-fourths of a mile in length, compactly built up on both sides with frame houses, many of them two stories high, with handsome exteriors, and all were occupied, and the most of them as stores and hotels."[344]

The population may have reached 6,000,[345] with perhaps 300 buildings in the town.

However, by the middle of 1859 the placer deposits were exhausted and no hardrock mines had been discovered. A fire leveled all but six of the town's buildings that year, and Rough and Ready was never able to effectively recover.

The I.O.O.F. Hall, an old schoolhouse, and a tollhouse (now a museum) are landmarks.

Rough and Ready in 1857 — *Nevada County Historical Society.*

The strangely constructed W. H. Fippen blacksmith shop at Rough and Ready.

Round Valley came into being near Greenville, probably in 1861. The Plumas County mining camp was short-lived.

Russianville was named for a colony of Russians who mined the area in the 1850s. The site was at the junction of the Little North Fork with the North Fork of the Salmon River.

Ruth first danced onto the southern Trinity County scene as **White Stump.** It seems that Clyde Barnes and Tom Elkins, two old-timers well fortified with "Oh Be Joyful," observed a bolt of lightning (not "white lightning") strike a pine tree, leaving behind a smouldering twenty-foot stump. They christened the new settlement for the lightning strike. Shortly after the turn of the century the town was renamed for Ruth McKnight, a relative of one of the town's postmasters.

The post office was apparently not the safest place in Ruth, for in 1910 three bullets were reportedly fired through the building. That post office was located about one and one-half miles north of present-day Ruth.

Ruth has mostly been an agricultural and cattle town, with sawmilling a part of its later history. However, some manganese mining has been carried on in the area for several years.

Ryan grew up near Death Valley as a model company town of the Pacific Coast Borax Company. The mines were operated from 1914 to 1928.

St. Louis was a Sierra County mining camp near La Porte. Hydraulic mining was undertaken here for several years.

Sageland sprouted up above Kelso Valley. Remains of past mining operations still exist, along with an old cemetery. However, the few houses that mark the townsite are not originals.

Salmon Falls was an El Dorado County gold camp on the South Fork of the American River. The camp was probably founded by Mormons about 1848. The place is marked by a historic landmark, but much of it is under Folsom Lake.

Salt Springs came into being as a stage stop on the Santa Fe–Salt Lake Trail. The camp on Salt Creek north of Baker in San Bernardino County later was known as a gold discovery site. First gold discoveries may have been made in 1856, but activity was apparently interrupted by Indian troubles. Mining was resumed in 1863 and has been carried on spasmodically ever since.

Salyer still exists, barely inside of Trinity County along Highway 299. It was named for miner Charles M. Salyer.

San Andreas began as an adobe Mexican town in 1848 or 1849 but was later taken over by Americans.

San Andreas may have a claim to fame as the site of an event that was memorialized in Mark Twain's *The Celebrated Jumping Frog of Calaveras County.* The jumping frog incident, in which a frog was reportedly filled with shot so that he could not jump, may have occurred in San Andreas' Metropolitan Hotel. On the other hand, the event may have taken place in Angels Camp or elsewhere. It has also been rumored that Joaquin Murieta began his career in San Andreas, but again, it is questionable if such a person ever existed.[346]

Poet-highwayman Black Bart (C. E. Bolton) was apprehended, tried, convicted, and sent to San Quentin Prison based on evidence found near San Andreas by sheriff Ben Thorn.

Southeast and southwest of San Andreas, limestone deposits suitable for making Portland cement have been located, and the mineral has recently been mined in the area.

San Antonio was on San Antonio Creek southeast of San Andreas in Calaveras County. It appears to have also been referred to as **San Antonia, Antoine, San Antone,** and **San Antone Camp.** It was probably first settled by Mexicans in 1848 or 1849. Mexicans also probably first found gold at San Antonio in Monterey County.

San Carlos was founded in the autumn of 1862 as a mining camp above Independence. But by 1864 mining had given out, and the town on the Owens River lost its lease on life.

The general store at San Andreas.

Ruins at San Andreas.

A camp called **San Diego** was immediately southeast of Columbia in Tuolumne County. A report from the February 16, 1878 edition of the *San Jose Pioneer* has it that a chunk of gold valued at $10,000 was discovered here.

Sawmill Flat was created southeast of Columbia along the banks of Woods Creek in the early 1850s. Wood from Sawmill Flat was used to build numerous other mining camps within several miles of the townsite.

Two large sawmills, using mostly Mexican labor, whined away at Sawmill Flat.

A fire in 1857 in nearby Columbia seems to have accounted for the demise of Sawmill Flat, because Columbians decided to rebuild their town with brick. A few ramshackle structures remain at the site of Sawmill Flat. The town has fared slightly better than its neighboring mining camp of **Martinez,** which has completely vanished.

Sawyer Bar, west of Yreka in the Salmon Mountains, began as a mining camp. It was named for miner Dan Sawyer.

The most notable reminder of the town's early mining days is the wooden, whipsawed Roman Catholic church dating to 1855. The church displays a large oil painting of the crucifixion.

Scales (Scales Diggings) was west of Downieville. It may have been named for a barkeeper or because gold was found in "scales" in the loose sand nearby.

Scott Bar, west of Yreka, was founded in the summer of 1850 by a prospecting party led by John Scott.[347]

The Scott party was driven from the area by Indians, but the men told of the gold waiting to be exploited. This naturally brought on a stampede of prospectors that the Indians could not contain. But by 1863 most people had departed, and half of the houses were left vacant.

Most remaining vestiges of mining operations are found east of Scott Bar, across the Scott River.

Sawyers Bar — *Siskiyou County Historical Society.*

Scott Bar, no date — *Siskiyou County Historical Society.*

The Scott Bar Community Association, Inc., building.

Scott Bar postal patrons get their mail from the porch of the Scott Bar post office.

The marker erected in memory of John Scott at Scott Bar. The monument overlooks the spot where gold was first discovered in Siskiyou County in the summer of 1850.

Second Garrote was named for the town's hanging tree.[348] Local lore claims that sixty men were hanged from the infamous tree, but the story has not been authenticated. It has also been rumored that two of the town's citizens — Jason Chamberlain and James Chaffee — were the basis for Bret Harte's *Tennessee's Partner.* The "Bret Harte Cabin" is at Second Garrote, but it isn't likely that the author ever came near the Second Garrote area.

Secreto (Secreta) was near Clinton in Amador County. It was settled by miners from Chile.

Secret Town (Secretown) was situated southwest of Dutch Flat in Placer County. It was probably first settled in 1849.

Seiad Valley still exists along Highway 96 in Siskiyou County. The town was once called by the Indian word "Sciad." It was a supply and transportation center for area miners during gold rush days.

Seneca was a Plumas County camp north of Quincy (near Greenville). It was along the North Fork of the Feather River.

Scottsville was an Amador County hydraulic and tunnel-mining camp near Jackson.

Scott Town was probably founded as a rival to Sonora by Charles Scott. The date was most likely 1848 or 1849, but the camp soon expired.

Scraperville was a Tuolumne County camp just west of Sonora.

Searles is along Highway 395 in Kern County skirting the China Lake Naval Weapons Center. It was a trading center for area silver and gold miners.

There were at least four California mining camps called **Sebastopol.** The Nevada County camp was southwest of North San Juan. The Sacramento County camp lasted only about five years. At the Sierra County camp near Downieville gold was scarce. The Trinity County camp was named by J. F. Chellis.

The site is now called **Shadow Creek** and is on a U.S. Forest Service campground, but at one time the Siskiyou County mining camp on a branch of the East Fork of Salmon River was known as **Shadricks.**

Shasta was first known as **Reading Springs** (or **Reading's Springs**), in honor of Major Pierson Reading. The settlement began as a tent city in 1849[349] and was renamed Shasta on June 8, 1850.

By 1852 Shasta boasted a population of several hundred and contained two wooden frame hotels. Peak years for Shasta were between 1852 and 1857.

The town was referred to as "the head of Whoa Navigation," because supplies were hauled from Sacramento to Shasta by team, and from there pack trains were used to reach the scattered mining camps. At one time perhaps 100 freight teams might stay overnight in Shasta and push off the next day to the northern mines.

During the winter of 1854–55, an estimated 1,876 mules were used in the packing trade out of Shasta.[350] Mules could carry between 200- and 300-pound packs.[351] In the fall of 1853, a 352-pound iron safe was packed from Shasta to Weaverville, thirty-eight miles away. The weight of the safe and the torturous mountain trail took their toll, for after delivering its load, the bellowing, weary hybrid offspring of burro-father and horse-mother lay down and died.[352]

After 1857 the mines began to play out, and by 1880 the camp's population was at 448, down from 1,500 in 1854. Fires in 1853 and 1878 destroyed most of the original buildings. In 1872 the California and Oregon Railroad bypassed the town, and in 1888 the fading village experienced its last rebuff — the moving of the county seat to Redding.

The town is now being made into a state historical monument, and many of the older structures are being restored. The 1853 Masonic Hall, the first in the state, is among the several attractions. Another landmark is the two-story house owned by Dr. Benjamin Shurtleff. The Greek Revival house, dating to 1851, was prefabricated in Boston, shipped around The Horn to San Francisco, shipped to Sacramento by riverboat, and freighted to Shasta by wagon.

The Masonic Hall at Shasta, erected in 1853.

Old Shasta, which some claim was once the longest row of brick buildings in California — *Shasta Historical Society.*

A view along the Shasta freighting trail — *Shasta Historical Society.*

An early view of Shasta — *Shasta Historical Society.*

Shaw's Flat grew up near Columbia in about 1850. The town may have been named for Mandeville Shaw, who planted an orchard there in 1849.

A pioneer observer called Shaw's Flat "a wide extent of perfectly flat country, four or five miles across, well wooded with oaks, and plentifully sprinkled over with miners' tents and shanties."[353]

Gold deposits from an ancient river channel were discovered in 1855, although the first placering probably occurred in 1848. Tarleton Caldwell's claim, Caldwell's Gardens, reportedly yielded $250,000.[354] It was here that shrewd, egotistical James G. Fair of Nevada Comstock Lode fame may have worked as a bartender.[355]

At one time the camp may have been called **Whimtown** because of the numerous whims, or windlasses, used in hoisting ore from shafts. However, there may have been a camp known as Whimtown that was separate and distinct from Shaw's Flat.

The Mississippi House built in 1850 or 1851 also served as a post office, store, and saloon. The structure still stands. But most of the original Shaw's Flat has disappeared except for a few crumbling walls.

Squabeletown was a nearby mining camp.

Sheep Ranch (also spelled Sheepranch) was established east of San Andreas as a quartz mining camp. It was here that George Hearst, father of newspaper magnate William Randolph Hearst, began to build his fortune.

Hearst owned the Sheepranch quartz mine, which was said to have been a moneymaker from the time the first shovelful was dug from its depths. Its total production has been estimated at $7 million.

Jimmy Sherlock was tracking a wounded deer to kill and sell to the miners at Agua Fria. He spotted gold nuggets and dug them out with his butcher knife. In time the news of a strike spread, and a town grew up northwest of Mariposa. **Sherlock Town** was named for the hunter-turned-miner.

The town boomed to about 500 miners and supported a combined schoolhouse and I.O.O.F. Hall, a hotel, and a bakery.

The heart of commercial activity in Sheep Ranch.

Sheep Ranch.

Sherlock Town went from a boom town in 1850 to a bust town. Nothing remains today.

Shingle Springs was named for a spring that flowed near a shingle mill built in 1849.

The Wells Fargo office and the Shingle Springs House are two original buildings that still stand. The original Planter's Hotel dates to 1861. Little else remains of the early mining days of Shingle Springs.

Shores Bar was a Butte County mining camp above Oroville.

Sierra City was founded in 1850 above Downieville.

Sierra City was the place where the E. Clampus Vitus society — an organization dedicated to pulling practical jokes on the uninitiated — surfaced in 1857. The group was organized in Pennsylvania in 1847 and came westward to California prior to 1853. The brotherhood became so powerful that newcomers found it impossible to conduct business until they joined the group.[356]

The Busch building, built in 1871, still stands, with the E.C.V. (E. Clampus Vitus) initials written above one of its doorways.

Silverado was a Napa County silver mining camp above Calistoga. The Robert Louis Stevenson Memorial is a reminder of the days when the author lived at the old, now-gone camp.

Silver Lake, located above Baker, was a trade center for miners in the surrounding mountains.

The settlement on the Tonopah and Tidewater Railroad was thriving in 1910, but now only adobe walls remain.

Simonville was south of Scott Bar along the Scott River in Siskiyou County. It was named for store owner Sigmund Simon.

Simpson Flat was near Oroville in Butte County. It was born in 1849, but its obituary seems to be missing from the record.

Six-Bit Gulch was on Six-Bit Gulch below Chinese Camp. It may have lasted about one dozen years.

Skidoo was populated mostly by miners from Rhyolite, Nevada, who trekked across

Death Valley and set up the new gold mining camp in 1906.[357] The population may have peaked at 700. The town even boasted a telephone line to Rhyolite.

Skidoo was the site of a hanging in 1908, when saloonkeeper Joe Simpson went on a rampage, robbed a bank, and shot and killed its manager, Jim Arnold. Photojournalists were sent to the remote mining camp to record the event, but they arrived after the fact. It has been reported, however, that obliging citizens exhumed the body and rehung it for the benefit of the cameramen.[358]

Perhaps up to $3 million in gold and silver came from Skidoo mines, but by World War I the town had died.

The cemetery and remains of a stamp mill are about the only discernable markers of this Death Valley camp.

Slabtown may have been named as such because its buildings were made from wooden slabs. It grew up east of Jackson, in Amador County in the 1850s and may have once been known as **Hoodville.** The miners soon hit borrasca, and the camp evolved from a mining to a farming settlement.

Slate Range straddled the San Bernardino–Kern county line. The camp east of Searles Lake had a post office for ten years or so and was the center of gold and silver mining.

There was a camp along Canyon Creek near its confluence with Slate Creek in Yuba County that may have been named **Slate Range Bar.** The first known gold mining occurred in 1849, but mining efforts were hampered because the gold was covered by layers of slate. The place has been a ghost site for so many years that its exact location is in doubt.

Slopeville was east of La Porte in Sierra County. It was an ephemeral gold camp.

Smartsville was a hydraulic mining center that began in the 1860s and ended in 1883. The population may have reached 1,500.

The camp is situated west of Grass Valley. Huge cuts made by hydraulic mining can still be seen.

During its heyday the camp boasted dance halls, general merchandise stores, a theatre, and sixteen saloons.

Smith's Bar was established west of Rich Bar on the North Fork of the Feather River.

The area may have yielded gold at the rate of $2,000 per hour[359] during one point in 1852.

Smith's Flat, east of Placerville, probably dates to 1849. Its post office was established in 1876 but closed in 1895.

Smithville was in Secret Ravine near Newcastle in Placer County. Its heyday was during the 1860s. It was probably named for storekeeper L. G. Smith.

Snake Bar is known as the birthplace of Sierra Woodall, the first white child born in Sierra County. The camp sprouted up above Goodyears Bar.

Extant **Snelling** was once a mining camp, and until 1872 it served as Merced county seat.

The alluvial plain of the Merced River between Snelling and Merced Falls was the scene of gold mining in the early days, but in 1907, when the Yosemite Mining and Dredging Company began operating the first connected bucket dredge in the nation, gold production shot upward. Several bucket dredges operated in the Snelling area for a number of years, with total gold production of perhaps $17 million. Federal mining regulations, including resoiling ordinances, and rising costs all put a brake on hydraulic mining in the area, and dredging steadily declined.

Soggsville was located somewhere near Nevada City in Nevada County. It was named for Nelson Sogg, who built a stamp mill there during the 1850s.

Somersville was a mid-1850s coal mining town near Mount Diablo. Very little physically remains, and very little is known of the camp's history.

The region's last mine was closed in the early 1880s.

A cemetery bearing the names of several Welsh miners squats on a ridge between

Somersville and its sister Mount Diablo coal mining settlement of Nortonville.

Somes Bar is located at the confluence of the Salmon and Klamath rivers. The camp began as a mining town but now is a fishing and camping center.

The community was probably named for George Somes, who found gold in the vicinity in the 1850s.

Sonora was settled by Mexicans in 1848 and was called **Sonorian Camp** because the Mexicans were from Sonora, Mexico. During 1849 men of many nationalities arrived, until 5,000 of them crowded the narrow canyon floor on which Sonora was built. By 1851 American miners had gained control of the claims and the camp. An observer in 1850 wrote of Sonora, "It is one of those towns that has sprung into existence by *magic — a system of building up towns unknown in any country excepting California.* It contains near a hundred stores, several fine hotels, mechanic shops, bakeries, &c., all of which have sprung up since the commencement of 1850."[360]

In 1851 the Big Bonanza mine was discovered. It became the richest pocket mine in the Mother Lode. The Golden Chispa gold nugget, weighing over twenty-eight pounds, was found within the city limits of Sonora — only one of several large nuggets to be found in the area. One gold lump weighing seventy pounds was said to have been found in the area, but that figure was later revised downward to twenty-two pounds.[361]

With so much money floating around, law enforcement was a problem. The July 4, 1859 *Herald* carried a warning to the citizens of Sonora from Justice of the Peace (Major) Richard C. Barry: "All persons are forbid firing off pistols or guns within the limits of this town under penalty; and under no plea will it be hereafter submitted to; therefore a derogation from this notice will be dealt with according to the strictest rigor of the law so applying as a misdemeanor and disturbance of the peaceful citizens of Sonora."

The town was ravaged by fires in 1849, 1852, and 1853 but each time was rebuilt. By 1865 the mines had given out, and by 1880 Sonora's population had fallen to about 1,500.

A short distance from the Big Bonanza mine is the 1859 St. James Episcopal church,[362] a reminder of Sonora's early days. Many other structures were destroyed by a fire in 1969.

Contemporary Sonora is a busy, thriving community.

Soulsbyville (Solsby, Solsbury, Soulsby Flat) was located eight miles east of Sonora. A rich vein parallel to the Mother Lode was discovered in 1856 by the Platt brothers while they were hunting for their cattle. Later, Benjamin Soulsby and his sons took up a claim north of the Platt claim and struck it even richer.

The Soulsby district, which includes the area around Soulsbyville, Tuolumne, and Buchanan, produced an estimated $20 million or more in gold. The most productive mines were the Soulsby, which yielded $5.5 million; the Black Oak, yielding $3.5 million; the South United, $1.7 million; the Grizzly, $1.5 million; the Gilson, $1.25 million; and the Draper, $1 million, according to information gathered by the Searls Historical Library of the Nevada County Historical Society.

At one time, Soulsbyville became known as the center of the temperance movement in the county.

South Fork was below Graniteville in Nevada County. It was a rich, but short-lived, gold camp.

Spanish Diggings (Spanish Dry Diggings) may have once been called **Spanish Bar,** and perhaps **Dutchtown.** Original discoveries were made by miners from Mexico, probably in 1848. The camp was northwest of Georgetown.

A camp called **Spanish Flat** was north of Kelsy in El Dorado County. Gold mining may have begun in 1848, although the town probably didn't exist until the following year. Another mining camp of the same name was southeast of La Porte on Rabbit Creek. Its heyday took place during the 1850s, but the town soon faded and died.

Spanish Ranch was a drift and hydraulic mining center west of Quincy. The first settlers were Mexicans. It is now a historic landmark.

Spanishtown was a Butte County mining camp near Yankee Hill. Whites, Chilenos, and blacks were all known to have worked the gravels at the site.

Spects Camp was on the main Yuba River in Yuba County. The here today-gone tomorrow gold camp was probably named for gold discoverer Jonas Spect.

Spenceville was situated along Dry Creek near the Nevada-Yuba county line. It was a copper camp discovered in 1862. House-to-house combat training took place there during World War II.

Springfield grew up in the shadow of Columbia. The town was named for a spring that gushes from limestone boulders and serves as the source of Mormon Creek.

Springfield exhibited concern for town planning; it had a central plaza, a town plat, and a number of shade trees.

Because the soil was mineral-rich at Springfield, many of the original houses were destroyed to reach the gravels beneath. One report relates that the entire town was torn up except the plaza.[364]

The only building left on the square is the old Methodist church, which also served as a school and courthouse.

One lime kiln dating to 1852 still remains.

Springtown was above Callahan in Siskiyou County. The miners were mostly Irish.

Squabbletown was along bubbly Woods Creek in Tuolumne County.

Two mining camps were named **Star City.** One was in Shasta County along Star City Creek. It was probably named for John Star, who owned a local trading post. The other camp was located in Mono County northwest of Cameron. The Shasta County camp hit its stride during the 1850s, the Mono County camp during the 1880s.

Startown seems to have been a Placer County mining camp near the North Fork of the Middle Fork of the American River close to Last Chance.

Stedman grew up around the Pacific mine, below Ludlow. John Sutter of the Santa Fe Railroad located deposits in 1898 or 1899. The town was first called **Rochester,** and later Stedman.

The Bagdad Chase mine south of town was discovered in 1903. Between 1904 and 1910 the Bagdad Chase produced $4.5 million in gold. The Stedman mining district has produced more than $6 million — over half the total recorded for all of San Bernardino County.

The townsite has been badly vandalized, and today little remains of this somnolent mining camp immediately north of the Twentynine Palms Marine Corps base.

Steelys Fork (Steeley) was in El Dorado County on the Consumnes River. It was named for Victor Steely, who discovered gold in the area in 1852.

Steiners Flat (Steinerville) was named for Benjamin Steiner, who started a ranch in 1850 along the Trinity River southwest of Weaverville. The camp became an important commercial center for area mines and miners.

Stent was a supply town for such mines as the App, the Dutch, the Jumper, the Sweeney, the Heslep, the New Era, and the Golden Rule. The settlement grew up about two and one-half miles below Jamestown.

However, as the story so often goes, the mines petered out, and in 1906 a debilitating fire destroyed more than 100 houses. It also destroyed Stent's hopes of reviving.

Only a pioneer cemetery near the schoolhouse remains to tell of Stent's early history.

Stewarts Flat was immediately east of Loomis. The Placer County mining camp may have reached a peak population of 1,500. The camp was born in the early 1850s and died in 1867. Only the graveyard remains.

Stewartville was a Mount Diablo area coal town. Born in the mid-1850s, it died in the 1880s.

Stingtown was near the Plumas-Sierra county line. The camp may have received its name from a miner who was badly stung by a scorpion.

Stone House Bar was a Butte County mining camp in the Big Bend of the North Fork of the Feather River.

Stoutenburg was named for William Stoutenburgh (Stoutenberg), a mining entrepreneur who had struck gold at Vallecito in about 1849. The camp's first store was operated by Stoutenburgh probably in 1850.

Strafford was in Placer County along the North Fork of the American River. It was probably so named because many of the miners had come to California on the boat named *Strafford.*

Strawberry Valley, near Quincy, was once a mining camp: The town may have been named for the wild strawberries that grew in the area, while others say that the title was a combination of the names of two pioneer miners, Straw and Berry. It is also possible that the original settlement was called **Berry's,** which was mutated to "Strawberry."

The town served primarily as a supply center for miners in the vicinity. The Columbus Hotel is the only remaining original building.

Stringtown was a Trinity County camp located along the Trinity River between Trinity Center and Carrville. It initially consisted of one ranch and a home. It is now covered by Trinity Lake, but about 1918 it was the site of mining by the Guggenheim Dredge Company. Several houses were later built on each side of a road in this dredge camp. The houses were "strung out" along the road, and thence came the name Stringtown.

After the mining had been completed, the steel hull dredge was dismantled and moved to Malasia for use in tin mining. It may be that yet another dredge plied the watery gravels between Stringtown and Carrville, built in 1938 and used until *circa* the end of World War II.[365]

The record seems to indicate that another camp called Stringtown was located in Butte County along the South Fork of the Feather River. The first mining occurred in 1849, but with fluming operations beginning in 1852, the camp began to grow rapidly. However, by 1858 the camp had lost its four-year-old post office.

The Strawberry Valley store.

Trinity County's **Sturdevants Ranch** was between Junction City and Weaverville. It was a mining camp beginning in 1849 or 1850. It was later named for a Mr. Sturdevant who owned a sawmill and farm in the area.

Sucker Flat was just above Timbuctoo. It was first called **Gatesville.**

Suckertown was an Amador County mining camp between Volcano and Fiddletown. The first historical reference to the town dates to 1855, when an observer wrote about two Chinese being murdered by Mexicans.

Sugar Pine was northeast of Columbia on Sugar Pine Creek. The Excelsior, Invincible, Sugar Pine, Monitor, and Mount Vernon mines were the best known.

Summersville was southeast of Soulsbyville in Tuolumne County. The camp probably began in 1858 when gold was discovered in the area. It was named for Franklin and Elizabeth Summers and is sometimes spelled **Somerville.** When the post office was established in 1888, it was called **Carters** for a local merchant.

Susanville's first cabin was built by Isaac Roop, who arrived at the site in 1853 and established an inn on this Sierra emigrant route. He named the site for one of his daughters. In June 1854[366] Peter Lassen and other prospectors arrived; they dug a ditch and struck gold. By the end of 1857 the town had shown moderate growth.

Early mining in the area was in the form of placer operations, but the area later became exclusively a lode mining district.

Today Susanville is a bustling community, but vestiges of the past, such as Isaac Roop's cabin, can be found.

Sutter Creek was bypassed in favor of Coloma for being the site of John Sutter's sawmill. Sutter first visited the Sutter Creek region in 1846 and mined the area in 1848. Sutter was only one of several famous people at Sutter Creek, center of some of the most active and profitable deep quartz mining in the Mother Lode. Leland Stanford invested capital in the mines,[367] while financial wizard Alvinza Hayward also figured prominently in the mining business at Sutter Creek.[368] At one time Hayward reportedly received an income of $50,000 a month from his mining interests.

Like elsewhere, Sutter Creek gold mines were shut down by government order in 1942. The Central Eureka mine at Sutter Creek joined the Homestake of Lead, South Dakota, and the Idaho-Maryland of Grass Valley and claimed a $100 million suit against the United States to determine if the government had the right to shut down the gold mines without compensation. The litigation dragged on, and finally, in 1958, the Central Eureka closed for good. But the pleasant community continued on, relatively unspoiled by commercialization.

Captain John Augustus Sutter — *California State Library.*

Sutter's Mill, 1851 — *Society of California Pioneers.*

The Wells Fargo Bank in Sutter Creek.

Swansea was located north of Keeler, near the old shoreline of Owens Lake. The community was named for the smelter town in Wales. Whether Swansea, California, ores were shipped to Swansea, Wales, via Cartago and San Pedro for smelting has not been resolved. Some sources say it was,[369] while others point out the ruins of a brick smelter at Swansea[370] and question why ores would be shipped to Wales for processing when Swansea had a smelter of its own.

James Brady stimulated the building of the town of Swansea after assuming the operation of the Owens Lake silver-and-lead furnace and mill in 1870. The structures, erected in 1869 by Colonel Sherman Stevens, were used until March 1874. The output of the Swansea and nearby Cerro Gordo furnaces is generally rated at about 150 eighty-three-pound bars of silver every twenty-four hours. Crumbling ruins of the furnace-mill remain near the townsite of Swansea.

Remains of relatively modern-day mining in the Swansea area.

Remains of the Owens Lake silver-lead furnace and mill built by Colonel Sherman Stevens at Swansea in 1869.

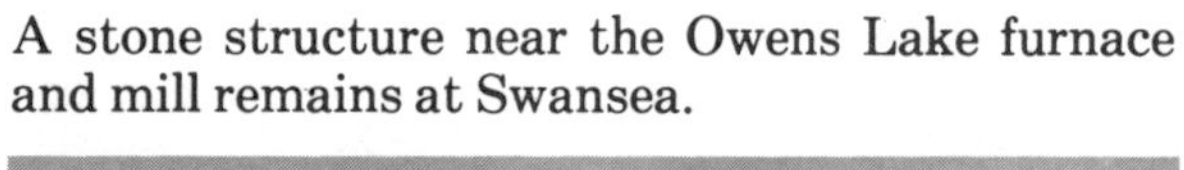

A stone structure near the Owens Lake furnace and mill remains at Swansea.

Sweetland, northwest of the North Columbia–Highway 49 intersection, is a placer mining camp dating to 1850. It was named for the three bachelor Sweetland brothers, who dug for gold in the area.

The town later became a hydraulic center, but the ban on hydraulic mining sounded the camp's death knell.

Taylor's Flat (Taylor Flat) was "blown in" about two miles west of Big Bar. One pioneer observer had some thoughts about the camp, writing: "The first mention that known history has of this locality is from 1853, when the name was given to it by a Taylor, whom the damsel hath thenceforth dropped."[371]

The writer thought that "life and stir" was imparted to Taylor's Flat by the Washington Fluming Company, which spent $60,000 on a three-mile flume system from French Creek.

By 1858 the camp had a hotel, three stores, a blacksmith and butcher shop, and about fifty miners.

Canadian Bar was nearby, consisting mostly of Chinese miners. Also nearby was **Martins,** but it isn't clear if it was an official settlement.

Taylorsville, located northeast of Quincy, was named for Jobe Taylor. Although little information is available on Taylorsville, the town does display one interesting vestige of the past: a schoolhouse dedicated to "Truth-Liberty-Toleration" by the Native Sons of the Golden West on August 29, 1954. The school stands, cobwebs clinging to its long-unused flagpole.

Gold mining operations at Taylorville. From an original daguerreotype taken in 1849 — *The Huntington Library.*

Tecopa, in southeastern Inyo County, was in the center of mining activity that began in 1865. However, little production occurred in the area until about 1910. From 1912 to 1928 the Shoshone mines produced perhaps $3 million in lead and silver; gold was also produced.

Tehachapi is now in the fruit-growing region west of Mojave. However, gold discoveries in the China Hill placers in 1854 started the town, originally located about three miles east of present-day Tehachapi.

In 1876, when the railroad bypassed the town, the buildings were moved to rest alongside the railroad right-of-way.

Telegraph City was southwest of Copperopolis. Copper prospects lured miners to the area, and a town was founded in the early 1860s. The town's naming may have had something to do with the telegraph line between Stockton and Sonora.

Texas Bar was north of Placerville. Other places of the same name were in Placer (two locations), Sierra, Trinity, Tuolumne, and Yuba counties.

Thompsons Flat was north of Oroville. The town was named in 1854 for George Thompson. By 1870 the camp had lost its post office and most of its population.

Timbuctoo may have been named for a black miner who was the first to pan for gold in the area. Because the man had come from Timbuktu, Africa, he asked if he might dub the place by that name. That was in 1850. By 1855 the town had grown only slightly.

With the advent of hydraulic mining, Timbuctoo boomed into the largest town in eastern Yuba County. It may have peaked at a population of 1,200. But again, with the outlawing of hydraulic mining, Timbuctoo died.

The neglected ruins of a Wells Fargo building mark the site.

The town, according to Thomas E. Farish in *The Gold Hunters,* may have also been known as **Sand Hat** in 1854.

The Wells Fargo & Co. building at Timbuctoo.

The faded sign on the front of the Timbuctoo Wells Fargo building indicates that gold dust is bought inside.

Tinemaha was an Inyo County trading center for area miners. Named for a legendary Paiute chief, the camp was between Bishop and Independence.

Tioga, first called **Bennettville,** sprouted up north of Tioga Pass on Mount Excelsior.

The first silver discovery probably occurred in 1860, but not until the Tioga Mining district was organized in 1878 did the settlement begin to grow.

Tioga was apparently the site of a large sawmill operation where charcoal was prepared for the smelting furnace to serve area mines.

Machinery and money flowed into the camp so that area silver ores could be treated. A tunnel was driven 800 feet through rock to reach the silver ledge. But the rock was so hard that three to five shifts were needed to put in a single round of dynamite holes for blasting.[372]

Costly litigation, delays, and other problems forced the order to close operations in 1884. The properties were later sold at sheriffs' auction. Money was spent to reactivate the operations, but nothing came of the effort. It has been claimed that not one ounce of silver was ever mined at Tioga, and that may be correct.[373]

Toadtown sprang on the mining scene north of Magalia in Butte County, but probably not until the late 1870s.

Todd Valley, named for Dr. F. W. Todd, a cousin of Abraham Lincoln's wife, was founded southeast of Colfax, probably in 1849.

The rich Jenny Lind mine at Todd Valley reportedly once produced $2,000 per day in gold. The Todd Valley mine and the Peckham Hill mine collectively produced about $5 million in gold.

Town Talk grew up midway between Grass Valley and Nevada City.

A tale persists that an old saloon sign bearing the words "Town Talk" was washed into the area by flood-swollen waters of Deer Creek. The sign was fished out of the water and stuck into the ground, and the camp that was situated at the site was thereafter called Town Talk.

Trinidad served as headquarters for the miners who toiled in Trinity County mines. During its peak years of 1851–52, the town may have had 3,000 people. Few vestiges of mining days remain.

Trinity Center is north and slightly east of Weaverville. This mining camp was founded in the early 1850s,[374] when small-scale placer operations were undertaken in the Trinity River basin. The town was so named because it was at the center of the Shasta–Yreka trail.

Huge dragline dredges and hydraulic giants were used in the area. But most Trinity County gold has been wrenched from placers.

Most creeks in the area were named during early mining days, including Coffee, Treasure, and Grave creeks. Coffee Creek was so named either because a mule loaded with coffee toppled into it, or because the stream had roily, muddy water. Treasure Creek was named for a Wells Fargo strongbox, still said to remain in the stream's

Trinity Dredge above the mouth of Baker Gulch in 1933 — *Trinity County Historical Society.*

depths. Grave Creek was named for an Englishman who drowned there and was buried nearby.[375]

The original townsite of Trinity Center was flooded out, and the settlement was relocated to its present site.

Tumco was a Cargo Muchacho Mountain mining town northeast of El Centro.

From 1865 to 1870 Mexicans had been quietly working deposits in the area. But when a railroad employee found gold in the early 1880s,[376] a stampede began near the Mexican diggings.

During the town's heyday, a 100-stamp mill was erected. The cyanide recovery process was used, and the town hummed along in prosperity. C. L. Hedges, a mining company vice president and the man who founded the town, saw his name temporarily immortalized as the camp became known as **Hedges.** The community may have grown to 3,000. Hedges later sold his interests, and the Borden Corporation took over. The company that operated the properties was the United Mining Company (or United Mines Company), and the town's name was changed to reflect the initials of the organization (*T*he *U*nited *M*ining *C*ompany). In 1909 the company began operations and closed them down the next year.[377]

The desert is reclaiming its domain, and today tired Tumco is a deserted, parched, barren ghost town.

Panorama of Tumco, 1905 — *Collection of Historical Photographs, Title Insurance and Trust Company, Los Angeles.*

Panorama of Hedges Desert mine on the Colorado River, about 1905 — *Collection of Historical Photographs, Title Insurance and Trust Company, Los Angeles.*

Hedges mine on the Colorado River, Tumco — *Collection of Historical Photographs, Title Insurance and Trust Company, Los Angeles.*

Miners in paydirt at Hedges (Tumco) on the Colorado Desert — *Collection of Historical Photographs, Title Insurance and Trust Company, Los Angeles.*

Tuttletown[378] was a trade and transportation center on the Slumgullion road. The town was named for Judge Anson A. H. Tuttle, who built a log cabin on the site in 1848.[379]

The Swerer Store, a stone building erected in 1852, was perhaps occasionally visited by Mark Twain and Bret Harte. Ruins of the store still stand.

Twentynine Palms (or **Palm City**) was founded in 1873 as a supply center for area mines that were located northeast of the Little San Bernardino Mountains. Gold production seems to have begun in earnest in 1893 with the opening of the Brooklyn mine. In the early 1900s the Supply and Nightingale mines were large producers, making the district one of the more prosperous in the nation. However, production fell off after World War II, and the district has been dormant ever since.

Tyler was established near North Columbia and was called **Cherokee** in the early 1850s. The town was a mining camp for a few years, but few specifics about its history are readily available.

Uniontown (Union Town) was southeast of El Dorado. The El Dorado County camp may have reached a peak population of 2,000 to 3,000. There also may have been a Union Town mining camp in Holcomb Valley in San Bernardino County.

Vallecito (Little Valley), located on the banks of Coyote Creek, was settled in 1850 by Mexican miners. The town languished until a gold strike in 1852, when the Americans muscled aside their Mexican predeces-

The former Dinkelspiel's Store and Wells Fargo Bank at Vallecito.

sors and soon had the plaza plowed up and buildings razed for the gold beneath.

A hotel, saloons, stores, a bank, an express office, a school, and a post office were established.

A ship's bell brought around The Horn was used to call congregations to Sunday services at the Union church. Because the church had no steeple, the bell was mounted on a nearby oak tree, where it stayed until a wind blew it down in 1939. The bell was later mounted in a monument in front of the church.

The church remains, along with other landmarks, including the 1851 rock and adobe Gilleado building and Dinkelspiel's store.

Valley View was northeast of Lincoln in Placer County. Area mines produced gold, silver, and copper.

Vanderbilt was built in the New York Mountains northwest of Needles, southeast of Mountain Pass.

The gold and silver mines that sustained the settlement were discovered in the 1870s, but the town didn't reach its heyday until the 1890s. Several old structures mark the site.

By 1893, 500 people called the gold camp home, but by 1897 the camp was dead. Even the coming of the California Eastern Railway in 1902 failed to revive the moribund camp.

The district is credited with gold production of $2 million or more.

Victorville was known as **Mormon Crossing** from 1878 to 1885, was then called **Victor**, and finally Victorville in 1903. The town was named for J. N. Victor, construction superintendent for the California Southern Railroad during the 1880s.

More than 200 films were shot in the area between 1914 and 1937.

The town is still very much alive today.

Virginiatown (Virginia) was east of Lincoln in Placer County. The camp was founded in summer 1851. A freight railroad was built through the town in 1852, and a post office (named **Virginia**) was established in 1858. But by 1860 the post office was closed, and the camp began to die.

Virner was near Georgetown in El Dorado County. Gold discoverer James Marshall built a cabin near here.

Volcano (Soldier's Gulch) was once one of the richest and largest towns on the Mother Lode. It was mistakenly thought that the town sat in the crater of an extinct volcano.[380] In 1848 John Sutter mined along Sutter Creek, and either that year or the next, men from Stevenson's regiment of the New York Volunteers found rich deposits in Soldier's Gulch.

By 1850 Volcano had become a boom town of forty-seven saloons, a jail, five hotels, two breweries, and even boasted a Thespian Society and a Miners' Library Association (probably the state's first miners' rental library). The town established the state's first astronomical observatory, and the Odd Fellows and Masons constructed lodges in the community.

The camp mushroomed to 5,000,[381] but by 1855 most of the placer deposits had played out. Shortly thereafter, however, hydraulic mining operations clawed at area gravels; it has been claimed that perhaps $90 million[382] in bullion was shipped from Volcano in the 1850s alone. The complete bullion shipment didn't reach San Francisco, because part of it was stolen in some spectacular robberies.

The George Hotel at Volcano.

When mining tapered off, Volcano lost part of its population but managed to survive, a shell of its former self. A goodly number of gold rush days structures remain.

The Union Hotel in Volcano. It housed a billiard parlor and saloon and functioned also as a boardinghouse.

The 1851 Hale Sash and Door factory in Volcano. One of the state's first private law schools was housed here.

Waldo was along Dry Creek near the Yuba–Nevada county line. The camp's beginning seems to trace back to 1852, when two blacks planted a field of cabbage at the site and the place was dubbed **Cabbage Patch.** When the post office was established in 1898, the name became Waldo.

Walloupa was between Nevada City and Dutch Flat. First gold discoveries were made in 1852, and that year the town was surveyed. The place was named for an Indian. The camp's demise came in 1860, when most miners and prospectors moved on to neighboring You Bet.

Warren Hill was northeast of La Porte in Sierra County. The camp probably lasted only during the 1850s.

Washington, located east of North Bloomfield, is a former mining camp that was converted to a lumber town.

Numerous boulders surrounding the settlement attest to mining activities.

Much of the camp can be seen from a marked viewpoint on Highway 20 east of Nevada City. The vista — the Alpha-Omega viewpoint — is located near the gold camps of **Alpha** and **Omega,** which date to the 1850s. Hydraulic diggings have engulfed most of both original townsites.

Alpha (first called **Hell-Out-For-Noon City**) was the birthplace of opera singer Emma Nevada. It was also the place from which Dan DeQuille (William Wright) wrote his brother-in-law, Dr. J. M. Benjamin of Iowa, about California's sequoia trees: "If one of the smallest of them . . . should be cut down, the butt would be lying on the ground so long as to be perfectly rotten before the top got to the ground."[383]

Mining was pursued at Omega (once known as **Delirium Tremens**) until 1949, but the town is now a lumbering center.

Weaverville was named for George Weaver, who discovered gold on Weaver Creek in 1849. The first log cabin was erected on the site by Weaver, James Howe, and Daniel Bennett on July 8, 1850, about the time the town was established. By mid-1852 Weaverville had grown to a town of 1,200 people and forty buildings. However, the air of permanence still didn't exist, for as one "pilgrim" to Weaverville wrote in his diary on June 9, 1852, "I have settled down once more and intend to stay settled if the town I have selected does not die out as a great many places do in this mushrooming country."[384]

But permanent or temporary, Weaverville was a lively town, described in July 1852 as "decidedly bad, gambling, drinking, and fighting being the amusements of the miners in their leisure hours. Saturday night is usually celebrated by such hideous yells and occassionally [*sic*] a volley from their revolvers which makes it rather dangerous to be standing around. At least a poor inoffensive jackass found it so the other night."[385]

Just because Saturdays were lively didn't mean that Sundays were sedate. It was written, "Last Sunday was the glorious 4th of July, and in this country people get most gloriously drunk generally."[386]

By 1852 about 1,500[387] Chinese lived in Weaverville — about one-half the total population. A tong war occurred at nearby Five Cent Gulch during July 1852.[388] The Yangwa (or Yang Wah) Company, dressed in red, consisted of 110 men.[389] Their foes, numbering 250,[390] were known as the Canton City Company.[391]

The Yangwa (sometimes referred to as "Red Caps" or "Hong Kongs") and Cantons (sometimes referred to as "Young Woes" or "Young Wos") were armed with pikes, spears, swords, squirt guns, and revolvers. Amid much pomp and noise, the battle finally began. The Red Caps attacked the Cantons, who broke ranks and ran. The fight may have lasted only two minutes,[392] and when the dust of battle had cleared, the Red Caps had lost two men, the Cantons six, and one white miner had been killed. The next day the dead were buried, and following ceremonies the Chinese passed out liquor and cigars to the whites. It was reported that "The wounded are doing well and quiet is again restored in China."[393] Not only did Chinese fight Chinese, but Indian fought white. In May 1852 a band of Indians killed the Weaverville butcher as he drove a herd of cattle. A sheriff's posse trailed the Indians to their village and massacred over 100 people — all but two or three of them chil-

The Trinity County courthouse at Weaverville.

The Chinese joss house in Weaverville. Constructed in 1864, the joss house was photographed here in 1936 — *Collection of Historical Photographs, Title Insurance and Trust Company, Los Angeles.*

The old Chinese joss house at Weaverville — *Trinity County Historical Society.*

dren. That autumn the Indian chief came to Weaverville and signed a peace treaty.

By autumn of the year of the "Tong War" there were two hotels in town and one under construction, although one hotel had but one private room and the other had but one room.

Weaverville was still a tough town in 1862 when the state geological survey team visited in October. They reported that gambling and fighting were favorite pastimes. But some Weaverville residents objected to their town's reputation, pointing out that as early as 1856 the town had held a church, a Sunday school, and even a dancing class.

Weaverville was the sometimes-home of Isabelle Hoffman Martin, sometimes referred to as "Queen of Dynamite." She and her son, John Martin, Jr. (whom she called "Baby John"), cut a wide swath around the area. It seems that Mrs. Martin beat her son with pokers and black snake whips and forced him to blow up mining equipment, houses, and ditches, as well as be an arsonist and poisoner of drinking water. Baby John maintained that if he didn't do these things, she'd take him to a mine tunnel, give him poison, put a charge of powder under him, and blow him to pieces, making it look like an accident.

Isabelle Hoffman Martin — *San Francisco Examiner and Trinity County Historical Society.*

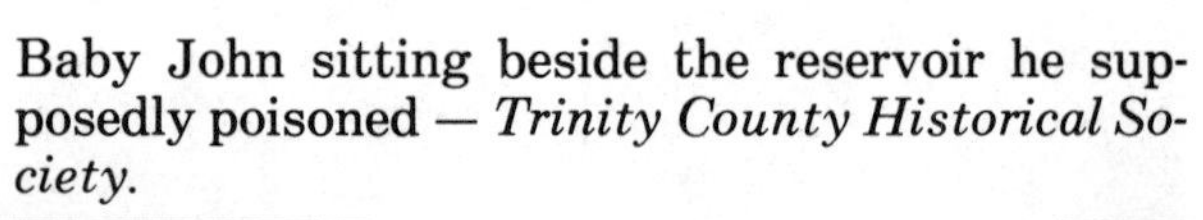

Baby John sitting beside the reservoir he supposedly poisoned — *Trinity County Historical Society.*

Mrs. Martin, it is assumed, killed her second husband and her former brother-in-law. While under sentence to life imprisonment for dynamiting the home of Judge Frank B. Ogden in March 1907, she went mad. John later became one of the town's most respected citizens.[394]

A number of older brick and adobe structures can still be found in this town, along with a newspaper office, a museum, and a Chinese joss house, preserved as a state historical monument.

Weberville was settled along Weber's Creek in 1848 by Captain Charles Weber, along with Indian chief Jose Jesus and his band. The camp below Placerville apparently was never the site of rich ore discoveries, for as early as 1850 it was reported that "It is a place of some business, but is not improving rapidly, the mines in its immediate vicinity having become pretty well exhausted."[395]

The town, however, became a bartering center, for here Weber exchanged beads and cloth for the gold brought him by the Indians. Weber gained a considerable fortune in his dealings, because the Indians didn't realize for quite some time that Weber was taking advantage of them in the exchange.

Ringgold is now a part of Weberville. At one time it was a separate camp of several hundred inhabitants.

Weeds Point was northwest of Camptonville. It was named for a miner named Weed.

West Point can be found on contemporary highway maps. It initially was called **Indian Gulch** but became West Point in 1854. Some say that it was named by Kit Carson. This was good pocket mining country, and several mills were in operation at various times.

Whiskey Diggings was the name of a short-lived mining camp on Little Slate Creek near the Sierra-Plumas county line. The camp was also known as **Whiskey** and **Newark.** Another Whiskey Diggings was located in Placer County northeast of Lincoln.

There were a number of places called **Whiskey Flat** in various counties in California. The only one that probably was a mining camp was in Mariposa County a couple of miles above Whitlock.

Whiskey Slide was northeast of San Andreas. The town was probably named for the Whiskey Slide Canal Company whose headquarters were at the town.

Whiskeytown is situated along Highway 299 west of Redding. The camp was settled in 1849 by miners in the Whiskey Creek area, on the trail to Oregon. The creek was so named because a barrel (or barrels[396]) of whiskey fell into it when a usually surefooted mule fell off a cliff into the rushing stream.

Granville Stuart[397] and his companions camped near the settlement the night of July 11, 1854. Stuart called the town a rather lively little village and concluded, "from the maudlin songs, yells, and cuss words that enlivened the night we decided that the place was rightly named."

It has been suggested that postal authorities have been prudish in trying to prevent the community from being dubbed Whiskeytown. They have instead called it **Blair, Stella,** and **Schilling.**

Twenty-five million dollars may have been taken from Whiskeytown area gulches and the Mad Mule mine.[398]

The government, which had seemed bent on destroying Whiskeytown from the very beginning, apparently succeeded when the Bureau of Reclamation diverted the waters of the Trinity River into the Sacramento through the newly created Whiskeytown Lake, formed by the Whiskeytown Dam. The dedication by John F. Kennedy in September 1963 occurred shortly before the president was assassinated.

Whiskeytown is now under water, but it lives on in a new settlement that has a post office built of lumber from an old saloon taken from the original Whiskeytown.[399]

White River grew up as a gold camp east of Delano, northeast of Bakersfield and south of the Tule River Indian Reservation. First called **Dogtown,** the name was changed to **Tailhold** (or **Tailholt**), then to White River. The town was founded about 1856 during the Kern River gold rush era.

The tavern in old Whiskeytown — *Shasta Historical Society.*

The post office and general store at Whiskeytown.

The settlement contains two cemeteries; one for "respected" citizens, and one for those who lived and died outside of the law.

Whitlock grew up northwest of Mariposa along Whitlock Road, near Whitlock Creek and the Whitlock mine and mill — all named for Thomas J. Whitlock.

The Whitlock mine produced about $430,000 between 1895 and 1901. It was English-owned and Cornish-operated.

About thirty houses and a two-story bunkhouse were spread along Whitlock Creek. There were no saloons and no jail. Today, nothing remains of the original camp.

Wild Goose Flat was in El Dorado County along the North Fork of the American River. It hit its heyday in the mid-1850s, languished by the mid-'70s, and was a ghost town by the mid-'80s.

Willow Springs was northwest of Amador in Amador County. Initial discoveries of gold were made, but later the camp became a copper producer. Another camp of the same name sprang into existence in Sacramento County immediately southeast of Folsom.

Winslow was along the North Fork of the Yuba River in Yuba County. The place was named for a Captain Winslow, who used Chinese laborers to mine his properties.

Wolverine was immediately northeast of Iowa Hill in Placer County.

Woodfords was established by errant Mormon bishop Sam Brannan in 1847. This transportation center, founded one dozen miles south of Minden, Nevada, was a temporary Pony Express stop for six weeks in 1860. During that decade the camp became a ranching and farming community to supply miners working in the area.[400]

The town still survives and has a few vestiges of earlier days, including two cemeteries.

Woods Crossing was a gold quartz camp that began in 1848 following gold discoveries by a man named Woods. The Harvard mine was the largest producer. Discovered in 1850, the mine was worked continuously until 1916. At least $2,036,697 was taken from the mine.

Woolseys Flat was north of North Bloomfield in Nevada County. It was named for an early prospector, probably in 1851. By the mid-1870s the camp died.

Wyandotte (Wyandot) was southeast of Oroville in Butte County. In 1849 the Wyandott Mining Company was organized by a Wyandot Indian from Kansas, and this may have had something to do with the town's naming.

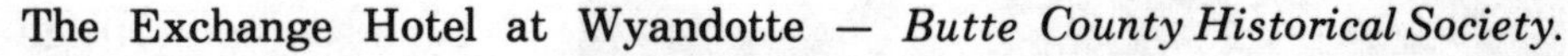

The Exchange Hotel at Wyandotte — *Butte County Historical Society.*

Mrs. Nancy Thatcher, at one time the proprietress of the Exchange Hotel in Wyandotte — *Butte County Historical Society.*

William Dunstone with the graduating class in the old Wyandotte Hall about 1904 — *Butte County Historical Society.*

Wynola grew up in the Julian mining district northeast of San Diego. Discharged Confederate soldiers discovered placer gold in 1869 near Wynola. The entire district evidenced very little activity after 1900, although occasional mining occurred in the late 1930s and early 1940s, producing about 1,500 ounces. The district has been idle since 1950.

A settlement called **W.Y.O.D.** may have existed near the Daisy Bell mine in the Grass Valley area.

Depending on the story you choose to believe, the initials may have stood for "Work Your Own Diggin's" or "Wear Your Own Drawers."[401]

Yankee Hill arose northeast of Columbia.

The camp was named for a "Yankee" named Hill or Hills when miners decided they didn't like the original monicker of **Knickerbocker Flat.**

Yankee Hill's main claim to fame is a 250-ounce gold nugget found by French miners and a twenty-seven-pound nugget found by a down-and-out Italian.

There is also a Yankee Hill in Butte County, north of Cherokee. Initial discoveries were made by Chileans and Mexicans, probably in 1850.

Yankee Jims was a trading center for hydraulic mining camps of the area. The town, located near Auburn, was apparently named for Yankee Jim (Jim Hill or a man named Robinson from Sydney), an Australian. Hill had a penchant for rustling horses. He was good at his work, but he almost got caught by a man from whom he had stolen a horse. He hightailed it out of the country just in time to avoid Judge Lynch. Stories tell that the corral in which Yankee Jim kept his stolen horseflesh was found to be lousy with gold.

The prosperous camp that sprang up near the corral was named Yankee Jims, and it grew to become Placer County's largest mining camp. But the town eventually shrivelled; today it consists of only a few weathered buildings.

Incidentally, folklore indicates that Yankee Jim was finally hanged, perhaps for being a road agent. It seems that about one month before Yankee Jim was caught and hanged, another man had mistakenly been strung up as the miscreant. The grisly tale relates that Jim's body and the other man's

Dr. I. L. R. Mansfield was a Wyandotte physician for more than half a century. These are his parents in front of their cabin at Wyandotte — *Butte County Historical Society.*

corpse were thrown into a common grave, with a marker pointing out, "Here lies the body of Yankee Jim. We made a mistake, and the joke's on him."

Yaqui Camp was southeast of San Andreas in Calaveras County. It may have been named for Yaqui Indians who perhaps mined the area.

Yatestown was a supply center for miners and was located along the Feather River in Butte County. It was probably named for James Yates, a former English sailor who worked for John Sutter.

Yornet (Yeomet, Forks of the Consumnes, Saratoga) began in 1849 or 1850 where the forks of the Consumnes River join. The life of the town's post office spanned only about seven years.

Yorktown was near Jamestown in Tuolumne County. The mining camp was probably settled in 1848 and may have been named for a man named York. The camp's life span was brief.

You Bet was contemporary with Little Rock, Walloupa, and Red Dog, around which 2,000 miners dug for gold in the 1870s. The town was located in the Dutch Flat-Gold Run-Colfax area.

Folklore has suggested that miners debated about giving the new settlement a decent name in place of its original obscene title. After much discussion, it was decided that the first stranger to straggle in to the camp would be asked what he thought of a name change. The man's drunken reply was, "You Bet!" . . . which became the camp's new cognomen.

Others claim that the camp was founded by Lazarus Beard from Beardstown, Kentucky.[402] Proponents of this idea remark that two of Lazarus' friends, Bill King and Jim Toddkill of neighboring Walloupa, frequently got Lazarus to spring for drinks as they discussed what to christen the new place. Since Lazarus was fond of saying "you bet," his buddies suggested that name for the fledgling camp. And so it was.

You Bet was the victim of hydraulic giants (monitors), for the town has disappeared, along with the hills on which it was built.

Youngs Hill was above Camptonville. The camp probably dates to 1851 and was named either for William Young or Nicodemus Young.

Yuba City was laid out in July 1849 by Sam Brannan, Major Samuel Hensley, Pierson Reading, and Henry Cheever.

The town took its name from the nearby Yuba River. Yubu, or Yuba, was the name of an Indian village opposite the mouth of the Yuba.

And that's something of California mining history as seen through an account of a few of the better documented of the state's ghost towns and mining camps. Both the bad and the good have been covered, although at times it's difficult to know for sure which is which.

Lucius Beebe and Charles M. Clegg wryly provided some food for parting thought when they wrote, "I may not be a competent judge, but this much I will say, that I have seen purer liquors, better segars, finer tobacco, truer guns and pistols, larger dirks and bowie knives, and prettier courtezans here, than in any other place I have ever visited; and it is my unbiased opinion that California can and does furnish the best bad things that are obtainable in America."[403]

The "You Bet" hydraulic mine in 1880 — *Nevada County Historical Society.*

The Borate mine about 1895 — *U.S. Borax.*

A tin mine in Trabuco Canyon, located in the Santa Ana Mountains of the southeastern part of Orange County — *Collection of Historical Photographs, Title Insurance and Trust Company, Los Angeles.*

The interior of an old stamp mill — *Collection of Historical Photographs, Title Insurance and Trust Company, Los Angeles.*

A 100-stamp mill — *Collection of Historical Photographs, Title Insurance and Trust Company, Los Angeles.*

Arrastre at Gun Barrel mine being built in 1907 or 1908 shows tub and discharge holes and table where the quicksilver plates were to catch the gold. Plates were three feet square, made of copper, and cost $45 each — *Trinity County Historical Society.*

Pipeline and steam hoist at the inverted siphon at Bridge Camp — *Trinity County Historical Society.*

An interior view of the Boomer stamp mill. Three 550-pound stamps each dropped about 100 times per minute — *Trinity County Historical Society.*

Footnotes

1. Richard Dillon, *Humbugs and Heroes,* Doubleday, Garden City, N.Y., 1970, p. 312.
2. Discoveries had been known to have been made in 1775 by Mexicans in the Colorado River and the Cargo Muchacho Mountains. In the 1830s gold was discovered in Los Angeles County, where other discoveries were reported in 1842. In 1825 Jedediah Smith probably discovered gold near Mono Lake. T. A. Rickard, in *A History of American Mining,* McGraw-Hill, New York, 1932, traces much of this early California gold discovery history.
3. Rodman W. Paul, in *The California Gold Discovery,* The Talisman Press, Georgetown, California, 1966, p. 18, points out that the problems in knowing answers such as precise discovery date stem in part from the fact that no one anticipated, few witnessed, and fewer still immediately recorded the event. Paul's *California Gold,* Harvard University Press, 1947, is a definitive study of the gold discovery.
4. Paul, in *California Gold,* p. 13, refers to Sutter as being "Munchausen-like."
5. Otis E. Young, Jr., *Western Mining,* University of Oklahoma Press, Norman, 1970, p. 103. However, as William Greever points out in *The Bonanza West,* University of Oklahoma Press, Norman, 1963, p. 7, the excitement didn't really start until May or June 1848.
6. One observer (Herman W. Albert, *Odyssey of a Desert Prospector,* University of Oklahoma Press, Norman, 1967, p. 181) wrote of Death Valley: "Winter is summer, and summer is but a few degrees from cremation."
7. The guidebooks of the day urged the gold hungry to seek gold, and to "cheer up and go ahead, and enjoy the trip and get all [the gold] you can; it will pay you if you do not get but little (Giles S. Isham, *Guide to California and the Mines,* facsimile of original 1850 journal, Ye Galleon Press, Fairfield, Washington, 1972, p. 61).
8. November 6, 1850.
9. Franklin Langworthy, *Scenery of the Plains, Mountains and Mines,* 1932 (from the edition of 1855), Princeton University Press, Cambridge, p. 170.
10. Lansford W. Hastings, *The Emigrants' Guide to Oregon and California* (reproduced from original 1845 edition), Princeton University Press, Cambridge, 1932, p. 31.
11. Bayard Taylor, *Eldorado,* George P. Putnam & Co., New York, 1850, p. 254.
12. M. T. McClellan to B. Leonard, Jackson County, Mo., *Independence Expositor,* quoted by the Missouri *Statesman,* April 27, 1849.
13. Evelyn Wells and Harry Peterson, *The '49ers,* Doubleday, New York, 1949, p. 57.
14. Daniel B. Woods, *Sixteen Months at the Gold Diggings,* Harper & Brothers, New York, 1851, p. 125.
15. *Ibid.*
16. G. Ezra Dane, *Ghost Town,* Alfred A. Knopf, New York, 1941, p. 2.
17. 1974 reprint of the 1871 Harper Brothers edition published by Promontory Press, New York, p. 306.
18. Adolphus Windeler, *The California Gold Rush Diary of a German Sailor,* Howell-North Books, Berkeley, 1969, p. 192.
19. *Ibid.,* p. 185.
20. D. L. Phillips, *Letters from California,* Illinois State *Journal,* Springfield, 1877, p. 152.
21. *Ibid.,* p. 87.
22. *Ibid.,* p. 141. J. Ross Browne (*J. Ross Browne,* edited by Lina Fergusson Browne, University of New Mexico Press, 1969, p. 219), in a letter to his wife from San Francisco in 1860, complained that intemperance was becoming the "great curse" of California.
23. Woods, p. 20.
24. Leonard Kip, *California Sketches,* K. A. Kovach, Los Angeles, 1946, p. 31.
25. John Frost, *History of the State of California,* Derby and Miller, Auburn, N.Y., 1850, p. 113.

26. Helen Rocca Goss, *The Life and Death of a Quicksilver Mine,* Historical Society of Southern California, Los Angeles, 1958, p. 126.
27. Charles H. Shinn, *Mining Camps,* Alfred A. Knopf, New York, 1948, p. 138.
28. Some sources (such as the *Fresno Bee,* March 5, 1931), give the date as 1874; others 1870 or 1871. But the Fresno County Historical Society (letter of November 26, 1976 and other reliable sources) give the 1872 date.
29. Woods, p. 121, and Wells and Peterson, spell the name "Agua Frio," as do Etienne Derbec in *A French Journalist in the California Gold Rush,* Talisman Press, Georgetown, California, 1964 and Robert Eccleston in *The Mariposa War, 1850-1851,* University of Utah Press, Salt Lake City, 1957. However, "proper" spelling would be "Agua Fria," as the Post Office Department had it written.
30. Woods, p. 121.
31. *Geologic Guidebook Along Highway 49 — Sierran Gold Belt, Bulletin 141,* State of California Department of Natural Resources, Division of Mines, San Francisco, 1948, p. 141; hereafter referred to as *Geologic Guidebook.*
32. Jack R. Wagner, *Gold Mines of California,* Howell-North Books, Berkeley, California, 1970, p. 231, gives the year as 1851.
33. *Geologic Guidebook,* p. 78. *California,* American Guide Series, Federal Writers' Project, Hastings House, New York, 1939 (hereafter referred to as *California*), p. 478, gives the year 1908. *Gold Rush Country,* Lane Books, Menlo Park, California, 1971, p. 90, gives an "opening" date of 1896. The confusion may arise from the fact that what is now known as the Sixteen-to-One is a consolidation of three mining properties — the Sixteen-to-One, the Twenty-One, and the Tightner, discovered and developed at different times.
34. Wagner gives total production figures of $35 million. A. D. Koschmann and M. H. Bergendahl, in *Principal Gold-Producing Districts of the United States,* U. S. Geological Survey Professional Paper 610, 1968, p. 79, only give production totals of about $9 million until 1928, but fail to give figures for the Sixteen-to-One.
35. Wagner gives the closing date as December 31, 1965. *Gold Rush Country* says 1966.
36. The former idea is from *Gold Rush Country,* p. 25; the latter from Lambert Florin, *Ghost Town Album,* Superior Publishing Company, Seattle, 1962, p. 113.
37. Probably dating to a couple of dozen years after the town's founding.
38. The population may have swelled to 4,500, according to Remi Nadeau in *Ghost Towns and Mining Camps of California,* The Ward Ritchie Press, Los Angeles, 1965, p. 84.
39. *Prospector, Cowhand, and Sodbuster,* United States Department of the Interior, National Park Service, Washington, D. C., 1967 (hereafter referred to as *Prospector*); Erwin G. Gudde in *California Gold Camps,* University of California Press, Berkeley, 1975, p. 19, used *The State Register and Year Book Facts,* San Francisco, 1857, 1859, to indicate that eight water-driven mills operated there in 1857.
40. *Mark Twain's Notebook,* prepared for publication with comments by Albert Bigelow Paine, Harper & Brothers, New York, 1935, p. 6.
41. *Ibid.,* p.8.
42. Nadeau, p. 259.
43. Otheta Weston, in *Mother Lode Album,* Stanford University Press, 1948, p. 140, calls him Claud Charnay.
44. *California,* p. 483. Muriel Sibell Wolle, in *The Bonanza Trail,* Indiana University Press, Bloomington, 1966, p. 109, indicates that two "Chilenos" found gold at Rich Ravine in 1849 where Auburn now stands, but that their properties were "expropriated" by John S. Wood, an ex-soldier who renamed the place Wood's Dry Diggings.
45. *Prospector,* p. 157.
46. *California,* p. 483.
47. Koschmann and Bergendahl, p. 68.
48. *California,* p. 611. Neil Morgan, in *The California Syndrome,* Ballantine Books, New York, 1971, p. 15, points out that Bagdad virtually has gone as long as two years without rainfall.
49. Koschmann and Bergendahl, p. 63. William B. Clark, in *Gold Districts of California,* California Division of Mines, Sacramento, 1970, p. 146, placed "total production" at over $1.3 million.
50. Lambert Florin, *Western Ghost Towns,* Superior Publishing Company, Seattle, 1961, p. 126.
51. Weston, p. 20, refers to Fremont's wife as "Jenny."

52. Jessie Benton Fremont, *Mother Lode Narratives,* Lewis Osborne, Ashland, Oregon, 1970, p. 14.
53. *Ibid.*
54. Fremont, pp. 14-15.
55. Florin, *Ghost Town Album,* p. 87.
56. Quoted in *California,* p. 500. On the other side of the coin, Fremont bought his original land grant for $3,000 and sold it in 1863 for $6 million. It's estimated that he may have netted $100,000 a year from various business interests.
57. Wells and Peterson, p. 144.
58. Nadeau, p. 216, calls it a silver camp. Thomas Moore, in *Ghost and Shadow Towns of the Glory Road,* A. S. Barnes and Company, Cranbury, N.J., 1970, p. 40, calls it a gold camp.
59. Moore claims that Benton was formerly known as Benton Station, and that it was the southern terminus of the Carson, Bodie Stage and the anticipated junction for the Carson & Colorado and the Bodie & Benton railroads. But Nadeau opts for the towns being separate and distinct and Benton being on the Carson and Colorado Railroad. The author's observation is that Benton is about four miles west of Benton Station. Highway maps bear this out.
60. Bidwell wrote a book about himself entitled *Echoes of the Past,* Citadell Press, New York, 1962.
61. Wells and Peterson, p. 93.
62. Louise Amelia Knapp Smith Clappe, *The Shirley Letters from the California Mines 1851-1852,* Alfred A. Knopf, New York, 1949, p. 10.
63. A California Department of Parks and Recreation brochure estimates peak population at "some 3,000" people.
64. It was displaced by Oroville.
65. Wells and Peterson, p. 93.
66. *California,* p. 557. Records seem to indicate that the Big Bar post office wasn't established until June 27, 1874.
67. The yearbook of the Trinity County Historical Society ("Trinity"), 1967, p. 18, indicates that it was settled by "one Jones" in 1849.
68. "Trinity," 1967, p. 18, and "Trinity," 1962, p. 40.
69. "Trinity," 1955, p. 18.
70. It seems likely that Big Bar includes the former camps of Manzanita Flat, Vance's Bar, and Cox's Bar.
71. Taken from "Trinity," 1962, p. 38.
72. *Ibid.*
73. "Trinity," 1962, p. 38.
74. "Trinity," 1966, p. 49.
75. Savage is also credited with having discovered Yosemite Valley.
76. Most accounts claim that the tree had an eleven-foot diameter. However, one account claims that the oak was forty-four feet in circumference at a height of fourteen feet from ground level.
77. Florin, *Ghost Town Album,* p. 96, has a slightly different version. He says that as miners dug close to the tree roots many branches were killed. A fire in 1862 spread to the dead branches and burned the tree; plus "unrestrained" digging around the tree's base toppled it in 1869. The limbs and most of the trunk were set afire in 1901.
78. *Geologic Guidebook,* p. 47.
79. The others were Sweetland, French Corral, and Bridgeport.
80. Koschmann and Bergendahl, p. 64.
81. *California,* p. 605. Colemanite was named for discoverer W. T. Coleman. It is volcanic clay with a crystalline borate of lime content, used for the production of borax.
82. Following a lengthy search for details about Dorsey, the temptation is to agree with Frederick Remington, who in *Following Crooked Trails* (1898, Harper and Brothers, New York, p. 116) observed, "One can thresh the straw of history until he is well worn out, and also is running some risk of wearing others out who have to listen."
83. Franklin A. Buck, *A Yankee Trader in the Gold Rush,* Houghton Mifflin Company, Boston, 1930, p. 270.
84. W. A. Chalfant, *Gold, Guns & Ghost Towns,* Stanford University Press, Stanford, California, 1947, p. 43.
85. *Ibid.*
86. Some reports indicate that his skull bedecked the back bar of the Cosmopolitan saloon for a time.

87. Moore, p. 20.
88. The newspapers were the *Chronicle,* also known as the *Alpine Chronicle,* which later united with the *Bridgeport Union* to become the *Bridgeport Chronicle-Union*; the *Free Press*; and the *Morning News,* which united with the *Bodie Standard* to become the *Bodie Standard News.* In 1882 the Bodie *Evening Miner* was established, succeeding the short-lived weekly *The Opinion.*
89. The town even boasted of a railroad — the Bodie and Benton — which an observer said was a railroad essentially between nowhere and nowhere (Lucius Beebe and Charles Clegg, *The American West,* Bonanza Books, New York, MCMLV, p. 277).
90. *Gazette,* October 1879.
91. *Gazette,* June 18, 1879.
92. Browne must not have been terribly impressed with Bodie, however. He writes (*Adventure in the Apache Country*), "A pair of boots, I suppose would have secured the right to a tolerably good [Bodie] lot; but having only one pair, and that pretty well worn, I did not venture upon an investment."
93. Taken from Chalfant, pp. 47-48.
94. In *The Ghost Town of Bodie,* Chalfant Press, Bishop, California, 1967, p. 20, Russ and Anne Johnson put the date at 1892. Apparently the power plant was completed in December 1892. But because of delays and accidents, power wasn't produced until October 1893.
95. The power line had been built as straight as possible, since its designers thought that power would jump off the line if it weren't straight.
96. Koschmann and Bergendahl, p. 70; although Wolle, p. 134, writes that about $50 million was taken from the principal producer alone — the Standard mine.
97. Nadeau, p. 209.
98. A brochure about Bodie is available at P.O. Box 2390, Sacramento, California 95811.
99. Nadeau, p. 245.
100. *Ibid.,* p. 247.
101. Cy and Jeannie Martin, in *Gold! And Where They Found It,* Trans-Anglo Books, Corona del Mar, California, 1974, p. 92, give the date as 1882.
102. Koschmann and Bergendahl, p. 60.
103. From *Annals of Trinity County,* Chapter 9, in "Trinity," 1967, p. 56.
104. *Ibid.*
105. *Ibid.,* p. 57.
106. Quoted in "Trinity," 1969, p. 44.
107. *Ibid.,* p. 45.
108. Records seem to indicate that the railroad station which served the mine was named **Delta**, but it was probably not an organized town, according to "Trinity," 1958, p. 40. There also appears to have been a camp near the furnaces where the Altoona mine mercury was retorted. Called **Cinnabar**, the settlement would have been about ten miles from the mine. A report of October 16, 1875 indicated that three families lived at Cinnabar, where an election had recently polled thirty-one votes, but the observer thought there were probably twice that number of men in the area, according to "Trinity," 1962, p. 28.
109. According to Wagner, p. 20, there were perhaps twenty other producing properties.
110. The Morgan mine was named for Colonel Alfred Morgan.
111. The nugget would be worth considerably more at today's prices.
112. Wagner, p. 69, indicates that her mother ran a miners' boardinghouse at Carson Hill.
113. Personal letter from Madge R. Walsh, Curator of Historical Collections, September 26, 1976.
114. Florin, in *Western Ghost Towns,* p. 122, indicates that he took over the Union mine. But apparently Belshaw had a legitimate partner in Victor Beaudry.
115. Nadeau, p. 190.
116. Koschmann and Bergendahl, p. 84.
117. *California,* p. 498.
118. C. M. Goethe, in *What's In A Name?,* Keystone Press, Sacramento, 1949, p. 15, claims they were English tea planters.
119. Weston, p. 36.
120. The church was built in 1855 and restored in 1949.
121. Franklin Street, *California in 1850,* R. E. Edwards and Company, Cincinnati, 1851, reprinted in *The Gold Mines of California,* Promontory Press, New York, 1974, p. 33.

122. *Ibid.*
123. Koschmann and Bergendahl, p. 73.
124. Rodman W. Paul, in *The California Gold Discovery,* has put together massive accounts of the discovery, many of them contradictory.
125. Wells and Peterson, p. 82.
126. *California,* p. 496. Lucius Beebe and Charles Clegg, in *U.S. West, the Saga of Wells Fargo,* Bonanza Books, New York, MCMXLIX, p. 55, assessed Columbia's early days. They write: "Columbia's early years were happy ones punctuated by a multiplicity of stabbings, garrotings, lootings, riots, holocausts, assaults upon female virtue when this commodity was infrequently available and other forms of noisy outrage which delighted the simple soul of the 'honest miner.' Columbia in the early fifties was, in a word, a caution."
127. A Charles Jarvis reportedly found a $28,000, 132-pound nugget in Columbia's Poverty Gulch, according to Robert Silverberg in *Ghost Towns of the American West,* Thomas Y. Crowell, New York, 1968, p. 83.
128. *Geologic Guidebook,* p. 54. Other estimates go to $90 million.
129. Paul, in *California Gold,* p. 162.
130. As a result of the 1857 fire, a delegation was sent to San Francisco to purchase a fire engine. They procured the handpumper "Pepeete," scheduled to be shipped to Hawaii.
131. *California,* p. 513.
132. *Prospector,* p. 158.
133. Beebe & Clegg, U.S. West: *The Saga of Wells Fargo,* p. 21.
134. Ralph Moody, *Stagecoach West,* Promontory Press, 1967, p. 316. This last holdup of Black Bart's career was the only one that reportedly netted him more than $500.
135. *California,* p. 499.
136. Wolle, p. 129.
137. *Gold Rush Country* claims that the year was 1849, but all other sources consulted give the 1850 figure.
138. The Coulter Hotel, later known as the Wagner Hotel, is commonly thought to be the site of this unusual arrangement. However, Ila Goss Barrett, in *Memories of Coulterville,* privately printed, 1954, p. 3, claims the City Hotel as the site.
139. Stephen C. Davis, *California Gold Rush Merchant,* The Huntington Library, San Marino, California, 1956, p. 94.
140. *Gold Rush Country,* p. 17.
141. A strike by the Workingmen's Club of Darwin, a quasi-labor union, against the New Coso Mining Company led to tragedy. The smelter workers struck against a pay cut from four dollars to three dollars a day. The company hired "scabs," the workingmen blocked them, authorities were called in, and they shot and killed a striker. That night the constable killed another striker. Later a citizens' group praised the peace officers and denounced the Workingmen's Club, which disbanded.
142. A plaque in Diamond Springs indicates that the town was settled in 1848.
143. Street, p. 36.
144. The building is said to be the oldest Odd Fellows Hall in constant use in California.
145. Granville Stuart, *40 Years on the Frontier,* Arthur C. Clark Company, Glendale, California, 1957, p. 57.
146. "Trinity," 1955, p. 14, indicates that Douglas City was originally called Douglass, but this "The Post office Department decided one 's' was enough."
147. These militiamen were sometimes also referred to as Douglas City "Rifles."
148. Buck, p. 195.
149. *Ibid.*
150. *Ibid.,* p. 196.
151. Anderson may have been accompanied by men named Haven and Culton.
152. Lambert Florin, in *Ghost Town Trails,* Superior Publishing Company, Seattle, 1963, p. 170 calls him Jack Cannon. *Gold Rush Country,* p. 91 agrees. Nadeau, p. 144 has it as Joe Cannon.
153. J. D. Borthwick, in *3 Years in California,* 1948, Howell-North, Berkeley, p. 182, claims that she stabbed the man without provocation.
154. William L. Manly, in *Death Valley in '49,* Wallace Hebberd, New York, 1894, p. 365 maintains that "A physician examined Juanita and announced to the mob that she was in a condition that demanded the highest sympathy of every man, but he was forced to flee from town to save his life."
155. Pointed out in Wells and Peterson, p. 258.

156. Florin, *Ghost Town Trails,* p. 172.
157. So named for the twelve-pound cannon ball used.
158. Another theory is that the settlement was named for German miners or prospectors Joseph and Charles Dornbach.
159. The publication is "Siskiyou Co. California with Sketches and Descriptions of Historic Points of Interest."
160. Another story relates that the town was named as such because its residents were "always fiddling."
161. Dredging operations ceased in the late 1950s, perhaps 1956, although reports of dredging as late as 1958 seem to be substantiated.
162. *California,* p. 537.
163. Named for Alfred Brown, former owner of the Table Mountain ranch.
164. Martins, p. 102. Koschmann and Bergendahl, p. 72, indicate that the Jenny Lind, Independence, and New Jersey mines produced $2.4 million in gold before 1868. Gudde claims on page 119 that the Independent, New Jersey, and Jenny Lind production figures should be $2.65 million, with total production at about $18.3 million.
165. Its name probably came about because it was at the fourth crossing of the Calaveras River, on the Stockton-Murphys road. The crossings were located at the Calaveras River, over the north fork of the Calaveras, across Calaveritas Creek, and across San Antone Creek.
166. *Geologic Guidebook,* p. 77, states that it was the first line ever built, but this is disputed. Some sources claim that this was the first cross-country phone in the state. What seems clear is that Alexander Graham Bell invented and patented the first telephone in 1876, and that the first telephone was installed in the home and office of Charles Williams, Jr., at Somerville, Massachusetts, in April 1877.
167. Lambert Florin, *Ghost Town Treasures,* Superior Publishing Company, Seattle, 1965, p. 22.
168. *Ibid.*
169. One theory is that the camp was so named from the heavy nuggets that "growled" in the miners' gold pans.
170. Edward G. Buffum, in *Six Months in the Gold Mines,* Lea and Blanchard, Philadelphia, 1850, p. 127, indicates that a man named Hudson, from New York, was the initial discoverer in summer 1849.
171. *California,* p. 545.
172. *Ibid.*
173. *Gold Rush Country* has the name as Andres Goodyear, but this appears to be an error.
174. Robert Welles Ritchie, *The Hell-roarin' Forty-Niners,* J. H. Sears, New York, 1928, p. 95.
175. The discoveries are generally credited as being made by George Knight; although Wagner, p. 166, gives the name as George McKnight.
176. Paul, *California Gold,* p. 258.
177. *Ibid.,* p. 260.
178. Koschmann and Bergendahl, p. 70.
179. This figure is suggested by Wagner, p. 213. Jim Morley and Doris Foley, in *Gold Cities,* Howell-North Books, Berkeley, California, 1965, p. 10, use this figure. Wagner, various pages, puts total production from only the Idaho-Maryland, North Star, and Empire mines at $167,508,277. The *Geologic Guidebook,* p. 74, points out that the Empire-Star Mines Company, Ltd. consolidated the North Star, Pennsylvania, and Empire mines, plus a host of other workings. This may account for discrepancies in production figures. The Idaho-Maryland Mines Corporation holdings included the Old Brunswick, New Brunswick, Idaho, and Eureka mines and other small holdings.
180. *Gold Rush Country,* p. 72, claims that the fire was in 1855. Although Editor H. J. Shipley was publicly whipped by Lola Montez, we find no reason to question Shipley, newspapers owners Warren B. Ewer and J. H. Boardman, nor former owners Oliver and Moore or subsequent owners Rufus Shoemaker or George D. Roberts. The September 18, 1854 "Extra" edition of the *Grass Valley Telegraph* clearly states that the fire was during September 1854.
181. Vardis Fisher, in *Gold Rushes and Mining Camps of the Early American West,* Caxton Printers, Caldwell, Idaho, 1969, p. 380, thinks it unlikely the house remains. It is strange indeed that a house on the corner of Mill and Welsh streets, within the fire area, would survive when all around did not.

182. Fisher, p. 463, calls her Maria Doloros Eliza Gilbert. He apparently bases this on writings of Robert Ritchie, Henry Jackson, Oscar Lewis, and others. A newspaper account (the *Shasta Courier*) called her, upon her marriage in California to Patrick Hull, Madama Marie Elise Rosanna Dolores, Countess of Landsfelt, Baroness of Rosenthal.
183. Dee Brown, in *The Gentle Tamers,* Barrie & Jenkins, London, 1973, p. 177, puts her wealth at $4 million.
184. Clark also promoted other mining camps, including Mill Canyon, in Eureka County, Nevada. See *Nevada Ghost Towns & Mining Camps* by Stanley W. Paher, Howell-North Books, Berkeley, California, 1970, p. 165.
185. Nadeau, p. 263.
186. Street, p. 34. However, one source indicates that the post office was established as Louisville in July 1851 and changed to Greenwood in October 1852. Another source claims that the town was first called Long Valley, but that the name changed to Lewisville (or Louisville) in 1850. Later, the town became known as Greenwood.
187. Garrote, meaning to execute or attack by strangling.
188. Gold was discovered there in 1849.
189. An example is nearby Sara Totten campground, where the U. S. Forest Service placed toilets and camping sites in close proximity to tailings left from mining activities dating to about 1850.
190. It was called the Grider Creek road.
191. Paher, p. 287. Gudde (p. 152) claims that, during its heyday, Hart had eight saloons.
192. The Siskiyou County Historical Society has an explanation about discovery dates. In 1851 **Frog Town** was settled near present-day Hawkinsville. In 1852 the Frog Town location was changed and the new name selected in honor of Jacob Hawkins.
193. A sidelight on Lee. He reportedly found buried skeletons of forty Indians.
194. Apparently graves were difficult to dig in the rocky soil, so Mexicans were buried on top of the ground, and little mounds were built over the tops to resemble bake ovens. Scholar and historian Erwin Gudde claims that the camp was named for Los Hornitas in Durango, Mexico.
195. As Joseph Henry Jackson in *Bad Country* and Dorothy M. Johnson in *Western Badmen,* among others, point out, the existence of such a person is, at best, questionable.
196. Fremont, p. 44.
197. Quoted in Wells and Peterson, p. 101.
198. Wells and Peterson, p. 104.
199. *California,* p. 500. *Gold Rush Country,* p. 16, states that the miners secured a rope around the Chinaman's neck and by violently jerking it dashed the man's brains out against the walls.
200. *Geologic Guidebook,* p. 38.
201. This figure is given by Joseph Henry Jackson in *Anybody's Gold,* D. Appleton-Century Company, New York, 1941, p. 305.
202. Perhaps as much as $40,000 in gold was shipped daily from the Wells Fargo Express Office by armed stagecoach.
203. This 1855 building was owned by Ghirardelli, who later became known as the "chocolate king."
204. *Geologic Guidebook,* p. 73.
205. Jackson, *Anybody's Gold,* p. 439.
206. Koschmann and Bergendahl, p. 78.
207. From *The Shirley Letters,* p. 50.
208. *Ibid.,* p. 56.
209. *Ibid.,* p. 78.
210. *Ibid.,* p. 57.
211. *Ibid.,* p. 104.
212. Winning sides were those that argued iron was more beneficial than gold, that women exerted more influence over men than money, and that Washington deserves "greater applause" for defending the nation than Columbus did for discovering America.
213. *Gold Rush Album,* p. 69, claims that $20 million was mined there between 1853 and 1858. *California* agrees with the total mined (p. 569), but says that it was from the years 1853 to 1880. But Koschmann and Bergendahl, p. 72, claim that the entire Iowa Hill mining district production until 1901 was about $10 million.
214. "Trinity," 1966, p. 8.

215. Wells and Peterson, p. 131.
216. *Mark Twain's Notebook,* p. 7.
217. Most authorities seem to agree with the latter motive, including Edward Wagenknecht, in *Mark Twain the Man and His Work,* Yale University Press, New Haven, 1935, p. 12.
218. Bernard DeVoto, in *Mark Twain's America,* Little, Brown and Company, Boston, 1932, p. 160, writes that Bill Gillis (William R. Gillis) appears briefly in Twain's "Autobiography" as the younger brother of Jim and Steve — "With an imaginative genealogy which Bill does not claim for himself." Bill Gillis wrote "Memories of Mark Twain and Steve Gillis," published in 1924 by the *Sonora Banner.* DeVoto describes it as a "pathetic specimen of an old man's garrulity."
219. The visits may or may not have been on the basis of a friendship between Jim Gillis and Bret Harte. Gillis apparently gave Harte money (probably twenty dollars) when he needed it; but when Gillis visited Harte a few months after the money-giving instance, while in San Francisco, Harte snubbed him. As Ivan Benson wrote in *Mark Twain's Western Year,* Stanford University Press, Stanford, 1938, p. 124: "Here was one of the many instances where Harte insisted upon considering as enemies those from whom he had borrowed money. Bret Harte became an unpleasant memory to kindly Jim Gillis, who, of all men, had not a trace of any aptitude for making enemies."

    Mark Twain, in his *Autobiography,* p. 360, paints a somewhat different picture of the Gillis brothers, but said that they all had fists that could whip anybody who walked on two legs, and that when a Gillis confronted a man and had a proposition to make, "the proposition always contained business."
220. Nadeau, p. 78.
221. *Gold Rush Album* says that it was named by "Chilean miners" impressed by the many bottles at the spring where passing miners obtained water.
222. Silverberg, p. 46.
223. Nadeau, p. 81.
224. *Gold Rush Country,* p. 46, says it was opened in 1850. On March 28, 1942, the mining ceased, but the owners, the Argonaut Mining Company, didn't officially dissolve until 1948.
225. Wagner, p. 111.
226. *Ibid.,* p. 93.
227. See Jackson's *Anybody's Gold* for an intriguing account of the contest between Jackson, Double Springs, and Mok Hill for county seat honors.
228. *Geologic Guidebook,* p. 62.
229. Nadeau, p. 83.
230. *Geologic Guidebook* gives the sixty-eight-foot figure on p. 62, and the figure of fifty-eight feet on p. 129.
231. Woods, p. 121.
232. Wells and Peterson speak of a $9 million figure (p. 136), but it isn't clear if they are speaking of only the Eagle-Shawmut, or of all mines in the Jacksonville area.
233. Weston, p. 44.
234. *California,* p. 498.
235. When the settlement was founded, singer Jenny Lind was touring the United States with P. T. Barnum.
236. Koschmann and Bergendahl, p. 74.
237. The camp may not have been officially founded until February 1870. Some credit Drury D. Bailey as founder.
238. Another inverted siphon was used at Cherokee.
239. The line was planned to ultimately connect Hawthorne, Candelaria, and Aurora, Nevada, with Bodie and Benton, California. For additional details see Lucius Beebe and Charles Clegg's *Virginia & Truckee,* Howell-North Books, Berkeley, California, 1963.
240. Not to be confused with the La Grange hydraulic mine, located in about 1862 four miles west of Weaverville.
241. These conflicting dates are given on monuments in La Porte.
242. Allen and friend Richard Bucke left the Washoe country on November 20, 1857. Snow, cold, and starvation threatened them, but they finally made it to Last Chance. However, Grosch died on December 19, 1857, primarily from exposure. His legs were frozen, but he refused to have them amputated. Amputation might have saved his life. But he was a vegetable, and never uttered an intelligible word while at Last Chance. His full name was Ethan Allen (some say Allan) Grosch, sometimes referred to as Grosh (as on his gravemarker). Allen's marker was

placed by Richard Burke, while that of his brother, Hosea, was brought by Schuyler Colfax, later Vice President of the United States, sent by the brothers' father from Philadelphia. Hosea's name is spelled Grosch on his marker.

243. "Trinity," 1969, p. 23.
244. "Trinity," 1955, p. 13.
245. "Trinity," 1960, p. 19.
246. The first known gold discoveries in the Yuba River in this area seem to have been made in 1848, and the camp may have existed by late that year. Some evidence seems to indicate that the camp had a population of about 1,000 in 1850.
247. Davis.
248. Koschmann and Bergendahl, p. 76.
249. Emil W. Billeb, *Mining Camp Days,* Howell-North Books, Berkeley, California, 1968, p. 89.
250. Chalfant gives a $2 million figure (p. 52), as does Nadeau, p. 217, although the total may have reached $3 million.
251. Nadeau, p. 216, and other sources.
252. Helen S. Giffen, in *California Mining Town Newspapers, 1850-1880,* J. E. Reynolds, Bookseller, Van Nuys, California, 1954, p. 46, says of Townsend's *Homer Mining Index,* that it was considered the best newspaper printed in Mono County, and an excellent source of information on early mining camps in the vicinity.
253. Moore, p. 40.
254. Chalfant, p. 97.
255. Quoted by Chalfant, p. 103.
256. Buck, p. 275.
257. It was named for the butterflies that inhabit the valley.
258. Wells and Peterson, p. 141.
259. *Geologic Guidebook,* p. 64.
260. They had been married on Christmas Day 1848.
261. Franklin Langworthy, *Scenery of the Plains, Mountains and Mines,* Princeton University Press, 1932 (from the edition of 1855), p. 169.
262. Henry C. Morris, *The Mining West at the Turn of the Century,* privately printed, Washington, D.C., 1962, p. 57.
263. There was another camp called Marysville north of Old Denny (New River City), in extreme northwestern Trinity County. It has disappeared. Please see the chapter on Denny.
264. For a comprehensive history, see Paul Fatout, *Meadow Lake: gold town,* Indiana University Press, Bloomington, 1969.
265. Paul, *California Gold,* p. 279.
266. Fatout, p. 70.
267. *California,* p. 495. The name may also have come from proper names such as Maloney, Meloney, or Melone. However, the temptation is to agree with Gudde that the origin of the name has not been determined.
268. Jackson, in *California Gold,* p. 335, claims that during one six-week period of the gold rush more than $10,000 in tolls were collected on the ferry.
269. Stanford was a millionaire railroad builder, a governor, a senator, and the founder of a university.
270. Stanford claimed that he slept on the counter of his store.
271. "Trinity," 1955, p. 9.
272. "Trinity, 1966, p. 49.
273. *Trinity Journal,* October 30, 1857.
274. Weston, p. 106.
275. Weston, p. 104, writes of the "Ledget" Hotel and includes a photo of the hotel on p. 102, where the hotel sign clearly indicates it's the "Leger" Hotel. Also, Mok Hill is not to be confused with Mokelumne City, a former San Joaquin County trade and transportation center located at the junction of the Cosumnes and Mokelumne rivers.
276. Moore, p. 106.
277. May 24, 1894.
278. Bancroft (VI, p. 486), claims that **Orleans Flat** was originally named Concord Bar. The camp was five miles northeast of North Bloomfield. It was active beginning in 1851, and by 1855 600 persons lived there. The diggings were shallow, and mining began to decline in 1857; in 1867 Mexican and Chinese miners worked abandoned claims. The town soon died. The existence of **Blue Diggin's** is debatable. It may have been an ephemeral Nevada County camp, perhaps not. Many camps had the word "Blue" in them, including Blue Bank in Sierra County, Blue Bar and Blue Gulch in Siskiyou County, Blue Bluffs and Blue Canyon in Placer

County, Blue Gulch in Tuolumne County, and Blue Belly Ravine in an unidentified mining locality. **Chinee Flat** is not to be confused with China Flat, three miles east of Downieville in Sierra County.

279. Goethe, p. 122.
280. Senator Benton was Jesse Benton Fremont's father.
281. *Geologic Guidebook,* p. 99, and several other sources.
282. Apparently during early 1851.
283. First known as Murphy's Diggings, then as Murphy's Camp, finally as Murphys.
284. Weston, p. 86, claims that it was known as the Sperry Hotel "in the early days." However, the photo of the hotel (p. 87) captioned "Sperry" Hotel clearly shows a sign naming it the Mitcheler Hotel.
285. The settlement was founded in the autumn of 1849.
286. Ritchie, p. 95.
287. Morley and Foley, p. 48. Wolle, p. 114, points out that the city had five major fires during its first ten years of existence.
288. Louis Chaboya may have been a co-founder.
289. Goss, p. 112, puts average annual production circa 1880 at 20-25,000 flasks. Until 1904, a flask of quicksilver contained 76½ pounds of mercury; from 1904 to 1927, 75 pounds; since 1927, 76 pounds.
290. *California,* p. 480.
291. *Prospector,* p. 167.
292. The mine was known variously as the Bloomfield hydraulic mine, the North Bloomfield, and the Malakoff.
293. Wagner, p. 33, puts the weight at 510 pounds avoirdupois.
294. Goethe, p. 128.
295. *California,* p. 479. Records seem to indicate that the South Yuba Canal Company telephone lines preceded those of the North San Juan area. The canal company lines followed by two years the granting of Alexander Graham Bell's first telephone patent. One year later the lines passing in the North San Juan area were strung.
296. *Prospector,* p. 168.
297. *California,* p. 479, and Wolle, p. 114.
298. Six were killed at an explosion at Chancellor on January 19, 1909. See H. B. Humphrey, *Historical Summary of Coal-Mine Explosions in the United States, 1810-1958,* U.S. Bureau of Mines Bulletin 586, 1960, pp. 6 and 23.
299. "Trinity," 1970, p. 24.
300. Official 1894 map of Trinity County.
301. Windeler, p. 98.
302. *California,* p. 536. Koschmann and Bergendahl, p. 59, indicate that in 1905 there were thirty-five dredges mining Feather River gravels, which they imply was the peak number.
303. Wagner, p. 43.
304. Koschmann and Bergendahl, p. 59.
305. The *Panamint News,* November 26, 1874, claims that the first discoveries were the "Stewart Wonder" and the "Jacobs Wonder," located in April 1873.
306. Wolle, p. 138.
307. Nadeau, p. 197.
308. A writer to the *San Francisco Alta,* January 25, 1875, visited Panamint and claimed the town had "recently sprung into existence by the magic influence of wealth, energy, perseverance and an unflinching confidence in the great future of Panamint."
309. Donald E. Bower, *Ghost Towns and Back Roads,* Stackpole Books, Harrisburg, Pennsylvania, 1971, p. 181.
310. Neill C. Wilson, in *Silver Stampede,* The Macmillan Company, New York, 1937, p. 312, wonders who dumped the last — 57th — man (Robert McKenny) in his grave in Panamint's Sour Dough Canyon "bone orchard," and concludes that only the bending junipers know.
311. Koschmann and Bergendahl, p. 74.
312. Street, p. 35.
313. Weston, p. 132, says he was a Mexican storekeeper.
314. Silverberg, pp. 50-51. Wells and Peterson, p. 127, have a slightly different version.
315. Borthwick, p. 94.
316. *Ibid.*
317. Browne, p. 312.

318. Joseph Henry Jackson (editor), *Gold Rush Album*, Bonanza Books, New York, 1949, p. 55.
319. Marvin Lewis (editor), *The Mining Frontier*, University of Oklahoma Press, Norman, 1967, p. 65.
320. Koschmann and Bergendahl, p. 61.
321. Give or take a couple of million.
322. Placerville was the western terminus of the Central Overland route from Salt Lake City.
323. Clappe, p. vii.
324. Some sources refer to the camp as Puckerville.
325. *Geologic Guidebook*, p. 62.
326. *California*, p. 487. Wagner, p. 153, puts the figure at $13.5 million.
327. Mrs. App lived in Quartz until she died in 1930.
328. The site was originally an old Indiàn campground. Quartzburgs are also located in Mariposa and Kern counties. The Kern County camp is under the waters of Lake Isabella. The Mariposa County town was overshadowed by Hornitos and is all but forgotten.
329. Other reports indicate that Quincy erected a frame building in the rear of his hotel and offered it free for county use.
330. Nadeau, p. 255.
331. Florin, in *Ghost Town Treasures*, p. 20, indicates that at one time there were 1,000 tents and a few board and canvas shacks in the bustling camp.
332. *Gold Rush Country*, p. 29, claims that the mine was open until 1909.
333. Goethe, p. 149.
334. See "Henry Lorenz: Biography of a Pioneer Businessman," in "Trinity," 1969, pp. 46–51.
335. The town was apparently called Osdick (or Osdic) at one time, for two brothers who once owned a stamp mill nearby.
336. *California*, p. 535.
337. *Gold Rush Country*, p. 86. George C. Mansfield in *The Feather River in '49 and the Fifties*, Oroville, 1924, p. 10, indicates that the figure should have been $36,000 and that the location was at the "other" Rich Bar mentioned in the last paragraph on Rich Bar.
338. Silverberg, p. 45.
339. Windler, p. 115.
340. Clappe, pp. 30-31.
341. *California*, p. 482.
342. The town was apparently the setting for Bret Harte's story, *The Millionaire of Rough and Ready*.
343. Fatout, p. x, says that it was an independent state "for decades."
344. Street, p. 32.
345. Wolle, p. 118.
346. Francis Farquahar and Joseph Henry Jackson (and others) have pretty much shown Murieta to be a legendary character. As Dorothy M. Johnson puts it so well in *Western Badmen*, "One thing certain is that . . . all the Joaquins and all the bandits of that generation are dead now." (p. 19).
347. The spot where the Scott party found the first gold in Siskiyou County is marked by a monument to John Scott.
348. The tree died in the mid-1930s, and little of it remains.
349. It wasn't a total tent town, for Milton Magree owned a log cabin, the only one in town.
350. "Trinity," 1969, p.6.
351. *The Book of the American West*, Jay Monaghan, Editor-in-Chief, Bonanza Books, New York, 1963, p. 93, claims maximum pack weight for mules at about 200, but this seems conservative.
352. The account was carried in the December 1856 issue of Hutchings' *California Magazine*.
353. Borthwick, p. 280.
354. *California*, p. 495.
355. Insights of Fair and others who virtually controlled Comstock mining can be found in *Silver Kings* by Oscar Lewis (Ballantine, New York, 1971).
356. When Lord Sholto Douglas brought his theatrical troupe to Marysville, the opening night audience was very small. He applied for E.C.V. membership, and the audiences significantly increased. Although members of the society were mischievous at times, they were well respected as people who aided the destitute, fed the hungry, and cared for the sick.

357. Martins, p. 94, claim that it was founded in January when "One-Eye" Thompson and Harry Ramsey, lost in a fog, discovered a gold ledge there.
358. Nadeau, p. 266. MacDonald, in *Ghost Town Glimpses,* p. 84, claims that the body was "rehung" for the benefit of the town's physician, Dr. Herbert MacDonald, who wanted a picture for his files.
359. Windeler, p. 215.
360. Street, p. 37.
361. Woods, pp. 108, 111.
362. This may be the oldest Episcopal church in California.
363. Martins, p. 103, put discovery year at 1855.
364. Wells and Peterson, p. 116.
365. "Trinity," 1960, p. 32.
366. It may have been 1855. See Nadeau, p. 152.
367. Stanford invested heavily in the Union (later the Lincoln) mine.
368. Sutter Creek figured prominently in the 1871 "Amador War," where for the first time in the West, mine owners called in the state militia to attempt to break up a strike. For more details, Richard E. Lingenfelter's *The Hardrock Miners,* University of California Press, Berkeley, 1974, makes good reading.
369. Florin, *Western Ghost Towns,* p. 124.
370. Nadeau, p. 194.
371. From Isaac Cox's *Annals of Trinity County* in "Trinity," 1965, p. 51.
372. Chalfant, p. 51.
373. Nadeau, p. 217.
374. It was probably founded in 1851 by Moses Chadbourne.
375. "Trinity," 1955, p. 8.
376. Martins, p. 105, state that area mines were first claimed by Peter Walters in 1884.
377. The Martins, p. 105, indicate that the mines closed in approximately 1914. The chronology of mine operation seems to be that the Gold Rock mines closed in 1909, the United Mining (or Mines) Company operations began about 1910 and closed in 1911, Seeley Mudd operated the Gold Rock mines from 1913-14, the Queen Mining Company began operations in 1916 and ceased in 1917, and the Sovereign Mining and Development Company operated area mines from 1937 to 1941.
378. Tuttletown was initially called Marmolitos, according to Dane, p. 127. The camp may have been called Mormon Camp at one time, according to the *Geologic Guidebook,* p. 54. Jackson, and Weston, claim that it was once called Mormon Gulch.
379. Some sources indicate that the camp was settled by Mormons in 1848, who had arrived before Tuttle.
380. Silverberg, p. 68. The camp was nicknamed Crater City.
381. Silverberg, *ibid.,* puts the figure at 8,000.
382. Silverberg, p. 69, Wolle, p. 121, and several other sources.
383. In *The Big Bonanza* by Dan DeQuille, Thomas Y. Crowell Company, New York, 1834, taken from the 1947 Alfred A. Knopf edition, p. viii.
384. Buck, p. 97.
385. *Ibid.,* p. 100.
386. *Ibid.,* p. 101.
387. *Prospector,* p. 180, says that there were 2,500 Chinese in the area. Jackson, p. 444, puts the figure at 2,000. One reason for these lower "guestimate" figures is that the *Trinity Journal* (Weaverville) on December 8, 1860, puts the entire Weaverville population at only 1,000.
388. The cause of the altercation is in doubt. Perhaps the battle was caused by one company insulting the other; a disagreement over seventy-five cents worth of gold dust, or other reasons. The Weaverville Elementary School is now located on the battle site.
389. *California,* p. 556, places the number at 300, and calls them the Ah You tong.
390. *Ibid.,* says that there were 500.
391. *California,* p. 556, says that they were called the Young Wo tong.
392. Buck, p. 140.
393. *Ibid.,* p. 141. "Trinity," 1957, p. 11, puts the figures at ten dead "on both sides." "Trinity," 1955, p. 16 indicates that twenty-six may have been killed and sixty wounded.
394. An interesting account of the Martin saga is in the 1958 issue of "Trinity," pp. 5-11.
395. Street, p. 36.

396. Florin Lambert, in *Western Ghost Town Shadows,* Superior Publishing Company, Seattle, 1964, p. 21, claims that it was two barrels of whiskey.
397. Vol. I, *40 Years on the Frontier,* p. 86.
398. Lambert, *Western Ghost Town Shadows,* p. 23.
399. Not only was there a Whiskeytown in California; there is also a Whiskey Slide, a lumber town near Jesus Maria. Whiskey Bar is a ghost town probably near the American River between Lotus and Coloma, but it has disappeared.
400. Paher, p. 61, speculates that the first billboard in the West may have been at Woodfords.
401. Goethe, p. 185.
402. Ritchie, p. 259.
403. Hinton Helper, *Dreadful California,* Lucius Beebe and Charles Clegg, editors, Bobbs Merrill, New York, 1948, p. 55.

Index

Note: All photographs appearing in *Ghost Towns of California* are courtesy of the author unless otherwise acknowledged.